Pulp Politics

SECOND EDITION

How Political Advertising Tells the Stories of American Politics

Glenn W. Richardson Jr.

ROWMAN & LITTLEFIELD PUBLISHERS, INC.
Lanham • Boulder • New York • Toronto • Plymouth, UK

ROWMAN & LITTLEFIELD PUBLISHERS, INC.

Published in the United States of America
by Rowman & Littlefield Publishers, Inc.
A wholly owned subsidiary of The Rowman & Littlefield Publishing Group, Inc.
4501 Forbes Boulevard, Suite 200, Lanham, Maryland 20706
www.rowmanlittlefield.com

Estover Road
Plymouth PL6 7PY
United Kingdom

Copyright © 2008 by Rowman & Littlefield Publishers, Inc.

An earlier version of chapter 1 was published as "Pulp Politics: The Genres of Popular Culture in Political Advertising." *Journal of Rhetoric and Public Affairs* 3(4): 603–26 (Winter), 2000.

An earlier version of chapter 2 was published as "The Popular Culture Context of Political Advertising: Linkages and Meanings in Political Information Processing." *Political Communication* 16(5) [special electronic volume on CD-ROM] G. R. Boynton and Kathleen Hall Jamieson, eds. 1998. Reprinted by permission of Taylor & Francis, Inc., http://www.routledge-ny.com

An earlier version of chapter 3 was published as "Looking for Meaning in All the Wrong Places: Why 'Negative' Advertising Is a Suspect Category." *Journal of Communication* 51(4): 775–800 (Winter), 2001.

An earlier version of chapter 4 was published as "Building a Better Adwatch: Talking Patterns to the American Voter." *Harvard International Journal of Press/Politics* 3(3):76–95. August, 1998. Reprinted by permission of Sage Publications.

An earlier version of chapter 5 was published as "Visual Storytelling and the Competition for Political Meaning in Political Advertising and News in Campaign 2000." *American Communication Journal* 5(3) (Spring), 2002.

All rights reserved. No part of this publication may be reproduced, stored in a retrieval system, or transmitted in any form or by any means, electronic, mechanical, photocopying, recording, or otherwise, without the prior permission of the publisher.

British Library Cataloguing in Publication Information Available

Library of Congress Cataloging-in-Publication Data
Richardson, Glenn W.
  Pulp politics : how political advertising tells the stories of American politics / Glenn W. Richardson.—2nd ed.
    p. cm.
  ISBN-13: 978-0-7425-5627-0 (cloth : alk. paper)
  ISBN-10: 0-7425-5627-1 (cloth : alk. paper)
  ISBN-13: 978-0-7425-5628-7 (pbk. : alk. paper)
  ISBN-10: 0-7425-5628-X (pbk. : alk. paper)
  eISBN-13: 978-0-7425-6452-7
  eISBN-10: 0-7425-6452-5
  1. Political campaigns—United States.   2. Advertising, Political—United States.
3. Television in politics—United States.   I. Title.
JK2281.R53 2008
324.7'30973—dc22   2008010139

Printed in the United States of America

∞ ™ The paper used in this publication meets the minimum requirements of American National Standard for Information Sciences—Permanence of Paper for Printed Library Materials, ANSI/NISO Z39.48-1992.

Pulp Politics

Contents

Preface		vii
Introduction		1
1	Communicating Culture: Audiovisuals in Campaign Advertising	11
2	Political Advertising and Political Thinking	31
3	The Attack on Attack Politics: Why "Negative" Advertising Is Good for Democracy	61
4	The Ad Patrol: Campaign Advertising and Ad Watch Journalism	89
5	Visual Political Communication in Campaign 2000	111
6	Terror TV: Political Advertising during the Bush Years	125
7	Conclusion: Reason, Passion and Democracy in the Digital Age	155
References		175
Index		191
About the Author		199

Preface

It has been nearly fifteen years since the seeds that would germinate into this book were planted. I continue to owe a deep debt of gratitude to those who helped cultivate those seeds, and without whose help, counsel, and guidance this work would not have been possible. The project had its genesis while I was a graduate student at the University of Iowa. I had taken an interest in political advertising during the 1988 presidential race, when candidate ads became the dominant element in the discourse of the campaign. I realized an opportunity to join and build upon what I saw as the intellectual projects of two of Iowa's most distinguished scholars, John S. Nelson and G. R. Boynton. Nelson had been exploring the political significance and meaning of the genres of popular entertainment, especially films and fiction. Boynton had been investigating political cognition, especially the networks of spreading activation that tie our thoughts, emotions, and experiences together. My insight was to see in the popular genres Nelson was focused on the cultural referents of the spreading activations Boynton was studying. In short, I thought, campaign ads worked largely by drawing upon our preexisting stores of culturally shared knowledge, gaining their persuasive power through their ability to use the recognizable audiovisual conventions of popular entertainment to evoke thoughts and emotions and attach them to the political struggle. Ads did so in a wholistic fashion, I reasoned, so it was the sum of the parts, rather than individual elements, that provided persuasive impact. Perhaps previous research had failed to find substantial effects of audiovisual content because researchers had isolated audiovisual elements, while they actually worked in tandem, generating the recognizable forms from which meaning was derived.

Along the way, my ideas benefited from the careful reading and suggestions of several colleagues, as well as the editors and reviewers of a handful of academic journals who reviewed my work. Among the latter are Marty Medhurst at *Rhetoric and Public Affairs*, Jon F. Nussbaum at the *Journal of Communication*, Stephanie Coopman at the *American Communication Journal*, Pippa Norris at the *Harvard International Journal of Press/Politics*, and the anonymous reviewers at these journals. I am also grateful to each of these journals, and to *Political Communication*, for their kindness in allowing me to include revised versions of work I originally published with them in this book.

I am also indebted to the pioneering scholarship of various students of political advertising, especially Kathleen Hall Jamieson. This book would have had far more original things to say if she had not already said them, and, moreover, much better than I could ever hope to.

I am particularly grateful to the fine folks at Rowman & Littlefield, especially Brenda Hadenfeldt, who was patient beyond reason and always encouraging during the long process of bringing the first edition of this work to fruition. It was a pleasure to learn more about good writing from her, and to the extent that this book reads well, it bears the imprint of her editorial pen. I am also grateful to Associate Editor Alden Perkins for helping me through the final steps toward publication, and to Daniel Brannen for his deft work on the book's index. This second edition of the book brings a new debt of gratitude to a new support team at Rowman & Littlefield, editors Bess Vanrenen and Niels Aaboe.

I have been blessed with more precious colleagues, friends, and acquaintances than I could ever hope for, and each has my thanks for their comradeship and support. I do not have the words to express my deep and heartfelt appreciation for the advice and support I have received from Professors Nelson and Boynton, and the late Timothy E. Cook of Williams College and Louisiana State University. My life is richer just for having known them, and all the more so because of the immeasurable support they have given me, not infrequently when it was not to be found elsewhere. Their examples, as scholars and human beings, light my world.

All of this and more is true as well of my dear friends and colleagues Karen Hult and Chuck Walcott. They have always been there for me, in every way, from my darkest moments to my most joyful. I hope that in some small way, this book (and my career) redeem their unshaken faith in me, which I treasure all the more for reasons they know only too well.

Such wonderful friends and colleagues all, far more than I (or anyone) could dream for, let alone expect. Yet even all of them could not save me from this book's errors and shortcomings, the one thing I managed to do all on my own!

Introduction

Sometimes, the legendary fictional investigator Sherlock Holmes reminds us, the most important clue can be found in something that didn't happen, as in the dog that didn't bark.[1] And so it is that we can learn a lot about televised political advertising by considering the case of a single ad that was barely run before its sponsors rushed to pull it from the airwaves during the final days of the 2000 campaign.

It was 1:28 a.m. on Friday, November 3, just four days before the election, when an urgent e-mail arrived at WTVJ-TV Channel 6. GHH Inc., the advertising firm hired by Charlie Crist, Republican candidate for state education commissioner, wanted the station to pull a Crist ad that had just begun running only hours before. The ad criticized Crist's opponent's "tragic DWI conviction." Why the urgent order to pull the ad? Crist said that he decided to stop the ad after receiving polling data (presumably that very evening and unavailable in the weeks of planning leading up to the decision to run the ad in the first place) indicating he should run a positive campaign during the race's closing days.

More skeptical observers thought otherwise. The evening of the day the Crist ad began airing, America first learned from news reports that Texas Governor George W. Bush, like Crist a Republican, had pled guilty to drunk driving as a thirty-year-old in the state of Maine. Crist denied the Bush news had anything to do with the decision to pull the ad. His opponent, George Sheldon, however, wondered, "If they considered it a good ad yesterday, I don't understand why they don't consider it a good ad today."

It's pretty easy to understand Sheldon's suspicion. Had the Crist ad continued to run, it very well could have drawn extensive statewide news coverage, inviting comparisons between Crist's argument that

Sheldon was unfit to serve as state education commissioner because of his DWI and Bush's own similar behavior. One can imagine the flurry of visual images populating the nightly news: the Crist ad . . . stock video of DWI arrests, possibly crash sites, victim testimonials, cynical comments from opponents . . . and, of course, Governor Bush. In the worst-case scenario, it could have even turned into a media phenomenon that Thomas Patterson and Robert McClure (1976) describe as a "meltdown," where viewers, bombarded with emotionally vivid and powerful images and stories from ads and news, begin to meld it all together, often mistakenly attributing ad content to news and news content to ads.

The 1988 presidential race featured perhaps the mother of all meltdowns, described in graphic detail by Kathleen Hall Jamieson, Dean of the Annenberg School of Communication at the University of Pennsylvania, in her book *Dirty Politics: Deception, Distraction and Democracy*. Vice President George H. Bush's campaign had used focus groups of key swing voters ("Reagan Democrats" who were thinking of voting for Bush's opponent, Massachusetts Governor Michael Dukakis) to identify the claims that would be most effective in eroding support for the Democratic nominee. What worked best was the story of a man convicted of first-degree murder, William J. Horton, Jr., who jumped a prison furlough while Dukakis was governor and went on to rape a Maryland woman and assault her fiancé. Horton was black; the Maryland couple was white.

Bush had been telling Horton's story on the campaign trail since June, but the story didn't catch fire until mid-September, when an ad telling the story produced by the National Security Political Action Committee (NSPAC) began to air. That ad was not broadcast widely, but excerpts were included in network news. Soon, journalists began telling the story in their reports. In early October, the Bush campaign itself began running an ad based on the Horton story. Yet more news coverage ensued. Then another independent PAC began airing ads focusing on Horton's victims. Still more news coverage. Indeed, now broadcast news segments were using clips from all three ads in their stories, along with clips from Vice President Bush's speeches. As Jamieson points out, "voters are like pack rats," gathering bits and pieces of information and storing them in one place in their minds. What is lost in the process is where particular bits and pieces came from in the first place. For many viewers, the Bush ad, PAC ads, and news all converged, vividly reinforcing a highly emotional tale (Jamieson 1992a:15–42).

Such a scenario involving Governor Bush's Maine DWI was unlikely in the closing days of the 2000 campaign, if only because it happened with but four days left before Election Day—far too little time for a sustained media frenzy to unfold. Nonetheless, if the 1988 campaign featured a full-on Chernobyl meltdown, Charlie Crist's ad might have precipitated something more along the lines of a Three Mile Island release of radioactivity. The potential here was that the Crist ad images, continuing news coverage of that ad, news coverage of Bush's DWI, and the graphic imagery regarding drunk driving already in viewers' minds would all latch onto Governor Bush's candidacy. They might forget where they saw what, but in their minds' eyes, they would have seen a blizzard of evocative visual imagery reinforcing the worst associations of drunk driving while the story of Bush's transgression was the hottest news item in the nation.

Would the election have turned out any different if the Crist ad had run in the election's closing days? Even under the worst set of circumstances, perhaps only a few voters would ultimately be swept up in such a media maelstrom. But in Charlie Crist's state, a few voters abandoning Governor Bush might in fact have made a *big* difference. That state was Florida.[2]

Why would the Crist ad, or any thirty-second political commercial, be such a big deal? In part, of course, in a tight campaign, *everything* is a big deal. No detail is too small if it has the potential to sway voters. But powerful campaign ads lie at the very core of modern political communication because they use audiovisuals to tell emotionally compelling stories about politics, and stories about politics help to define the political environment itself. To understand why this is so, we need to consider some of what we know about how people think, how our brains work, and how we tell and listen to stories. In so doing, we may also come to discover the power for enlightenment, as well as the power for manipulation, embedded in audiovisual communication.

In some ways, the central challenge to human cognition (or information processing) is, in the words of political scientist Doris Graber, "taming the information tide" (Graber 1988). Our brains are constantly bombarded with an overwhelming array of stimuli. Fortunately, much of the brain's work can be set on "autopilot," as it were, such as the control of basic functions like breathing. But even in the limited sphere of political thinking, the information tide can be quite daunting. With so many issues and so many sides to each issue, how can one ever find meaning through the madness?

Perhaps the most fundamental way our brains can approach excessive information is to search for patterns and compare them with those already stored in our memory. Once a pattern or form has been recognized, our brains can engage in what cognitive scientists refer to as "top-down" or "wholistic" processing. In short, as Graber notes, "people create and store mental maps, which serve as the general guidelines for reconstructing specific types of events" (Graber 2001:15). These maps or forms (also known as "schema") speed up perception and help us to reconstruct and interpret the details of the information being processed. When information appears to fit an existing map, our brains can process it quickly and with little effort.

The key to understanding how political advertising works is to recognize that many of the cognitive maps that viewers use to process campaign communication are drawn not just from our stores of knowledge about politics, but also, in very important ways, from our stores of knowledge about popular culture. Using our rather extensive knowledge of popular culture to guide our political thinking is an example of a process political scientist Samuel Popkin describes as "low-information rationality." He writes:

> Despite the many kinds of information voters acquire in daily life, there are large gaps in their knowledge about government and politics. To overcome these limitations they use shortcuts. (Popkin 1994:44)

He indicates that these shortcuts can be based on past experiences, daily life, the media, and political campaigns. Popkin is writing in the context of the process by which voters decide whom to cast the ballots for, a task which compels at least some attention, increasing the likelihood of more conscious effort. In processing political advertising, however, that incentive is muted. To make sense of the political commercials we see on television, our stored memories of all the other programming on television provides a readily accessible and powerful cognitive shortcut. If a candidate can use evocative audiovisuals to successfully tap into our extensive catalogs of cultural knowledge, a picture, story, or soundtrack can literally be worth a thousand words.

The appeal of invoking associations drawn from popular culture was not lost on George H. Bush's advisors in 1988 when they considered what turned out to be one of the most important phrases the vice president would ever utter. In August, Bush's speechwriting team was sharply divided over whether to include in his acceptance speech at the Republican National Convention the now infamous line, "Read my lips: no new taxes!" "Read my lips" was a catch-phrase of the hyper-macho action-film hero, "Dirty Harry" Callahan, played by actor Clint Eastwood. "Stupid and irresponsible," argued Richard Darman, who had been designated editor-in-chief of the speech. Speechwriter Peggy Noonan admonished the informal speech committee: "Whatever you guys do, don't screw with these lines." Darman claimed that huge budget deficits would be a drag on the economy and that the no taxes pledge would make governing very difficult. Ultimately, what media advisor Roger Ailes called the "Clint Eastwood factor" prevailed: politics for Ailes was theater, Bush needed to bury forever the "wimp factor," and mimicking Dirty Harry would do it (Woodward 1992).

By merely aping the language of a familiar Hollywood icon, the vice president was able to activate a deep web of preexisting associations in his audience. Campaign ads can do this even more effectively, by using audio, visual, and narrative elements to tap viewers' cognitive maps, literally evoking entire neural networks in our brains to communicate campaign themes with emotional force. Consider the ad the Bush campaign created in 1988 to dramatize the risks of the Massachusetts prison furlough program (titled "Revolving Door"), which possessed the audiovisual conventions typically found in popular horror stories. It featured an eerie and ominous soundtrack, including "slasher" sound effects and foreboding musical scoring. It used dark black-and-white visuals to underscore its disturbing storyline. Viewers of "Revolving Door" are literally invited by the evocative audiovisuals to attach the associations with horror stories they have stored in their memories to the Massachusetts furlough policy. And so it is that a dry tale of public policy can be turned into a frightening thirty-second trailer for the "nightmare on Elm Street" that America would face if Bush's opponent were to become president. In 2004, a different Bush (George W.) would evoke a different fear (of terrorism) by drawing upon the audiovisual conventions of a different popular genre (the action/suspense thriller) to score points against a different Massachusetts Democrat (Senator John F. Kerry), with similar effects. Bush ads, adopting the look and feel of the Fox action-thriller series *24*, drew upon viewers' existing associations with the anti-terror exploits of Special Agent Jack Bauer facing down terrifying threats that require a steely determination to do *whatever it takes* to keep America safe to contrast Bush and his opponent.

If campaign ads rely on the audiovisual conventions of popular culture for much of their persuasive effect, what does this say about informed citizens and electoral democracy? At first glance, it would appear nothing much good. Indeed, such a view would be consistent with much of the academic research literature on public opinion in general. The indictment against campaign spots, however, goes further. Not only do political ads contribute little to informing citizens, critics say, but the most negative of them actually drive people away from politics.

Perhaps this is to confuse the medium with the message. In fact, the evidence that negative advertising discourages citizens from voting or political engagement is sketchy at best. Some studies suggest negative ads can *increase* voter turnout and citizen engagement. More to the point, the brief against negative advertising points to a deeper current in our political culture: a profound unease with the emotional bases of politics. In essence, this current runs, if there is anything worse than an uninformed voter, it is an emotional voter.

The rationale behind this position is reasonable enough. Emotions, so the argument goes, cloud judgment. Yet beneath this analysis is a common but false assumption: that emotion and intelligence are incompatible. Graber (2001:36) notes that emotions are a common trigger for thoughts (and vice versa) and cites several studies indicating that the connection between emotions and reasoning is much closer than previously thought (Blakeslee 1994, Damasio 1994, LeDoux 1996). Emotions, Graber argues, do not cloud reasoning; in fact, they are a vital part of the ability to reason (Graber 2001:36, citing Sniderman et al. 1991; Damasio 1994 and Marcus, Neuman, and MacKuen 2000).

Abandoning the bias against the emotional underpinnings of politics invites us to begin anew our assessment of the potential of audiovisual campaign communication. It may very well be that up to this point, political communicators have used political advertising in ways that leave much to be desired. Yet the inherent potential of the medium is much greater. If we allow for this possibility, we may be taken down very different paths in our explorations of mass communication and democracy. This book is a beginning step in that direction.

Chapter 1 explores the ways popular culture can frame political communication. A brief tour through some of the cultural referents found in campaign spots in the recent past reveals the contours of our changing political concerns. Viewing political advertising through the lens of popular culture may improve the way scholars approach and categorize campaign spots, providing insights that more clinical approaches may lack.

Chapter 2 probes more deeply into the cognitive underpinnings of political information processing. Exploratory data from small-group experiments are used to illustrate the ways that the generic evocation of popular culture can affect the way people think about the ads they see. This data documents an intriguing indicator of top-down or wholistic processing: the way people embellish their reconstructions of an ad with details that fit quite well with the generic form but which were actually not present in the ad itself. People remember seeing things that weren't there because they fit with the recognizable pattern their brains used as a shortcut in information processing. The exploratory data also suggest that audiovisuals can both draw upon the existing patterns of associations in our minds and help shape or activate new patterns of associations.

Chapter 3 addresses the driving concept behind much of the academic literature on campaign advertising (and a good deal of public disdain as well): negativity. This concept is fundamentally flawed as an analytical tool—in part because it is actually quite difficult to distinguish ads simply in terms of the positive/negative dichotomy. More importantly, the pursuit of negative advertising is a project that does not lead to politically useful insights. Negative or attack politics not only has been with us since the nation's founding, but it is in fact one of democracy's most cherished expressive freedoms. While there may be much to criticize in contemporary campaign commercials, negativity does not warrant the sustained focus it has enjoyed over the past two decades.

Chapter 4 considers alternative ways that analysts, especially journalists, can more productively approach political advertising. The ad watch journalism that has emerged to police the content of campaign ads can be enhanced in two ways. More serious attention to audiovisuals would bring into focus key elements of campaign communication that often remain underappreciated. Emphasizing the broad patterns of policy and performance of candidates and parties (rather than dwelling on the technical errors or exaggerations that seem to obsess many journalists during the course of political campaigns), would better assist voters with their fundamental responsibilities and stem the tide of petty criticism that helps sour the public on politics. Journalists should help citizens by putting the pieces of the puzzle together, not cut the puzzle up into smaller and smaller pieces.

Chapter 5 revisits the presidential campaign of 2000, noting how the carefully choreographed use of audiovisual imagery allowed the Bush–Cheney campaign to relentlessly tar Vice President Al Gore with the stain of scandal that viewers associated with Bill Clinton, all the while never explicitly mentioning Clinton's name. Bush's ads also appropriated some of the very techniques devised to help broadcast journalists visually critique campaign advertising in their attacks on Gore.

Chapter 6 examines political advertising in a time of terror, exploring the systematic juxtaposition of fear and aggressive foreign policy that have come to define the Bush years. Scholars have suggested that terror invites a pattern of cognitive and emotional response, and notably, a fear of "others." In 2002, Senator Max Cleland (D-GA), a Vietnam War hero who lost three limbs overseas, was attacked in ads for being weak on national security. The same script would be deployed in 2004 against Vietnam vet John Kerry with decisive effect by the infamous "Swift Boat Veterans for Truth" ads. Even terror, however, would not completely displace the long-standing uber-narrative of otherness in America, race. From Karl Rove's 2002 experiments in "narrowcasting" to rural white males in Georgia (fanning racial resentment over the confederate battle flag's removal from the Georgia state flag) to the GOP's 2006 attacks on Senate candidate Harold Ford (raising the specter of miscegenation), the politics of race remain alive and well in the age of terror.

Chapter 7 confronts the central issues in democratic politics that the first five chapters of the book raise. A better understanding of how political advertising works is part of a larger effort to place campaign communication in the context of mass democracy in a twenty-first-century republic. Despite the desires of many well-intentioned reformers, the notion of American politics as driven fundamentally by a deeply engaged and informed citizenry is at odds with both the design of the constitutional framers and with the population's limited capacity for political involvement. Seen in this light, most of the fundamental criticisms leveled at campaign advertising do not warrant the degree of concern with which they are frequently imbued. In fact, vigorous audiovisual campaign communication performs a critical role in linking citizens and government, and is more worthy of celebration than condemnation.

America is a diverse country, and people are going to disagree. It is also a free country, and people will express their views, often with great passion. It is also a democratic country, where the people must make choices about government. Campaign advertising, from the coarse to the elegant, is not something that Americans need view with horror, shrink from, or view with disdain. It is, in fact, part of our essential legacy as a free and democratic people in an age of audiovisual communication.

NOTES

1. In the short story "Silver Blaze," by Sir Arthur Conan Doyle, Holmes solves a mystery by deducing that a dog in the barn where a crime occurred must have known the intruder because the dog didn't bark.

2. The narrative and quotations regarding Charlie Crist's ad in the preceding paragraphs are drawn from Rado 2000 and March 2000. Governor Bush's official margin of victory (537 votes) rested upon a combination of (1) a minimum net gain of 245 votes through illegal absentee ballots (thousands of other illegal absentee ballots had been corrected by local Republican officials); (2) the fact that even though *tens of thousands* more Floridians left the polls believing they had cast votes for Vice President Al Gore, vote disqualifications (owing to factors including poor ballot design, defective voting machinery, and a lack of poll workers) were decisively more common in Gore strongholds than in areas that largely supported Bush; and (3) a net to Bush of 435 votes from the favorable decisions of state and local officials during the recount process. (On Sunday, November 26, Republican Secretary of State Katherine Harris refused to include the results of Palm Beach County's manual recount of ballots which had netted Gore 215 votes because they arrived shortly after 7:00 P.M., missing her 5:00 P.M. deadline, and also excluded the results of a partial recount in Miami-Dade County that netted Gore 168 votes; the Republican canvassing board in Nassau County reported as official their original vote count, not the results of the machine recount as mandated by Florida law, netting Bush 52 votes. Had illegal absentee ballots been excluded, as they had been during previous elections, the mandatory machine recount in Nassau County included, and had the valid votes identified in the manual recounts not been excluded by Ms. Harris, Gore would have won by 143 votes.) Gore supporters could find bitter irony in the fact that while Bush prevailed before the United States Supreme Court in arguing that the different standards in different counties would violate his rights under the equal protection clause of the Fourteenth Amendment, on the ground Bush operatives were *encouraging* local officials to employ different standards in different counties in the treatment of absentee ballots (pressuring them to reject ballots in Gore counties identical to those they argued should be accepted in Bush counties—including rejecting *military* ballots in Gore areas). Indeed, media recounts of all Florida ballots indicate that if illegal absentee ballots (as identified by the *New York Times*) were excluded and a single, statewide standard was used to count the ballots, *Gore would have won no matter what standard was used.* (See especially Barbanel and Fessenden 2000 on voting machinery; Barstow and Van Natta 2001 on absentee ballots; Calmes and Foldessy 2001, and Fessenden and Broder 2001 on the media recounts; see also Kellner 2001.)

Chapter One

Communicating Culture: Audiovisuals in Campaign Advertising

This book seeks to advance a handful of claims about political advertising and American politics. The first is that political advertising is very effective at telling the stories of American politics. This is principally a function of how our brains work, how our culture works, and how we understand politics. Against the ideal concept of a reasonably informed, rational voter, politics through audiovisual storytelling may seem to leave much to be desired. It is important to keep in mind, however, that America's founders did not rest their vision of popular government on so demanding an ideal as the reasonably informed rational voter. They deliberately insulated citizens from government through representative institutions. In this context, politics through audiovisual storytelling may begin to appear far less disturbing, perhaps even appropriate, and worthy of the celebration of a free people.

The first step on our journey will be to consider the audiovisual threads of American culture. From these threads are woven the stories of American politics: stories that are told, heard, and envisioned so easily because they resonate so deeply, even for those who have little formal knowledge of government and politics. The key to understanding why this is so is appreciation of the familiar forms that comprise the tapestries of popular culture. These forms are collections of narrative and audiovisual elements that, when they occur together, our brains can recognize as part of a larger family of meaning. Such recognition is the material from which effective political communication can be sewn. The narrative and audiovisual conventions of popular forms of culture and entertainment are extremely attractive to political communicators because they embrace meanings and understandings already shared by ordinary citizens. These conventional understandings are the linchpins of what culture and film critics call genre.[1]

Arthur Asa Berger defines genre as "a type of text characterized by a particular style, such as soap opera, news show, sports program, horror show or detective story" (Berger 1995a:174; see also Berger 1992).[2] In visual media, genres are characterized by several reinforcing stimuli, where the music, sound effects, rhythms, and tones of narration exist in synergistic combination. More importantly, as Berger notes, "we quickly learn the conventions of a genre and expect to find them" (Berger 1995a:45). Viewers come to recognize what the pictures "should be," from their sense of how an announcer's voice sounds and how the music goes. Viewers of a horror story, for example, are aware of imminent danger as the musical score becomes tenser and the scene darkens, even before the monster appears, because they know how the pieces fit together. Similarly, a sparse, high-tech soundtrack combined with an appropriate narrative can evoke science fiction and the future. Words, sounds, and pictures work together in evoking a "genre." These are the shared audiovisual conventions of popular culture in our time.

It is because of this that an ad like the "Revolving Door" spot produced for George H. Bush's 1988 campaign can so effectively create a sinister impression of Michael Dukakis's crime policies: it virtually placed him in the starring role of a thirty-second slasher film, replete with ominous and foreboding musical scoring, dark visual imagery, and horrifying sound effects. Leo Braudy, the contemporary American film and literary critic, described genre this way:

> Genre films affect their audience especially by their ability to express the warring traditions in society and the social importance of understanding convention. The genre film lures its audience into a seemingly familiar world, filled with reassuring stereotypes of character, action and plot. . . . Because of the existence of generic expectations—how a plot "should" work, what a stereotyped character "should" do, what a gesture, a location, an allusion, a line of dialogue "should" mean—the genre film can step beyond the moment of its existence and play against its own history. (Braudy 1985: 416–17)

At one or another level, generic evocation is one of those things that "everybody knows." It is not surprising, then, that political advertisements often invoke genres to convey their messages or achieve other effects (Nelson 1993; Richardson 1995). Indeed, for an analysis based in genres to provide valuable insights into the nature and meaning of campaign spots, it is not even necessary that admakers be consciously aware of generic conventions as such. When they think about how they can best convey the themes they want to communicate, their sense of what looks and sounds "right" is likely to be shaped by the same pervasive cultural expectations (based on genre) that the viewing audience shares—whether they recognize it as a formal set of conventions or not.[3]

In certain ways, the idea that televised political advertising is driven by the conventions of television and film seems obvious. Yet, for several very understandable reasons, one of the central conventions of television—that meaning is derived not merely from individual audio and visual components but in the way they fit together—has largely eluded students of political advertising.

In part, this may be a function of the analytical enterprise itself. Scholars are taught to break complicated phenomena up into their component parts in order to better analyze them. Yet, even if doing so runs the risk of, as the aphorism suggests, failing to "see the forest for the trees," there are even deeper reasons why analysts have overlooked the audiovisual elements of campaign advertising. Audiovisual information is frequently seen as aesthetic or poetic in nature, rather than logical. Poetics, almost by definition, elude logical analysis. And politics, especially, is often seen as too important to be determined by such elusive considerations. This is not to suggest that scholars have failed to study persuasion. They have done so with great force. But even here, the presumption has been that persuasion grounded in aesthetics or emotion is somehow less true than persuasion governed by pure reason. If we trace both of these threads—the analytical impulse to break things into parts to study them and the suspicion of emotional persuasion—back to their point of origin, we find ourselves face to face with the great ancient Greek philosopher Aristotle. John S. Nelson and G. R. Boynton (1997:207) summarize the point this way:

> Aristotle addressed musical aspects of persuasion only as a matter of the vocal pitch and rhythm in delivering speeches. Then he separated story and drama as topics for poetics, rather than rhetorics. His famous theory is that dramas (and stories?) practice and purge our passions (in catharsis) by giving the audience a vicarious experience of events plus their attendant emotions. By purging passions, dramas can make us ready for rational persuasion, but they play no legitimate part in persuasion as such. Western rhetoricians mostly follow Aristotle in these matters.

From Aristotle forward, then, students of political communication have been inclined to focus their efforts on what Aristotle considered the "substance" of communication (its facts and logics) rather than those things he saw as "accessory." In terms of political advertising, researchers have created a large body of work probing the effects of "negative" (as opposed to "positive") advertisements and a slightly less sizeable effort to examine differences in "issue" and "image" advertising. A smaller but hardy body of work has explicitly examined audiovisual production techniques and styles, and it is to this work that we now turn.[4]

Scholars have long recognized that the audiovisual and narrative components of campaign spots were important in how ads conveyed meaning (Jamieson 1984; Kaid and Davidson 1986; Kern 1989; West 1997). Among the individual elements that have attracted academic interest are camera angles, music, editing techniques and special effects (Kaid and Davidson 1986), facial and kinesic codes, iconology and mythology, colors, spaces, and light (Biocca 1991b). Yet, in general, those who have shown the greatest sensitivity to the nuances of audiovisual production have isolated production techniques and have not dealt with the wholistic way they evoke associations (see for example Kepplinger 1991).

Frank Biocca is an astute analyst of political communication and political advertising in particular. He goes further than most when he discusses the "orchestration of codes and discourses" in political advertising and acknowledges that processing is "somewhat holistic (parallel)." Still, he offers an analytically segmented rather than wholistic perspective. He suggests that "each item in a commercial has certain semantic features," and that viewers "decode" scenes in an ad by identifying individual signs among the many codes present in the scene, deriving a "momentary meaning" (Biocca 1991b:67). While no doubt true in a technical sense, perhaps if viewers actually saw themselves as engaged in "decoding" an ad by identifying individual "signs" and "codes" to derive "momentary meanings," Biocca's depiction would ring more true. In his zeal to relate the way viewers respond to political ads to the language of technical semantics and semiotics, Biocca's emphasis seems a bit misplaced, losing the substance for real viewers in the quest for an ideal process.

He moves closer to the mark in discussing how viewers frame an ad's message. For Biocca, ads provide a semantic frame through one of five types of linkages: contextual, classificatory, oppositional, causal and narrative, and metaphoric and hierarchial links. Yet presumably all of the above can occur within a given ad, leaving a viewer with quite a large plate of information processing to digest. And left unacknowledged is where viewers obtain the ability to "decode" such semantic linkages in the first place. Consider, for example, Biocca's discussion of the 1988 Bush campaign's attempt to combat the "wimp factor."

> Bush started appearing in political ads or in news bites talking "tough" and engaging in rugged outdoor sports—Bush at the helm of a speed boat, Bush the jogger, Bush "kicking the ass" of Dan Rather in their infamous live news confrontation. Ads depicted Bush "the oilman" and Bush "the young fighter pilot." (Biocca 1991b:65)

Perhaps it is so obvious as to be overlooked, but why did these alternative presentations of Bush so resonate with ordinary citizens? It is because they were so thoroughly grounded in popular culture. Viewers already possessed the cultural knowledge necessary to attach to the images the associations the Bush ads sought to evoke.

One particularly telling example from the 1988 campaign illustrates how evocation of popular genres conveys meaning and how other analytical approaches fail to fully describe how ads work. "Tank Ride" is one of the most famous political commercials, memorable almost entirely because of its satirical portrayal of Michael Dukakis in a tank. Analysts focusing exclusively on the policy claims of an ad (as many practitioners of ad watch journalism did in this case) would completely overlook the ad's satire and effect on viewers.

The ad featured video footage of Dukakis in a tank that was motoring around the General Dynamics tank facility in Sterling Heights, Michigan. Dukakis had hoped to dramatize his support for strengthening conventional weapons such as tanks, in contrast to the Reagan–Bush policy of neglecting conventional forces in favor of building up strategic nuclear weapons. Instead, reporters viewed the tank ride as indicative of a desperate candidate who had to struggle with an image of being soft on defense. Thus, Dukakis's tank ride was ridiculed in the media while Bush's own tank ride photo-ops were not subject to the same searing interpretations. Bush was ahead in the polls, and the media's focus on strategy and the "horse-race" between the two candidates colored the reporting (Jamieson 1992a:4–5).

Soon, Bush began running an ad featuring the footage of Dukakis in the tank. The ad's policy claims eventually drew scrutiny from reporters, who noted that three of the charges were false. Dukakis did not oppose "virtually every defense system we developed"; he opposed two, not four weapons systems (the MX and Midgetman); he did not oppose the Stealth bomber (Jamieson 1992a:7). For most viewers, however, the ad's charges were not what stuck with them. Instead, it was the audiovisual images of Dukakis and the tank.

Biocca considers the audiovisual elements, but in his quest for the microsopic "units of meaning" he fails to correctly spot the wholistic way the ad works.

> The footage of Dukakis looking self-conscious and foolish, rolling about aimlessly and playing tank commander, is overlayed by a serious male voice listing all the military items that Dukakis had opposed. An additional layer of meaning was provided by the sound of a tank engine noisily shifting gears and sputtering. In this case the interaction between the codes of the audio and video track provides contrast and irony. (Biocca 1991b:77)

By focusing only on the "interaction between the codes" Biocca arrives at an erroneous assessment of the ad (it is more precisely satire than irony) while imparting meaning to the visual images ("foolish," "aimless") without elaborating the context necessary for these semantic linkages.

These are not negligible matters. There is a meaningful difference between satire, with its connotation of ridicule, and irony, with its connotation of detachment. A key component to how such communication occurs, moreover, is not acknowledged. The reason the components of "Tank Ride" combine or "interact" to create the impression of foolishness is that ordinary viewers have learned to recognize the sound, rhythm, and pacing of satire from popular culture. It's not that there is some inherent meaning in the sound of a tank sputtering or even the image of a politician interacting with the sound of a sputtering tank. Describing this as mere interaction underestimates the wholistic way in which such combinations reverberate with the shared narrative and audiovisual conventions of popular genres with which viewers are already familiar. Over the years, I have had the opportunity to talk with audiences across the country about this ad. Invariably, almost no one remembers the specific charges made by the "serious" male narrator. What almost everyone remembers is the ad's satirical portrayal of Michael Dukakis.

Genres draw upon the conventions, associations, and understandings that permeate our culture. In ads, they are the most notable manifestations of "the social construction of reality" (Berger and Luckmann 1966). As such, they provide the student of political advertising with a powerful yet accessible tool for understanding the substantive meaning of campaign spots. Genres communicate to audiences precisely because audiences know what the package of conventional associations stands for. And unlike arguments, that package spans both logic and emotion. A genre approach to campaign spots invites us to explore the ways in which visual images, aural cues, and narrative combine in culturally conventional fashion to convey substantive meaning, meaning that is often found beneath the surface veneer of political argumentation and in the deep grains of unspoken cultural knowledge. Such meaning must be at the core of what Judith Trent and Robert Friedenberg (1991) call the "only important reason to categorize types of political commercials": "to gain some understanding of their rhetorical purpose."

Veteran admaker Bill Hillsman pointed to the power of popular culture in political advertising in an interview with *Insight* magazine. Hillsman had prepared a 1998 ad for Jesse Ventura, candidate for governor of Minnesota, which was styled as an ad for a new action figure toy. "New from the Reform Party!" begins the narrator. Two young boys are seen outdoors running toward a Ventura doll standing on the leafy ground in between a miniature American flag and a Minnesota state flag. They shout "Yeah!" as they drop to the ground to place their heads at eye level with the bald-headed doll in a suit and tie. "It's the new Jesse Ventura action figure," continues the narrator. "You can make Jesse battle special interest groups. . . ." The child holding the Ventura doll gently shakes it as if to animate its speech while saying, "I don't want your stupid money." ". . . And party politics," says the narrator. The other child, holding another doll, says, "We politicians have powers the average man can't comprehend." Then the narrator continues, "You can also make Jesse lower taxes, improve public education and fight for the things Minnesotans really care about." The camera shows one of the boys holding the Ventura doll at a miniature podium with a gavel in its hand. "This bill wastes taxpayer money! Re-draft it!" Then the narrator says, "Don't waste your vote on politics as usual," as a graphic with Ventura's name and picture appears on the screen. "Vote Reform Party candidate Jesse Ventura for Governor." (See figure 1.1.)

"It took Ventura two-and-a-half seconds to approve the action-figure ad," Hillsman told *Insight*. "Unlike many other candidates," Hillsman said, "Ventura understands popular culture and knew this would resonate with the public" (Edwards 2000). The key to that resonance is the shared generic knowledge of action figure toy advertising. Subtly, the ad invites viewers to associate the genre's emphasis on

Narrator: New, from the Reform Party! It's the new Jesse Ventura Action Figure.
Kids: Yeah!

Narrator: You can also make Jesse lower taxes, improve public education and fight for the things Minnesotans really care about.

Child: This bill wastes taxpayer money. Re-draft it!

Figure 1.1. Jesse Ventura Action-Figure Ad (1998). Photos courtesy of North Woods Advertising

super-heroic traits with candidate Ventura—himself a former pro-wrestler. That it does so with disarming humor only enhances the ad's effectiveness. Ventura's election was widely seen as one of the biggest political upsets of the year.

Of course generic evocation is hardly the only effective way campaign ads can communicate their messages, and not all political ads use the genres of popular culture to communicate with viewers. The fact that so many ads don't resonate culturally, however, is one reason that admaker Hillsman believes that most political ads today aren't effective. "They are filmed with poor equipment and are not creative, so the average American leaves the room when political ads come on," he told *Insight* (Edwards 2000). Genre-based appeals cannot only draw viewers in with recognizable production values, but they can also connect with preexisting understandings in the audience.

Not only can recognition of how genres work offer insight into why certain political ads work, but examining incongruent generic appeals can also help explain why other ads were *not* effective. A number of Dukakis ads in 1988, for example, may have been inept because of their pairing two opposing generic evocations in the same thirty-second spot. In each of these ads, the first part used the audiovisual conventions of horror to portray George Bush, while the second part employed bright colors and upbeat music to portray Michael Dukakis. The jarring incongruence of the pairing caused the ads to fall flat in effectively communicating a coherent theme (Nelson and Boynton 1997:82–83). It is possible to evoke a genre very quickly. If the proper elements are present, it can easily be done in a matter of seconds. But while viewers might readily recognize a succession of three-second video clips by genre, a series of such clips, each evoking a different genre, would translate into an unfamiliar and incomprehensible whole, leaving viewers with little to structure their interpretation of the ad's message.

Some might see the Dukakis ads as product comparisons. If this was the intention, however, the ads could have much more effectively embraced the type of audiovisual conventions that would underscore comparison. A Bush ad from the same campaign ("Crime Quiz II"), for example, juxtaposed side-by-side pictures of each candidate with a narrator posing questions such as "which candidate opposed the death penalty?" The Dukakis picture would then be "pulled" forward and enlarged on the screen, visually reinforcing the comparative claim. No such explicitly comparative visual grammar marked the Dukakis ads.

The incongruence of generic evocations was not lost upon musician Bruce Springsteen, whose 1980s rock anthem "Born in the U.S.A." attracted the attention of Ronald Reagan's 1984 reelection team. The campaign sought to convey the sense of the reawakened pride of the nation, and the song's chorus refrain seemed to capture that well. Yet the song's bright, up-tempo rock beat and power riffs belied its narrative of a down-and-out Vietnam vet. The soldier, who was "born in the U.S.A.," endured an abusive childhood and got into a "hometown jam" that led to his service in Vietnam, where he was sent "to kill the yellow man." He returns home, is unable to find work, and relives the memories of his fallen brothers in arms. In the end, he is left with "nowhere to run" and "nowhere to go . . . born in the U.S.A."

In the late 1990s, Springsteen released a far more haunting version of the song that featured only the singer and his acoustic guitar, sounding much like folk singer Woody Guthrie during the Great Depression. That version would definitely not have been attractive to President Reagan's campaign.

In contrast, the Fund for a Conservative Majority did find appropriate musical scoring for the Reagan ad it sponsored: Lee Greenwood's "Proud to Be an American." The song and the ad effectively captured the resurgent pride and "retro" orientation Reagan sought to communicate. Indeed, the broad narratives of American politics over the past two decades can be discerned in some of the shifting generic referents in campaign spots. In 1988, the Bush–Quayle team used the popular genres of horror and dystopia through spots such as "Revolving Door," (Boston) "Harbor," and "New Jersey at Risk," to blast Michael Dukakis on crime and the environment, while also countering his claims of competence. "Revolving Door" (the Bush campaign's prison furlough ad) evoked the genre of horror through stark black-and-white pictures of prison watchtowers matched to the soundtrack of a slasher film. "Harbor" also used the conventions of horror, including ominous and foreboding music, stark visual imagery, and a tone of narration and narrative strongly consistent with horror. In 1992, the Bush team reprised many of these same themes in the dystopia "Arkansas," which featured a barren landscape and ominous storm clouds to signal the imminent danger of Clintonism.

In 1994, the genre of tabloid TV news, with its emphasis on the salacious and the scandalous, had become recognizable enough that evocation of its generic form powerfully communicated the charges of womanizing, fraternizing with drug dealers, and not telling the truth in Oliver North's attack on rival Charles Robb's character in the Virginia U.S. Senate race. In 1996, Richard A. Zimmer, Republican candidate for the U.S. Senate in New Jersey, aired an ad designed to look like a conventional television newscast. It featured a news anchor reading copy (including "Fox news reports that . . .") charging his opponent with corruption and mob association, grafting onto his ad the credibility of local news.

Also during 1996, a Pat Buchanan ad used the "real-life" look and feel of the TV show "Cops" to evoke fear and urgency over the dark side of illegal immigration. Had viewers not been familiar with the herky-jerky camera motion and night vision imagery, the ad would have appeared to be some weird, poorly produced creation. Instead, it tapped the credibility of law enforcement, attaching greater legitimacy to Buchanan's plea.

In the 1996 presidential campaign, the Clinton–Gore team's strategic focus on "soccer moms" and suburban voters found a powerful voice in the adoption of the generic form of family melodrama (a type of program often seen on the Lifetime TV network), which was used to portray "Dole–Gingrich" as the sinister threat to family life and Bill Clinton as the caring and benevolent father figure (conveniently countering charges of Clinton's own character flaws). The ad (I call "Protecting Our Values") employed the same genre conventions (including melancholy solo piano to underscore the threat and bright soft focus—to underscore benevolence) as an actual melodrama (in which the President made a cameo appearance) that aired during the winter following the campaign on the Family and Medical Leave Act. The '96 Clinton–Gore campaign offered its own take on the leave act in an ad featuring an emotional plea in support of the legislation by an ordinary family done in the style of a TV talk-show testimonial. By evoking the genre of family melodrama (tales of abused children, alcoholic parents, and so on), "Protecting Our Values" could combine both threat and response in a way that Bush's earlier "Grandchildren" ad (which combined a soundtrack of swelling strings with soft focus close-ups of a family picnic) could not. This proved especially useful in dodging charges of "negative" campaigning that clung to the more one-dimensional Dole spots.

The Ventura ad described earlier is difficult to analyze save in terms of genre. It featured two children playing with action figures (Jesse Ventura and "Special Interest Man"). An awareness of cartoon action dramas allows one to favorably fill in the details the ad seeks to convey: that Mr. Ventura will be a heroic independent voice for Minnesota. Absent such knowledge, two children playing with dolls would seemingly fail to convey a political message at all.

The year 1998 also saw a clever third-party ad run during the California gubernatorial campaign that drew upon the irreverence of Comedy Central's *South Park* to convey the notion that major party candidates Gray Davis and Dan Lundgren were well-financed drones, mouthing the same bland political platitudes, and that Libertarian candidate Steve Kubby was a true alternative.[5] The ad begins with animated figures comprised of cut-out photos representing the Democratic and Republican nominees debating on a stage. Their faces appear in black and white and the cut-out images of their mouths bounce up and down to simulate speech. The voice-overs for the candidates reflect a typical *South Park* motif, an exaggerated sense of authority creating an undertone of silliness. "As governor, I'll reduce crime, educate your children and lower taxes," mouths Lundgren. "What?! If I were governor, I'd reduce taxes, educate your children, and lower crime," replies Davis. The *South Park* schoolchildren note the similarity between the statements of the two parties' nominees and bemoan the lack of choice. A color animation of Kubby then appears, entering the debate stage from the side. Lundgren asks, "How'd you get in here?" Davis adds, "You don't have $40 million!" Kubby then makes his pitch, emphasizing that people need choices in education, health care, and helping their communities. "Dude," says Stan, one of the children, "Kubby kicks ass!" Seated next to Stan is Kenny attached to an IV drip labeled "215" (the number of California's ballot initiative legalizing medical marijuana).[6] The Davis figure grabs one of Kenny's arms, saying sternly, "That medicine is not government approved." The Lundgren figure yanks on the IV, Kenny whimpers, a short beep is heard, and blood starts to pour out forming a puddle on the table in front of him. Kenny dies, which he usually does on episodes of *South Park*. "Oh my God!" says Kyle, "Lundgren and Davis killed Kenny." Normally, the words "those bastards" follow the identification of Kenny's killers on *South Park*. While those words are absent here, viewers familiar with the show's conventions might make that connection anyway. The ad's final frames shift to another child, Cartman, with the Kubby campaign website address superimposed below as he points to it and says, "Screw you guys, I'm voting for Steve Kubby." (See figure 1.2.)

For third-party candidates like Kubby, targeting younger voters makes some sense. Young voters typically have weaker attachments to the major parties; younger voters are also likely to be familiar with the *South Park* characters. The irreverence of *South Park* is a natural fit for Kubby's appeal to voters to dismiss the major party nominees.

In 2000, politicians sought to convey authenticity in their spots, and they did so by evoking the look and feel of home video or "real-life" TV, not infrequently staging the candidate at the proverbial kitchen table or on the living room couch. Such audiovisual conventions can be readily distinguished from those that evoke integrity—a related yet distinguishable theme also prominent in Campaign 2000. Senator John McCain's heroic biography (emphasizing his five years as a prisoner of war in Vietnam) proved an appealing antidote at a time when politicians have proven all too mortal.

Spoiler candidate Ralph Nader's advertising in the 2000 campaign

After hearing almost identical statements from the major party candidates for governor, Stan, a *South Park* student, complains about the lack of a real choice. "Dude! Didn't that other guy just say the same thing?"

"Hi, I'm Steve Kubby and I'm also running for governor. . . ." The sign on the podium in front of Davis reads, "Paid for by huge unions." The sign on Lundgren's podium reads "Paid for by huge corporations." Davis and Lundgren appear in black and white; Kubby is shown in color.

As Davis says, "That medicine is not government approved," Lundren pulls the green IV drip labeled "215" (the number for California's medical marijuana ballot initiative) out of Kenny's arm. Kenny slumps over and dies, as he does in virtually every episode of *South Park*.

Kyle says, "Oh my god! Lundgren and Davis killed Kenny." (Normally on *South Park*, Kenny's killers are identified, followed by the words "those bastards." Familiar viewers might draw that connection here even though the words are absent.) "Screw you guys," Cartman says, " I'm voting for Steve Kubby."

Figure 1.2. Kubby *South Park* Ad (1998)

also sought to convey integrity, though by harshly contrasting his opponents as tools of wealthy special interests and himself as the devoted protector of the public interest. Bill Hillsman, who created Jesse Ventura's 1998 advertising, produced a spot for Nader modeled after the long running and highly recognizable Mastercard corporate ad campaign, which would list a variety of emotionally endearing items and their prices (tickets to baseball games: $75.00, souvenir pennants for the kids: $35.00, their first hot dog at a ballgame: $15.00, etc.), then conclude with a tagline like, "the smile on their faces: priceless." Some things are priceless, the ad would tell us, "for everything else, there's Mastercard." Nader's ad begins with the sounds of a brass band playing "Hail to the Chief" and videotape of Governor Bush greeting a contributor at a fund-raiser, patting him on the back as the narrator says, "Grilled tenderloin for fund-raiser: $1000.00 dollars a plate" (the text is also superimposed over the images on the screen). Then the ad cuts to choppy video of Vice President Gore addressing a campaign rally that appears sped up at first, because of the somewhat ridiculous, hyperkinetic quality of the handclapping behind the vice president, then slowed down as Gore moves his head to emphasize his point. "Campaign ads filled with half-truths: $10 million." "Promises to special interest groups:" says the narrator as the video alternates between fund-raiser glad-handing by Bush and Gore, "over $10 billion." The sounds of "Hail to the Chief" grind to a halt as if the plug had been pulled. "Finding out the truth:" says the narrator as an image of a diligent Nader working at a small desk cluttered with paperwork appears, "priceless." "There are some things money can't buy," the narrator says, as the ad shifts to a fast-paced montage of video clips of Nader accompanied by a spirited drum-based techno soundtrack. Nader, the ad invites us to believe, is the real thing, priceless, just like the smiles on children's faces in the Mastercard ads are the real things, priceless.

One of the reasons why integrity was such a hot commodity in the 2000 campaign was that the media's incessant all-Monica, all-the-time bender (and to a lesser degree focus on other Clinton "scandals") had served to indelibly mark upon the public's memory a series of unflattering audiovisual, emotional, and narrative linkages. One GOP consultant remarked that press coverage of Clinton scandals amounted to the longest running negative ad in history. Televised images of tense White House press briefings, and alternatively scandalous, embarrassing, and revolting reports and revelations flickered across TV screens around the country. What the Bush–Cheney campaign was able to do in their ads was to visually graft this sordid and long-running national soap opera firmly onto viewers' associations with Al Gore, by placing Gore, when he appeared in Bush ads, in Clintonesque settings and always represented as being "on TV." In chapter 5, we will note how the Bush ads used the very techniques designed to help broadcast journalists produce their ad watch segments to link Gore with the dark side of Bill Clinton.

The 2002 congressional elections were the first national campaigns to occur after the attack of September 11, 2001. Some campaign ads that year featured images of Saddam Hussein and Osama bin Laden, but it would not be until 2004 that candidates would be able to draw upon generic audiovisual conventions made to order for the "global war on terror." Chapter 6 documents how Bush–Cheney ads evoked the audiovisual conventions of the Fox action-thriller 24 to convey their message of a nation facing formidable terror threats on the home front. Nor is it surprising that during a time of war, the generic form of military documentaries would appear in candidate ads. An ad aired by John Kerry's campaign during the run-up to the Iowa precinct caucuses featured Del Sandusky, a crewmate of Kerry's during the Vietnam War, describing how Kerry "saved our lives." Perhaps the most significant of all the ads in 2004, however, were the military documentary-styled spots produced by the "Swift Boat Veterans for Truth." Over time, the charges made by the "Swifties" would be largely discredited, but not before they had done lasting damage to the Kerry–Edwards campaign.

The 2008 presidential campaign was well under way by the summer of 2007 when a series of "viral videos" began circulating across the Internet. The first to draw major attention was titled "Vote Different," a take-off on Apple Computer's "1984" spot (based on George Orwell's dystopia of the same name). In "Vote Different," however, it was not big brother but Hillary Clinton projected on the telescreens. The ad cleverly played off the Clinton reputation for smooth, well-oiled political machines and placed Barack Obama squarely as the candidate of change. When the "Obama Girl" music video also went "viral," it signaled the dawn of an era when candidates would be less able than ever to fully control the way they were portrayed in the public eye. Attempting to stay current, Hillary Clinton released a web ad reproducing the ending series-ending scene from HBO's *The Sopranos*, with Bill and Hillary in the roles of Tony and Carmela. Even in the "new" media, generic evocation continues to prove an extremely attractive approach for political campaigners.

The great contribution of generic analysis lies in providing analysts an effective tool with which to discern and interpret the meaning of campaign spots. Yet this interpretive project carries with it a measure of complexity and ambiguity. For while scholars have presented precise definitions of what a genre is, reality does not prove quite so tidy. Not only may the various components of a specific genre be found (in isolation) in different generic forms, the very boundaries of genre are fluid and permeable. Jacques Derrida put it this way in "The Law of Genre": "every text participates in one or several genres, . . . yet such participation never amounts to belonging" (Derrida 1980). Multiple, subjective, and even potentially contradictory realities may be irritants to the social science project (Simons 1978). The serious limits to neat and tidy demarcations that might facilitate our academic projects but that ultimately prove inconsistent with reality must be acknowledged. Viewer response to political advertising is itself complicated and contradictory, and this necessarily constrains our analytic endeavors. It does not, however, preclude them. Viewers recognize genres, and ultimately it is more what they do with them than what researchers say about them that is politically relevant. Within the context of specific audiences and environments, viewing political advertising through the lens of genre can be used in conjunction with other approaches to provide a fuller understanding of the nature and meaning of political advertising. To illustrate this, let us turn to the issue of taxonomy.

In order to illustrate how a genre approach can offer enhanced description and categorization of campaign spots, I have selected nine advertisements from various campaigns since 1988. Each of these ads meets the criteria for prominent ads defined by Jamieson (1992b) and applied by West (1997): newsworthy, flamboyant, entertaining or effective. The ads do not exhaust the population of prominent ads since 1988, but they are well known and serve to illustrate a range of generic forms.

Five classificatory schemes can be found in the extant literature. I have attempted to code each ad by each approach. Table 1.1 summarizes the results. Virtually all of the ads are what many call "negative," though Perot's "Purple Heart" ad and Ventura's "Jesse Ventura Action Figure" did not fit into any of the classifications offered by Johnson-Cartee and Copeland (whose focus was exclusively negative ads) so I have labeled those cells not applicable (n/a). Criteria for genre categories were informed by an extensive literature on genre.[7]

Each of the typologies brings something important to bear on the study of political advertising. West's categories alert us to the relative

Table 1.1. Selected Campaign Ads and Academic Typologies Compared with Popular Genres

Ad	West	Gronbeck	Kern	Johnson-Cartee and Copeland	Devlin	Genre
"Revolving Door" (Bush–Quayle 1988)	specific domestic policy	assaultive	fear-unpleasant	transfer (events that happened on your watch)	negative	horror
"Tank Ride" (Bush–Quayle 1988)	specific foreign policy	assaultive	uncertainty	being your own worst enemy (voting record)	visual	satire
"Tongues Untied" (Buchanan 1992)	specific domestic policy	assaultive	anger	transfer (events that happened on your watch)	negative	pornography
"Arkansas" (Bush–Quayle 1992)	domestic performance	assaultive	uncertainty	transfer (events that happened on your watch)	negative	dystopia
"Purple Heart" (Perot 1992)	personal qualities	implicative	trust	n/a	testimonial	testimonial
"Character Counts" (North VA Senate 1994)	personal qualities	assaultive	guilt	being your own worst enemy (political character)	negative	tabloid TV scandal
"Protect Our Values" (Clinton–Gore 1996)	domestic performance	comparative	anger	being your own worst enemy (voting record)	negative	family melodrama
"The Stakes" (Dole–Kemp 1996)	specific domestic policy	assaultive	fear-unpleasant	transfer (events that happened on your watch)	negative	altered states (drugs)
"Jesse Ventura" (Ventura MN Governor 1998)	personal qualities	implicative	trust	n/a	production idea	action hero

Note: Typologies were applied by the author and are based on the following sources: West 1997; Gronbeck 1994; Kern 1989; Johnson-Cartee and Copeland 1991; and Devlin 1986.

emphasis on domestic and foreign policy as well as on candidates' personal qualities. Gronbeck's tripartite typology of negative ads is most useful in gauging the potential social effects of the ads as ads. He argues that assaultive ads bring unsavory consequences to the body politic where comparative ads do not (Gronbeck 1994). Kern offers insight into the specific emotional conditions ads provoke, while Johnson-Cartee and Copeland provide a thematic framework for analyzing an ad's claims. One weakness common to all of these typologies (perhaps save Gronbeck's), however, is the substantial potential for overlap between the categories. This is most obvious with Kern's affect-based categories, arguably reflecting not a shortcoming in analysis but rather the complexity of human emotion. Even in West's classification, an ad like "Arkansas" can be seen as either focused on domestic performance (which it is directly) or on Bill Clinton's personal qualities (which it is implicitly). Note also how very different ads can be coded exactly the same by particular authors' typologies. By the Kern categories, "Arkansas" and "Tank Ride," are examples of uncertainty ads. By the West categories, "Character Counts" and "Jesse Ventura Action Figure" are both examples of personal qualities ads.

The strength of a genre approach is that it is based on categories grounded in the wellsprings of popular culture, providing special insight into the culturally resonating substance of campaign spots. As such, it allows one to more finely distinguish one spot from another. For example, both "Revolving Door" and "The Stakes" are coded the same way using the Kern and West classification schemes (fear-unpleasant for Kern, specific domestic policy for West). By genre, one evokes horror and the other drug-induced altered states, both of which carry substantive meaning for ordinary viewers that cannot be gleaned from the other approaches. The threat of drug use by the children of suburban America is far more than an abstract matter of domestic policy for many voters. The hallucinogenic visual imagery is central to understanding the unnerving emotional impact of the ad, something that merely noting the ad is about drugs would fail to articulate. Similarly, it's not just that "Revolving Door" was about crime, but that it painted the crime issue with the audiovisual connotations of horror. Admakers know this, and this can help their work to reflect and heighten the deep emotional issues at stake.

The exercise above shows that knowledge of how ads evoke the genres of popular culture can provide analytical leverage that extant approaches cannot. Most importantly, the insights provided go to the very core of the meaning of the communication embedded in political spots.

Among the advantages of a genre approach are that it can integrate the various levels of meaning within real forms of social experience and that it can connect those forms with how individual viewers experience the ads. This enables the genre analyst to speak in many of the same terms as viewers. Rather than classifying ads with terms like "being your own worst enemy" and "disparagement humor," the use of existing genres such as biography, horror, and romance links analysts to rich networks of conventional language familiar to large portions of American culture. Indeed, in their analysis of focus groups exposed to a variety of campaign communication, Marion Just and associates found not only viewers who processed ad content in terms of genre (the Bush dystopia "Arkansas" about Bill Clinton's record as governor "frightened" one respondent), but also those who conveyed their reactions by creating generic referents such as "Laurel and Hardy" and "Abbott and Costello" to characterize the candidates (Just et al. 1996:168, 189–90). At the same time, the use of genre also enables the analyst of ads to go beyond the culture's ordinary talk to engage the technical and political subtleties that configure the campaign activities of candidates and consultants. Finally, genre analysis can be firmly grounded in cognitive theories of how our brains process information, the subject of chapter 2.

NOTES

1. Rhetoricians dating back to Greek antiquity have engaged the study of forms. In *Form and Genre*, Karlyn Kohrs Campbell and Kathleen Hall Jamieson (1978) describe genres as "groups of discourses which share substantive, stylistic, and situational characteristics," and note that "a genre is a group of acts unified by a constellation of forms that recurs in each of its members. These forms, *in isolation*, appear in other discourses. What is distinctive about the acts in a genre is the recurrence of the forms *together* in constellation." Yet, it is not the more formal genres of rhetoric but their kindred spirits in popular culture that have been neglected in the quest to unpack the meaning in campaign commercials. Indeed, as Herbert W. Simons notes, the central thrust of the primary tradition of generic conceptualization in rhetoric points to the fact that "the study of rhetorical genres is discontinuous with the study of artistic, literary or dialectical genres." For Simons, the core of that tradition is the recognition that similar situations and purposes constrain a diverse array of rhetorical forms. While political advertising itself can be seen in such a light, the role of popular genres in ads is not to shape the structure or form, but rather to provide condensed communication of the sub-

stantive content of campaign appeals. Accordingly, we must turn to the work of film, entertainment, and cultural critics, who see genre as "a type of text characterized by a particular style, such as soap opera, news show, sports program, horror show or detective story" (Berger 1995a). These are the forms that will help provide clues to the substantive meanings embedded in political ads.

2. Berger contrasts this use of genre, preferred by analysts of popular culture, with the broader generic categories (history, comedy, tragedy; see especially Frye 1957) favored by literary critics (Berger 1995b:45). For an application of one such literary taxonomy to political ads, see Smith and Johnston 1991.

3. See also Biocca (1991b:84) for a similar argument.

4. Within the voluminous scholarly investigation of political advertising, much attention has been devoted to how ads convey their messages (see Jamieson 1984; Kaid and Davidson 1986; Nimmo and Felsberg 1986; Kern 1989; Johnson-Cartee and Copeland 1991; Biocca 1991a, 1991b; Gronbeck 1994; Just et al. 1996; West 1997; Hart 2000) and how viewers respond to those messages (see for example Cundy 1986; Garramone 1986; Biocca 1991a; Jamieson 1992a, 1992b; Ansolabehere and Iyengar 1995). This work has produced a rich collection of insights into the workings of campaign spots through a wide range of theoretical perspectives. Yet, perhaps because of the very nature of the analytical project, much of the existing literature has sought to split the political advertising atom into its subatomic component parts, at the cost of underappreciating the wholistic way in which ads actually work for many viewers.

5. I am particularly grateful to the students of Public Opinion and Propaganda (POL 220) at Kutztown University of Pennsylvania during the spring semester of 2002 for their insights on how this ad evoked *South Park*.

6. Kubby was a twenty-three-year survivor of a rare form of adrenal cancer and a vocal supporter of medical marijuana, which he credits his survival to. He was later arrested for growing marijuana in his Olympic Valley, California, home just a few months after the 1998 election. He was unanimously acquitted by a jury on all marijuana charges, but has continued to face marijuana charges since then (*Oakland Tribune* 1999, Bonanza News Service 1999, Suprynowicz 2002).

7. John S. Nelson, "Genres in the Rhetorics of Political Ads," *Argument and the Post Modern Challenge,* ed. Raymie E. McKerrow (Annandale, Va.: Speech Communication Association, 1993), 379–87; John S. Nelson, "Horror, Crisis, and Control: Tales of Facing Evil," North American Society for Social Philosophy, Annual Meeting of the American Political Science Association, New Orleans, La., 1985; Arthur Asa Berger, *Popular Genres: Theories and Texts*; John Fiske, *Television Culture;* Marjorie Perloff, ed., *Postmodern Genres* (Norman: University of Oklahoma Press, 1988); Paul Hernadi, *Beyond Genre: New Directions in Literary Classification* (Ithaca, N.Y.: Cornell University Press, 1972); Stuart M. Kaminsky, *American Film Genres: Approaches to Critical Theory of Popular Film* (Dayton, Oh.: Pflaum, 1974); Stuart M. Kaminsky and Jeffrey H. Mahan, *American Television Genres* (Chicago: Nelson-Hall, 1986); Gerald Mast and Marshall Cohen, eds., *Film Theory and Criticism*, 3rd edition (Oxford: Oxford University Press, 1985).

Chapter Two

Political Advertising and Political Thinking

From the very beginning, the movies have been a powerful prescription for America's blues. But the antidote has become a syndrome: what began as an escape from reality has stealthily usurped it. The very language is clotted with film idiom. Our personal scenarios unspool in a sequence of flashbacks, voice-overs, and cameos. We zoom in, cut to the chase, fade to black. As metaphor, movies are better than ever. In the eighteen-thirties, Tocqueville came here to encounter democracy; in the nineteen-eighties, Jean Baudrillard, France's leading philosophe of postmodernism, came here to encounter the movies. "You should begin with the screen and move outward to the city," he writes in "America." For Baudrillard, illusion is America's reality. He searches out the society not in the people but "in the speed of the screenplay, in the indifferent reflex of television, in the film of days and nights projected across an empty space." New York "is the world of 'Blade Runner'"; the Mormon Tabernacle in Salt Lake City is "straight out of 'Close Encounters'"; and Monument Valley is "the geology of the earth, the mausoleum of the Indians, and the camera of John Ford." The demented, too, see themselves on America's flickering screen: after the attempt to assassinate President Reagan, John Hinckley told psychiatrists that it was all "a movie starring me," with the President a featured player and "a cast of doctors, lawyers, and hangers-on."

—*The New Yorker*, March 21, 1994, p. 12

Chapter 1 explored the way popular culture can help provide the substantive meaning of political advertising. We now turn our attention to the way our brains work to help explain why this is so. Our task will unfold in two parts. First, we will probe the physiological underpinnings of thought and perception, the ways our brains try to make sense of the political world. Then we will consider exploratory data from a quasi-experiment to assess whether or not the audiovisual evocation of genres drawn from popular culture affects the way viewers process and interpret political advertising.

COGNITIVE CONNECTIONS: THE TINY CHIPS OF THE MENTAL MOSAIC

The human brain is composed of many billions of cells called neurons. Cognition (or thinking) occurs with electro-chemical communication at the synapses (or spaces) between neurons. The key to efficient thinking, the key to the ability to function in the world without having to process each and every stimuli the brain encounters anew, is to rely on neuro-chemical patterns that have already been etched onto our brains to guide us in processing incoming information. The stimuli we become familiar with are processed by our brains quickly and with little effort because a pathway has already been established. More novel stimuli that we are unfamiliar with require greater cognitive effort. By evoking the recognizable patterns of popular genres like horror stories or heroic biographies, campaign ads can be processed quickly. These genres also provide substantial emotional content, which provides an additional channel that further influences memory and evaluation.

Our minds store a large amount of information, spread over various locations in the brain. The pathways linking the locations where memories are stored shape our responses to incoming stimuli, determining which preexisting memories will provide the context for the interpretation of new information. Graber (1997, citing Hilts 1995) points out that the

> process of connecting neurons—the tiny chips of the mental mosaic—appropriately so they can form a recognizable mental schema is guided by mental maps or indexes that are developed by storing memories of past experiences.

Researchers have described the linkages of memory as cognitive maps, associative networks, stereotypes, and schema. There are some subtle but important differences among these various conceptualizations, but they share much in common. All recognize that memory is grounded in the physiology of the brain, and that how we process new information is shaped by existing linkages of memory and emotion. From these basic premises, researchers have been able to develop several important insights into the strengths and weaknesses of human information processing.

MENTAL MAPS: SCHEMA AND PATTERNING

It is probably not surprising to learn that the brain's strengths and weaknesses are different sides of the same coin. Our use of pattern matching speeds up the processing of new information, but it can also lead to misperceptions. Sometimes, in an effort to reconstruct information from memory, we will falsely identify elements that fit with the patterns already in the brain but that weren't present in the information we are trying to recall. The commonsense understanding of the dangers of stereotyping reflects this phenomenon in a socially important context. When a political advertisement evokes a particular genre, it invites us to reconstruct details consistent with that genre. Hence, the attractiveness of the horror genre in buttressing charges that one's opponent is soft on crime.

Information processing research in political science has emphasized schema theory.[1] Schemata can serve two important functions: first, they guide the processing and storage of information; second, they guide recall and interpretation of information in memory (Lau and Sears 1986:350–51). They operate in a *top-down* fashion, a point crucial in explaining how genres work in political advertising to affect meaning, memory, and recall. Lau and Sears (1986:352) describe the "reconstructive" nature of schemata this way:

> Recall of some specific instance of a schema is often guided by the generic principles of the schema rather than by the particulars of that specific instance (Rothbart, Evans, and Fulero 1979; Snyder and Uranowitz 1978). For example, once a person has been categorized as having a particular trait or fitting into a particular category, people will falsely recognize that trait or category because schemata provide "default values" to fill in the blanks (Minsky 1975).

Doris Graber notes that "norms that are prevalent within cultural communities ... provide a unifying mechanism" in cognitive processing and that individuals describe their own thoughts "in terms of what they believe these shared norms to be rather than in terms of their own unique perceptions" (1997:4). She also notes:

> When people are asked to recall very specific situations, such as details from a news story, memory is apt to be weak or absent because details have not

been stored in memory. Rather, people have stored general meanings as part of already existing schemata. (1997:6)

Evoking popular genres provides the form that viewers use to reconstruct the details of content in political advertising. It is therefore crucial in shaping viewer "recall" of campaign spots. In fact, in what may have been the first attempt to specifically address cognitive schemata, Frederic Bartlett found that when asked to retell an Indian folk tale "The War of the Ghosts," subjects routinely altered the story's details to fit better with the Western ghost stories they were more familiar with (Bartlett 1932).

The use of genre recognizes the important ways in which memory can be characterized as the "spreading activation" of cognition along neuronal networks of association (Anderson 1983). Spreading activation is "motion in an associative network" (Boynton 1995:234). Instead of assuming a fixed pattern of connections between stored memories, spreading activation suggests that the patterns of association vary across different contexts. Depending on what stimulus we encounter or what the purpose of our thinking is, different nodes may be activated, and different patterns of activation may spread out from them.[2] Perhaps more significantly, the nodes in associative networks have "affective tags," or emotional evaluative components. Boynton and Lodge (1998), following Abelson (1968), describe this as "hot cognition." This is a particularly important insight, as emotionally charged memories are easier to recall.

GENRE AND ASSOCIATIVE NETWORKS

It is at this point that the power of the evocation of generic conventions in campaign advertising can be seen both in terms of communication and understanding. Through spreading activation, ads can communicate effectively because they draw upon preexisting memories and emotions, speeding up processing. As Boynton (1995) notes, activation is measured in milliseconds (Anderson 1983); learning (the addition of new nodes of memory), by contrast, is measured in seconds (Simon 1979). Activation spreads in response to the cues in ads, which can forge new linkages that are often not obvious or logically related. Attention to genre can also help our understanding of the substance of communication and memory by offering what is, in essence, a social parallel to these associative operations of individual cognition (see also Biocca 1991b:62). When viewers process an ad such as "Revolving Door" in terms of horror, they are activating a network of neuronal associations (some emotionally charged), prompted by the top-down recognition of a generic form. These associations are likely to be similar across different viewers, each of whom is aware of the shared conventions of horror and its associated emotional response. The ultimate goal of political campaigns—generating support for or opposition to particular candidates—can be achieved through the hard work of new learning, or, perhaps just as effectively, by steering the linkages between concepts already in place. Linking candidates to our preexisting packages of memory and affect by evoking the recognizable audiovisual conventions of popular genres, therefore, would seem to be a very effective communication strategy.

As a theoretical orientation, spreading activation may allow us to avoid some of the analytical baggage attached to schema theories. Kuklinski, Luskin, and Bolland (1991) fault extant schema research for "vagrant measures," "cosmetic applications," "familiar theory," and a limited depiction of cognitive processes. They suggest much of this work could have been done in the absence of schema, utilizing extant constructs such as cognitive maps and attitude theory. They offer a five-point research strategy: use the whole gamut of cognitive theories, emphasize information processing, focus on process, use experiments, and begin with the problem.[3]

The research discussed below attempts to meet some of those criticisms. First, it explicitly recognizes a range of cognitive processes involved in the viewing of political ads. Therefore, data were collected on audio and visual perception, affective response, and the reconstruction of meaning, in addition to data on associative linkages. Our brains process political advertising in different ways and different places. We see and hear, we evaluate, and we feel. To get a better grasp of these processes, our research must both probe each element separately as well as attempt to gauge their combined effect.

Second, this work deviates from much extant schema-based research in that it does not focus exclusively on a limited number of specific politically relevant "nodes" in memory. Typically, researchers have been interested in how voters think about candidates, issues, groups, or political parties.[4] Yet, we have strong reason to believe that other factors must be taken into account as well. If we want to understand how political advertising works, we need to also consider other nodes in our minds that pertain to the various other elements embedded in the audiovisual communication found in ads. By probing for viewers' free recall by asking questions like, "What does the ad you just saw bring to mind?" this research attempts to include the variety of associations viewers may experience when watching a political ad without focusing exclusively on things like candidates, parties, and issues. This is likely to be especially important in discerning the role popular genres play in viewers' processing of political ads.[5]

This research is designed to reveal some of the potential nodes in memory that may be activated in the processing of political advertisements. Viewers are asked, "What are the first five things that come to mind about the ad you just saw?" But it also attempts to probe beyond the initial level of associative memory. Viewers are asked to list a set of five additional associations of five terms each, one set for each of the original associations.

HOW ADS EVOKE GENRE: A QUASI-EXPERIMENTAL DESIGN

The basic way we will seek to uncover the role of the audiovisual evocation of genre in processing political advertising will be to compare the responses of two groups of viewers. One will view an ad with a certain audiovisual or genre profile, the other will view an ad with exactly the same script but a different audiovisual profile. Approximately seventy undergraduate students enrolled in different sections of an introductory American government course (and one section of students enrolled in a political communication course) at a large midwestern state university served as the sample population.[6]

Students in each section were shown two ads, each of which was part of a different pair of ads being studied. The first pair of ads was designed to probe the effects of the audiovisual evocation of the popular genre of horror, a frequent motif in political commercials. A "Horror" ad was created specifically for this research, on the subject of global warming. Roughly half of the viewers would see this ad, while the other half saw an ad with exactly the same script and the same text superimposed on the screen, but lacking the audiovisual evocation of horror. Originally, I set out simply to create an ad that wasn't a horror ad. In doing so, I learned something about the wholistic way that the individual elements of a genre work together.

By taking away the sense of urgency and acute fear generated by the audiovisual evocation of the horrors of global warming, I was left with a more diffuse anxiety. In trying to find musical scoring that would fit the ad's narrative but not create horror, I chose to look for music evocative of science. Rather than the visual evocation of global warming and pollution, I chose to use an image of planet Earth viewed from space. Taken together, these elements suggested a genre themselves: science fiction. Genre theorists might be quick to note that science fiction and horror share much in common (see Berger 1992:133). Nevertheless, as we will see, the two ads generated noticeably different responses in viewers, responses consistent with the generic evocations in each.

The second pair of ads was taken from the 1990 Michigan U.S. Senate campaign of Republican Representative Bill Schuette. The ads provide a contrast between the generic evocation of satire (much like the anti-Dukakis ad, "Tank Ride") and the same policy arguments in an explicitly comparative context, filmed in front of the Vietnam Memorial in Washington, D.C. These two ads were chosen because they made virtually identical policy arguments but differed in the ways they went about doing it. Let me now describe each of these ads in detail.

The "Horror" Ad

Not every political story can be told in terms of horror. A particular tale must lend itself to such a telling. The case of prison furloughs certainly did, as did the story of environmental degradation embodied in the 1988 Bush campaign's (Boston) "Harbor" ad. I chose to use an environmental theme, global warming, in creating the ads I used.

I devised a script for a thirty-second ad that was compatible with horror, yet would also work with a different generic interpretation. The script read:

> Bob Simmons takes global warming seriously and John Hanson doesn't. Hanson voted against plans to shift to cleaner-burning alternative fuels. He voted to weaken emission standards designed to curb global warming—even though global warming threatens to return the American heartland to the "dust-bowl" days of the 1930s, turning human dreams into ecological nightmares.
> We don't need John Hanson shaping our planetary future. Bob Simmons supports measures to fight global warming and revive our environment.
> Vote Simmons, November 3rd.

The subject of global warming lends itself to a presentation as horror. Many people are aware of predictions of catastrophic devastation projected by some climatologists. Indeed, environmental decay in general is amenable to a horrific interpretation (as the [Boston] "Harbor" ad illustrates). The script itself specifically invoked horror through language such as the words "threatening" and "nightmare." The reference to the "dust-bowl days of the 1930s" also serves to underscore the frightening nature of the claims.

Political advertisements evoke genre through the combination of audio and visual elements (as well as text) in a way that appeals to the conventional understandings of mass audiences. In evoking horror, several such conventions stand out. My sense is that the soundtrack may actually be the most crucial component in the evocation of horror.[7]

Horror soundtracks are comprised of both music and special effects. The music is tense and dramatic. The deep organ tones that characterized early horror music have been supplanted by a variety of electronic and synthetic sounds in contemporary horror productions. Tension is maintained through the juxtaposition of quick-paced rhythm and sustained droning tones. Melodically, a short phrasing is often repeated over and over; think of the musical theme from television's original *Twilight Zone*, a show featuring segments that, while not narrowly horror stories, may be closely related to them, or the music from the film *Jaws*. Both high-pitched and low-pitched sounds are used, occasionally in counterpoint to each other. A tense, rhythmically pulsing synthetic musical chord is virtually a stand alone indicator of horror.

The use of music to convey emotions such as horror has a long institutional history in audiovisual production. Indeed, in creating the advertisements used in these experiments, I was able to rely on a series of approximately twenty compact audio discs marketed especially for A/V production. The discs were made up of short pieces of music with titles designed reflecting the emotions each piece is supposed to evoke. In seeking to convey horror, I could choose from titles like "Haunted House" or "Creepy Creatures." For the "Horror" ad, I used two such musical selections. The first was used to open the ad and featured a high-pitched, sustained synthesizer chord that plays under the narrator's charge that "Bob Simmons takes global warming seriously and John Hanson doesn't." At this point a second much deeper synthetic chord comes in, underscoring the musical tension and punctuating the narrator's claim.

The second musical selection consisted of two notes alternating back and forth, punctuated by the toll of a bell which overlays the sound of stringed instruments which rise in tone, again underscoring tension. The musical selections themselves seem to include sound effects in the way that the sound of the bells and the chords ebb and flow. An additional sound effect was added toward the end of the ad, the whistle of the wind. The music and sound effects fade out at the end of the ad as the narrator speaks of candidate Simmons's plans to "revive our environment and fight global warming."

The narrator's voice must also be consistent with the evocation of horror. It needs to be deep and serious. In producing this advertisement, I employed a deep-voiced student narrator who had previous radio experience. Numerous "takes" were required before the voice seemed to sound right throughout the duration of the ad. While I often warn viewers before I show them these ads that they will know after watching them why I am in the business of writing about ads rather than making them, despite whatever professional shortcomings they may have had, the ads did serve their fundamental purpose: they provided a plausible contrast of generic evocation.

The visual component of the ad was comprised almost exclusively of film footage borrowed from documentaries. There were seven different video segments in total, each lasting approximately three seconds each (two of the clips were repeated). The ad begins with an orange-cast picture of the sun on the horizon of a farm field. The picture conveys heat. The phrase "global warming" is superimposed at the bottom of the screen in white block lettering. The next visual image is that of an oil refinery viewed in slow motion from the air. Plumes of smoke and the burning flames of spiral towers like those seen at an oil refinery are visible. The phrase "John Hanson: weak on alternative fuels" is superimposed over this frame. This image gives way to another picture of the sun, this time obscured by rolling black clouds of smoke. The phrase "John Hanson: weak on emission controls" is placed over this image. All of these clips were taken from documentaries about the earth and its environment. As such, they represent the attempts of the producers of those films to convey ideas with symbols widely understood to represent environmental decay—again, the shared understandings upon which genres are based.

The second series of images are black-and-white film clips depicting the bleakness of the dust-bowl days of the 1930s through images of a dust-storm ravaged and barren prairie landscape. These, too, were borrowed from a documentary, this one addressing the life of a particular conservationist. Superimposed over these clips are another series of phrases: "John Hanson: weak on global warming," "John Hanson" and "the future?" Shortly after I had completed the creation of this ad, I saw for the first time a 1992 Bush campaign ad, "Arkansas," which featured remarkably similar black-and-white images of desolation designed to depict a bleak American future under Bill Clinton. I couldn't help but think I was onto something! (See figure 2.1.) The final images are of a black screen with white lettering urging viewers to vote for candidate Simmons. The lettering was the simple block style that is somewhat common to political advertisements.

As a whole, then, the ad combines a series of widely recognizable visual images depicting environmental degradation with a narrative, musical scoring, and sound effects evocative of a horror story. From what we know about political thinking we may be inclined to believe that viewers will recall and reconstruct the meaning of the ad but will forget many of the details. And that meaning will be constructed in part from the horror genre that frames the viewer's experience.

The Science Fiction "Earth" Ad

A second ad was created using exactly the same script and superimposed text as the horror ad. It differed in its audiovisual elements. The ad uses a single visual image throughout its duration, the slowly revolving planet Earth as viewed from outer space (see figure 2.2). The ad's soundtrack can perhaps best be described as "space music."

The "Horror" ad was created in the spring of 1992. That fall the Bush–Quayle campaign aired the ad "Arkansas" using the audiovisual production values of a horror story to paint a bleak picture of what America would be like under Bill Clinton. The two images are virtually interchangeable.

Figure 2.1. The "Horror" Ad (left); "Arkansas," Bush–Quayle 1992 (right)

It is comprised of a short series of high-pitched electronic "beeps," the last of which is sustained for several measures before the pattern repeats itself. Such music is frequently associated with science or science fiction. Indeed several viewers described the music as similar to that of *Star Trek* or other works of science fiction, or the kind of thing you might hear in an educational film on a scientific subject.

Science was something of a natural choice in trying to develop a second ad based on the same global warming script. The tone of narration (though not the script) was also changed, in order to provide the kind of emphasis more appropriate for the more intellectual concerns of science and science fiction rather than the ominous tone of horror.

Levin of Arabia

The second pair of ads was taken from the 1990 Michigan U.S. Senate election. Both of the ads make essentially the same substantive charges: that incumbent Democratic Senator Carl Levin opposed both the Maverick anti-tank missile and funding for the battleship USS *Wisconsin*. The first ad, "Levin of Arabia," does so by evoking satire in a fashion reminiscent of the "Tank Ride" ad used by the Bush campaign against Michael Dukakis in 1988 discussed in chapter 1. The second ad features Republican candidate Bill Schuette speaking in front of the Vietnam Memorial in Washington, D.C.

The "Horror" ad uses dark visual images and ominous musical scoring and sound effects to characterize John Hanson's opposition to emission controls. The "Earth" ad features exactly the same script and superimposed text, but replaces the audiovisual evocation of horror with that of science fiction.

Figure 2.2. The "Horror" Ad (left); the "Earth" Ad (right)

The script of "Levin of Arabia" read:

Carl Levin's anti-defense record is so bad the *Detroit News* actually demanded he resign from the Armed Services Committee. As your senator he opposed virtually every strategic defense system. Carl Levin opposed the Maverick anti-tank missile now on duty in the Arab desert. He voted against the battleship *Wisconsin*, now protecting our troops against Saddam Hussein. Yet Carl Levin flew to the *Wisconsin* at taxpayers' expense for a press release and TV cameras. If Levin had his way, he wouldn't have a ship to stand on and neither would our troops.

The ad begins with a full-screen picture of the front page of the *Detroit News*. Immediately, a quote from the April 11, 1982, edition is shown. That the quote was eight years old at the time the ad ran is, by the way, exactly the kind of detail viewers routinely overlook. The quote appears in white type on a black background that has ragged edges, perhaps to convey the sense that the quote was "cut out" of the paper. The front page itself is now largely obscured, save for the masthead and the headline of a story next to a picture of President Bush that is visible beneath the "cut-out" quote. The headline reads, "'Saddam Hussein will fail,' Bush promises." The excerpted quote reads, "Sen. Levin . . . *owes it to his country to resign* from the Senate Armed Services Comm.," and in smaller print, "Detroit News 4/11/82" (emphasis in ad).

The second visual image of the ad is a video clip of Levin standing in front of a gun turret on a battleship. The caption at the bottom of the screen reads "Carl Levin on the USS *Wisconsin*." Levin appears disheveled. His hair is blowing wildly in the wind, long and curly. He is smiling, though it is not immediately apparent why. This image is the first part of the functional equivalent of Governor Dukakis's smiling visage aboard the tank during the 1988 presidential campaign.

The second part is the next image seen in the ad. As the narrator charges Levin with opposing the battleship *Wisconsin*, we see, through superimposed crosshairs, a black-and-white picture of a ship at sea, presumably the *Wisconsin*. The black-and-white image of the ship appears inside a narrowing circle. The area outside the circle is red, though transparent enough for the underlying image to show through. The circle narrows in two increments (while the image of the ship draws closer and larger, in rhythm with the circle's contraction) after which the entire screen is now shrouded in red, with the *Wisconsin* sitting straight in the middle of the crosshairs. Then the process repeats itself.

In contrast to the "Tank Ride" ad, special sound effects are conspicuously absent in "Levin of Arabia." Where "Tank Ride" used mechanical squeals and the tank's sputtering engines to rhythmically punctuate each charge against Dukakis, in "Levin of Arabia" there is nothing but the narrator's voice. Sound effects are instrumental in providing the humorous overtones that satire requires, and they may do so subtly. The absence of any background noise at all, moreover, contributes to a certain unreality regarding the pictures themselves. In the context of "Tank Ride," for example, the very rumble of the tank in the parking lot helped convey absurdity—quite apart from the squeals and sputters added in after the fact for dramatic effects.

As the narrator says ". . . yet Carl Levin flew to the *Wisconsin* at taxpayers' expense . . ." we return to the windswept image of Levin on the ship. A reporter with a microphone can be partially viewed momentarily as Levin continues to grin. The final image of the ad returns to the aerial shot of the battleship and its wake trailing in the water. The narrator says, "If Levin had his way," (the ship now fades to become invisible, though the wake remains) "he wouldn't have a ship to stand on and neither would our troops." A disclaimer appears at the bottom of the screen next to a small color picture bearing the profile of candidate Schuette.

Taken as a whole, this ad works by invoking the genre of satire. Like a skit from *Saturday Night Live* or *The Simpsons*, the superficially serious setting (here a United States senator aboard a Navy battleship) actually serves a comedic effect. The effect is magnified to the extent that the object of the satire is oblivious to it. I would note in passing, however, that the ad also plays upon the associations viewers have regarding the authenticity of the print media in politics. The ad uses the "form" (the picture of the newspaper) to gain credibility and shape processing of the details (the charges against Levin) despite the fact that the quote used is eight years old while the narration speaks of current tensions in the Persian Gulf as does the front page shown on the screen.

Argumentatively, this is an advertisement about weapons voting in Congress and political hypocrisy. Generically, however, it is satire. Carl Levin is made to look silly and the graphic targeting of the battleship *Wisconsin* underscores the humor. In my view, the ad would have been more effective in evoking satire had it employed more of the conventions of the genre, in particular, special sound effects. Nonetheless, I expected that a fair percentage of the audience would still process this ad in terms of its satirical elements.

Never Again

Essentially the same argumentative claims (Levin's opposition to the two weapons systems) are found in an ad entitled "Never Again." The script of that ad is as follows:

> Americans differed over the Vietnam War. But we all agree never again will our soldiers fight without the support they deserve. In the Arab desert, our troops face another Hitler. Our soldiers are armed with the Maverick anti-tank missile. I voted for it, Carl Levin opposed it. They're protected by the battleship *Wisconsin*. I voted for it, Carl Levin opposed it. As a Republican congressman, I support a strong national defense. As your senator, I'll work with George Bush, so if we need to fight another war, we'll be ready.

The ad begins with a waist-up shot of Schuette slowly walking toward the camera in front of the Vietnam Memorial in Washington, D.C. The congressman is wearing a light blue shirt and red tie. The wall of the memorial is visible in the background, though it may not be immediately obvious to some viewers that that is what it is. The dominant color is the green of the grass visible both above and below the wall. Superimposed at the bottom of the screen are the words "Bill Schuette U.S. Senate."

As Schuette continues talking, the next image appears, fading into the image of Schuette speaking. It is a close-up taken over the shoulder of a Marine standing immediately in front of the wall. There is no hair visible on the back of the soldier's head beneath his white cap. The black wall of names is shiny enough to reflect back at the Marine as Schuette's image from the previous shot fades under.

The next image to fade in is that of a small blonde child touching the wall. His fingers touch their own reflection in the wall at a spot where the image of the Marine's head can be seen as it fades out of the picture. As the image of the Marine fades, a woman's leg is reflected in the wall. She wears knee length shorts and light blue shoes, which in this context suggests young motherhood. The remainder of the ad features Schuette walking toward the camera. He stops momentarily before stating his support (and Levin's opposition) to the Maverick, and again after noting Levin's opposition to the *Wisconsin*.

The ad's soundtrack features a somewhat somber musical theme of sustained whole notes punctuated by various drumbeats. The first punctuation is a single deep beat, which occurs immediately after Schuette says "never again" as the clean-shaven Marine views the shiny black wall of the Vietnam Memorial. The second punctuation is a higher-pitched short drumroll that occurs immediately after Schuette says "another Hitler." Two more deep beats follow the phrase "I voted for it, Carl Levin opposed it" (referring to the Maverick). A similar punctuation occurs after Schuette charges Levin with opposing the *Wisconsin*. A cymbal roll marks the end of the phrase "strong national defense." As the ad ends, the music becomes decidedly more upbeat.

A second form of musical punctuation occurs in the ad through the use of deep bass notes. They are in counterpoint to the drumbeats and add emphasis to the phrases "troops," "missile," "battleship," "Republican," and "senator."

The ad is difficult to categorize in terms of genre. It might be seen as an excellent example of a "comparative" ad (Gronbeck 1994). Some call ads like this "talking head" ads because of the prominence of the simple image of the speaker.[8] What is clear is that the ad stimulates associations and emotions—both in those sympathetic to Schuette and in those opposed to him. The reason, however, has little to do with the talking head or the ad's explicit policy comparison. Instead, the central emotions of the ad are stirred up by the images of the Vietnam Memorial and the somber military-sounding background music. The ad also seems to fail as an explicit comparison of the two candidates. That message too is drowned out by the emotions of patriotism and sadness associated with the Vietnam War.

In any event, the ad is clearly not a satire. Its strongest generic connections may be with the scores of films and television programs about Vietnam. Still, the similarities of the policy claims in "Never Again" to those found in "Levin of Arabia" provide the basis for an experimental comparison. Simply put, if the argumentative policy claims of the ads drive viewer response to advertising, the responses to these two ads should be similar. If the audiovisual and generic evocations drive viewers' processing of political ads, the responses to these two ads should be noticeably different.

MEASURING VIEWER RESPONSE TO GENRE

To gauge viewer response to these ads, respondents completed a questionnaire after being shown each of the two ads they saw. Each viewer would see one ad from each pair, either the "Horror" or "Earth" ads and either "Levin of Arabia" or "Never Again." The response document included several open-ended probes: "What do you remember seeing (pictures, colors, lighting, motion, etc.)?" "What do you remember hearing (voices, music, sound effects)?" "Please describe any emotions you felt," and "If a friend or classmate asked you what Advertisement #1 was about, what would you tell them?" It also probed respondents' associative linkages by asking viewers to list the first five things that came to mind when they thought about the ad they had seen. Subsequent items probed viewers' secondary associations by asking what were the first five things that came to mind about each of the things they had listed as primary associations.

The questionnaire also included a set of fixed-response items, modeled after the Boynton-Lodge research (Boynton 1995:238). Viewers were presented with twenty-one terms, each placed over the center of a line. At the top of each page on the left, the phrase "not at all applicable" appeared, while the phrase "highly applicable" appeared in the right corner. Respondents were instructed to mark the point along the line which best indicated how much that term applied to them.[9] The terms included "anxious," "frustrated," "sad," "fearful," "horrified," "relaxed," "thoughtful," and "cynical." Other terms included in the response document referred to physiological states: "muscle tension," "stomach sickness," "head pain," "hot," and "accelerated heartbeat." While obviously crude, the inclusion of these physiological items at least recognizes that there is a biological basis to the processing of political advertising in addition to its cognitive bases.

Viewer Response to Genre: Horror

Let us turn first to viewer response to the "Horror" ad. The affective and physiological response items illustrate the effects of genre in the processing of political advertising. Figure 2.3 presents the median response for four conditions associated with the horror genre (anxious, fearful, horror, and tense) for each of the four ads used in this study.[10] Please keep in mind that these data are exploratory. They are not designed to formally test hypotheses, but rather to demonstrate the plausibility of the arguments suggested so far.

For each of the response conditions associated with horror in figure 2.3, the "Horror" ad does indeed obtain the highest median level of response. These levels may somewhat understate the actual response of viewers, because the distribution of responses is skewed by those reporting no response at all. A similar pattern occurs for viewers of the satire ad who report no amusement at all. In fact, they may be very well aware of the message, and how it seeks to invoke fear, amuse-

Political Advertising and Political Thinking 47

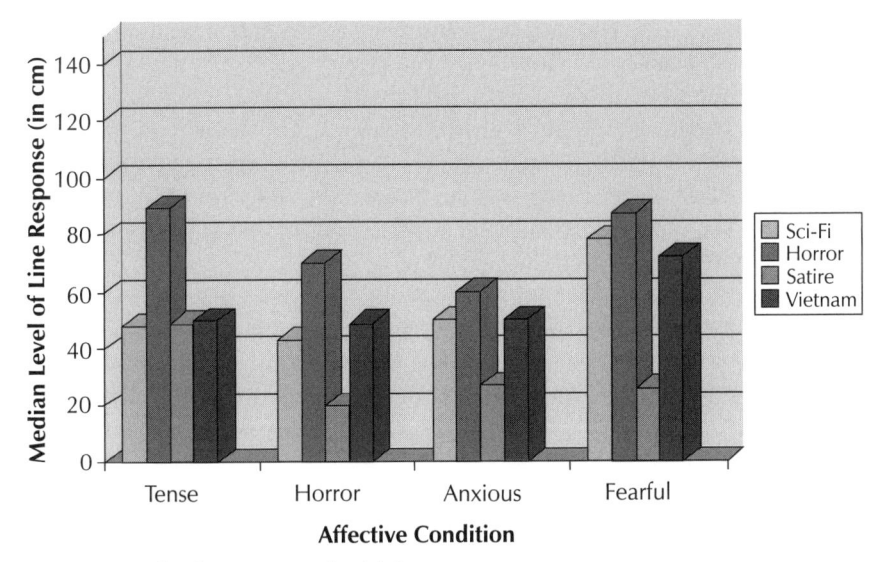

Figure 2.3. Affective Response by Ad Genre

ment, or other emotions, and may be consciously resisting such influences. This would seem to reinforce the notion that genres communicate meaning. Even those unreceptive to the message can most likely discern its contents. (This study was not, however, designed to produce direct evidence on this point.)

The different genres of ads appear to be experienced by viewers in a consistent pattern across different response measures. The horror ad evokes the highest level of affective response, with the science-fiction and Vietnam genre ads following behind, all three set apart from the satire responses. Given the substantive similarity of the three genres, that is not surprising. If anything, the fact that we can observe differences in response to genres evoking such similar conventions suggests that viewers are fairly sophisticated in processing genre.

The response document also included crude measures of physiological responses to ads. Respondents were asked to indicate how much the terms stomach sickness, head pain, muscle tension, and accelerated heartbeat applied to their reaction to the ads they saw. Again, while only indirect, these items are designed to shed some light on the vital role played by emotion and biology in the processing of political ads.

Figure 2.4 presents a comparison of physiological response by ad genre. Again, the pattern is consistent with expectations based on genre. In the case of three of the conditions (stomach sickness, muscle tension, and accelerated heartbeat) the responses to the horror genre ad are higher than those for the other ads. For one condition (head pain) the median response from the Vietnam genre ad slightly exceeded that of the horror ad. Despite the primitive measures employed here, there is no reason to dismiss the role physiological factors play in the processing of political advertising, an issue that future research may be able to address.

Turning to the open-ended response items, we find that in general, viewers of the "Horror" ad made repeated references consistent with the horror genre in their open-ended responses to the ad, and there can be little doubt that many of the viewers of "Horror" understood the ad as conveying "horror" in the Hollywood-genre sense of the term. They identified the music, special effects, and visuals of the ads in ways fully consistent with the genre. Some did not do that but nevertheless retold the story as horror. Such retellings provide evidence of the use of genre in "top-down" cognitive processing as details are reconstructed so as to be consistent with the generic form. Let us consider some of the responses to the open-ended probes in more detail.

When asked what they remember hearing, many identified the music. The music in the ad was described by various respondents as "ominous," "eerie," that "which can be found in a scary movie," "like

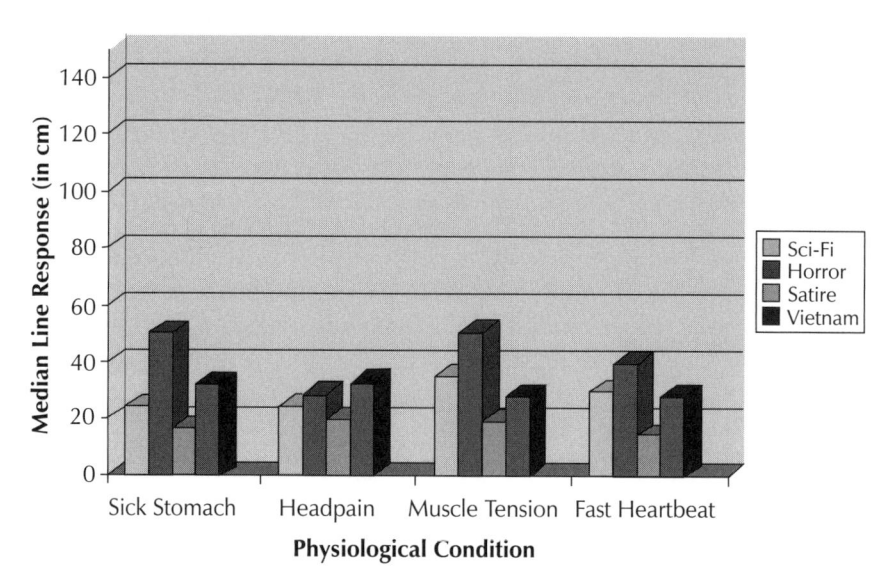

Figure 2.4. Physiological Response by Ad Genre

in a horror show when something bad happens," "eve of destruction background music," "music that came out of the Friday the 13th series," "dark," "foreboding," and "troubling." Some identified the sound effects in horror terms as well, for example, "creepshow high-pitched sound" and "dramatic doom harsh sound effects wind blowing."

In response to the item probing what the respondents remembered seeing, a number of people also explicitly described the visual images contained in the ad in terms of the language of horror. One respondent wrote, "The pictures were rather spooky," and added in their secondary associations: "The images created a picture of inevitable doom if something is not done about global warming." Another described what they remember seeing in the ad this way: "Many pictures of desolate awful places after a war or bombing. Colors bleak and plain—no life. Motion—wind, smoke, blowing dirt." Yet another described what they remember seeing in the ad as, "Dark pictures w/red or orange—all looked destructive. . . ." Other descriptions of what viewers remembered seeing in the ad consistent with horror included "bleak," "stark and gloomy," "desolation," "awful" "unnerving dark images . . . very harsh and unsettling," and "scenes of what looked to be the end of the world."

Perhaps even more telling than the respondents' recollections of what they remember hearing or seeing, many viewers used the language of horror in their retellings of the ad to describe feelings they had as a result of viewing the ad, or in the initial and secondary associative linkages they reported. One respondent provided this retelling of the "Horror" ad: "It was about John Hanson's poor record on the environment. Bob Simmons painted a very dismal future under Hanson's leadership. It was a troubling spot. . . ."

Another respondent, who took issue with the ad's approach, offered this "retelling":

> It was about fear. An attempt was made by Simmons to paint his opponent as some *monster* bent on destroying the earth. Using environmentalism, Simmons was attempting an attack from dubious moral high ground (emphasis added).

A number of respondents used language consistent with horror to describe the feelings they had upon viewing the ad. "Fear" was perhaps the most common. Among the other terms used were "despair," "dread," "worry," "grief," "desolate," "eerie," "scared," and "disturbed." One respondent wrote the following in response to the "feelings" probe:

> Fear & concern—I definitely would not vote for a person who would not try to help save the land. I've grown up in a farming community & that is all those people know. Many of them saw the Dust Bowl & wouldn't want to see it twice.

Another described feeling this way: "The music and tone along with the grim pictures created a scared feeling inside me." Another wrote simply, "I felt despair about the future." One respondent was slightly more intense: "Scared for the sake of the earth. Nervous that Simmons will lose and the earth will be destroyed."

Some respondents explicitly recognized but rejected the ad's appeal to fear. One's response to the feelings probe was: "The ad alone would not move me to vote for Simmons. I didn't feel it was a very good ad. It didn't scare me into worrying about pollution."

Another was considerably more emphatic in voicing the same feelings:

> Intense feeling of negative advertisement. The feeling of "Vote for Simmons or die." I resent that type of advertisement very much. Concern for the environment is important, important enough for serious concern, but the "vote for me or die" attitude has got to go.

Although these respondents rejected the ad's message, there can be no doubt that the genre of horror figured prominently in their perceptions of what that message was, and in their reconstructions of the message after the fact.

The response document also provided evidence suggesting that the networks of associations in viewers' minds stimulated by the ads were also a rich source of horror imagery, both in initial and secondary associations. Among the initial associations consistent with horror that were offered by viewers of the "Horror" ad were "death and destruction," "fear of a barren and ravaged earth," "how one man portrays the other to be a murderer," "big time scare tactics," "danger, doom, threat," "apocalypse," "death," "destruction," "dismal," and, simply, "fear."

Viewers' secondary associations can provide evidence of the effect of the evocation of the horror genre in two ways. First, we can explore secondary associations for initial assocations that were explicitly consistent with the horror genre. One respondent, for example, listed "apocalypse" as an initial association and provided these secondary associations: "Destruction. Desolation. The end of an age. Wrath of God (punishment, as separate from judgement . . .). Judgement." Another respondent listed "Environment is in danger" as an initial association and also "Hanson wants environment to be destroyed." That person then offered these secondary associations: "Global warming. Act now! Earth will be destroyed soon. Only a few ways to save earth. We are going to be killed off by global warming. . . . Hanson is evil. He is our enemy. He is responsible for global warming. Earth will have continuous storms. Earth is almost gone."

A second way secondary associations provide evidence of the role of genre occurs where respondents listed among their initial associations terms that were not themselves explicitly based in horror, but offer secondary associations for those terms that were consistent with the genre. One respondent, for example, listed "effective images" as their first initial association, which generated these secondary associations:

> The pictures were powerful. They created a need for worry. That barren land was a little bothersome. The images created a picture of inevitable doom if something is not done about global warming.

Another respondent listed "the environment" and "going back to the dust bowl" as initial associations, and provided these secondary associations:

> It needs to be saved. We need candidates that support saving it. We don't want another dust bowl. The ozone depletion is scary. What will people do to save it? Strong imagery. Shows real problem. Gives past example. Proves environmental damage is devastating.

Another listed "the pictures" as an initial association and these secondary associations: "Scary. Horrifying. Extreme cases. Dark. Not comforting."

Taken as a whole, viewers' recollections of what they remember seeing and hearing in the ad, the way they retell the story of the ad, and their initial and secondary associations all provide ample evidence that, at least for some viewers, the audiovisual conventions of the popular genre of horror do in fact shape the way the "message" of this political advertisement was processed. Viewers are, of course, free to discount the evocation of horror, as many did. Nevertheless, these responses indicate how political questions can be imbued with emotional content, and how through the evocation of horror an environmental threat or prison furlough program can take on the meaning of the deeply dark, ominous, and foreboding ambience of horror. Let us now contrast these responses to those of viewers of the science-fiction "Earth" ad.

Viewer Response to Genre: The "Earth" Ad

As a genre, sci-fi shares seriousness and uncertainty with horror, and adds a focus on the future. In various ways, viewers of the "Earth" ad seemed to process this spot in terms consistent with its generic evocations. They did so in recalling the soundtrack and in retelling the ad's story. Perhaps more to the point, though the ad used exactly the same script as the "Horror" ad, the pattern of responses we saw among viewers of that ad did not obtain among viewers of "Earth."

Viewers of the "Earth" ad frequently described the ad's musical soundtrack in terms consistent with science fiction. The following quotations are drawn from responses by several different viewers to the question, "What do you remember hearing?":

> "Twilight Zone"—esque music; Very weird, wayout music . . . felt like I was in some futuristic space show; Sort of a 2001: A Space Odyssey type blips to give the feeling of being in outer space; Music that seemed very spacey; Space age music; Music—soft, "planetary" music; The music was eiry [sic]—kind of like something from 2001—The Space Odessey [sic]; . . . space age music [two respondents]; Star Trek type music; The music or sound effects reminded me of Star Trek. It got me thinking about space; "scientific" music. The type of music you'd hear on an education show showing the process of mitosis under a microscope.

Some responses to the "Earth" ad were consistent with horror, but far fewer than in the responses of viewers of the "Horror" ad. The phrases consistent with horror in the responses of viewers of the "Earth" ad were: "felt kinda creepy," "eerie voice," "plays on fear," "destruction . . . drastic effects . . . disaster," "speaker's voice . . . threatening . . . fear of global warming," "human dream—ecological nightmare," "fear . . . evil," and "He made it sound as though . . . we would all die a horrible death. . . . I heard ominous music that suggested impending disaster." Even many of these responses could be easily seen as consistent with the generic evocation of science fiction. What is clear, though, is that such responses were far less prevalent among viewers of "Earth."

Moreover, in contrast to the responses of viewers of the "Horror" ad, where references consistent with the generic evocation of horror were found in the associative linkages, retellings, and recollections of viewers, references consistent with horror among viewers of "Earth" were relatively few and far between, and found mostly in reference to the soundtrack. Further, the major recurring themes articulated by "Earth" viewers focused on environmentalism and, for many viewers, its use in a "negative" campaign ad. (I was surprised that the "Earth" ad actually generated more references to "negative" advertising than the "Horror" ad with its harsh and more threatening generic evocations.)

In sum, given the similarities between the two genres, and especially between the two scripts, the differences between viewers' response to the two ads are impressive. That is, despite their similarity, there were observable differences in the patterns of viewer response to the two spots. These patterns were highly consistent with the audiovisual generic evocations of horror and science fiction, respectively. Let's now turn to the second pair of ads, the satire "Levin of Arabia" and the ad evocative of Vietnam, "Never Again."

Viewer Response to Genre: "Levin of Arabia" (Satire)

To my eye, "Levin of Arabia" could have been far more effective in evoking satire than it was if it had been more aggressive in its use of audiovisuals. Unlike "Tank Ride," which employed audio special effects (the squealing and sputtering rumble of the tank, rising in volume after each of the ad's charges scrolled down the screen), there are no special audio effects in "Levin of Arabia" that can help to underscore the ad's satirical theme. The lion's share of that work is accomplished visually, through both the unflattering image of Carl Levin "looking dumb" and the graphic "targeting" of the USS *Wisconsin* culminating in the ship's image dissolving at sea as the narrator intones, "If Carl Levin had his way, he wouldn't have a ship to stand on and neither would our troops."

The ad clearly did succeed in painting an unflattering physical image of Carl Levin, with nearly a third of viewers specifically referring to his disheveled appearance. Levin's "bad hair day" was summed up by one viewer this way: "Looked stupid . . . silly; unauthoritative." In some ways, this is a rather remarkable observation. Carl Levin is a United States senator, presumably possessing at least average intelligence. Yet, merely by being shown with his hair flying wildly about, he can appear to many to be stupid or silly. Maybe bad hair days are a little more traumatic than we give them credit for!

Other aspects of the ad worked to underscore the ad's approach as well. The punch-line conclusion of the ad ("he wouldn't have a ship to stand on . . .") invites a satirical response. Among the other responses offered by viewers that are consistent with satire are many expressing "humor" or "amusement," and several recognizing "disdain" or "contempt" in the narrator's voice. Overall, the median line-response level for the term "amused" among viewers of "Levin of Arabia" was seventy-six, while for viewers of "Never Again" it was seventy-one.

Further evidence of the generic processing of "Levin of Arabia" can be found in those respondents who indicated hearing special sound effects (consistent with satire) that weren't actually there. One respondent, for example, described what they heard this way:

> Voices—it was a very monotone voice that repeated the problem with the candidate—annoying. Sound effects—at the end it was the sound kind of like a bomb or gun went off and removed the ship.

Such embellishment is fully consistent with top-down processing, where the form is used to construct the details. Sound effects would have amplified the satire; they are consistent with the audiovisual elements of the genre, and this viewer remembered hearing them even though they weren't actually there. In a related vein, one viewer expressed the thought that the ad would have been better if it had included patriotic music. At first, I thought that this observation missed the point—the ad wasn't supposed to be about patriotism. Yet, while this suggestion could have been a response to the ad's military subject, the actual juxtaposition of patriotic music with this ad would almost surely amplify the satirical effect.

Viewer Response to Genre: "Never Again" (Vietnam)

If the relatively simple "Levin of Arabia" failed to fully evoke the generic associations of satire because it didn't take advantage of all the audiovisual cues available, "Never Again" suffers from no such problem. Indeed, the message of that ad is drowning in generic evocations—albeit in ways that subvert the ad's ostensible attack on Schuette's opponent, Carl Levin.

While overtly a comparison of two candidates' stands on defense issues, "Never Again" is in fact much more. The ad employs a solemn, "patriotic" musical score and images of the Vietnam Memorial in Washington, D.C., on a pleasant summer afternoon, serving to stoke viewer associations with that war.

Says candidate Schuette in the ad, "Never again will our troops go to war without the support they deserve." Because of the wholistic effect of the evocation of Vietnam, that argument filters through the contextual linkages of viewers' own assessments of the war. Fifteen of the thirty-four viewers of "Never Again" explicitly mentioned patriotism, either to describe the music or as a more general comment on the tenor of the ad. While the Vietnam War Memorial itself, the U.S. Marine shown standing in front of it, and the patriotic background music might each individually have generated responses like these, their combined, wholistic effects may be more effective than each alone.

The ad also evokes a sense of patriotic pride and identification by its use of other "All-American" imagery: a young child, green grass, and blue skies. In some cases, viewers made such connections explicitly. For initial associations, one respondent wrote: "Seeing war vets, the Vietnam Memorial, little kids, baseball diamond." This person included "baseball" as an initial association (though in fact there is no baseball diamond in the ad) and offered the following secondary associations for that term:

> Hot dogs, apple pie, Chevrolet—all American dream. Summer—time spent with family. Young men should be playing baseball instead of fighting. Children—let them be concerned w/a game, not a war.

Another respondent described the ad as featuring an ". . . outdoor scene, mother, America and Fourth of July flavor." Another listed "little blonde boy fingering the names—all-American child" as one of their initial associations, and provided, "All-American. Must protect." among the secondary associations.

Another respondent was even more implicit in attributing "All-American" imagery to the ad, listing "America First" as the first initial association with the ad, and offering the following secondary associations: "Trade protection. Red/white/blue. Flags. Apple pie. War mentality." While this person listed "flags" as a secondary association (and better than 10 percent of the viewers of this ad [four of thirty-four] indicated that they saw flags), *none actually appeared in the ad*. Still, one respondent described seeing the ad this way: "The background contained buildings, it was a sunny day. There was a child looking at the memorial of the Vietnam War. There was a flag." Another saw in the ad simply, "Vietnam wall memorial, flags." In response to the "seeing" probe, this person wrote:

> I saw the candidate near the Vietnam Memorial, pictures of soldiers and a flag. The spot was filmed on a sunny day. The candidate walks slowly to the camera thru the course of the ad.

That viewers would associate the flag with the patriotic themes evoked by "Never Again" is not surprising, and is a good example of how top-down processing identifies a form (here, patriotism and Vietnam) that is then used to "reconstruct" the details (here, flags that didn't actually appear in the ad). Even a viewer decidedly hostile to the ad and its message reported seeing a flag. A respondent wrote about what they saw this way: "Lighting was bright. Flags. Nazi walking toward the camera."

Yet, if all-American imagery is one layer of association prominent in "Never Again," it is neither the only one nor even the most common. In invoking war, and Vietnam in particular, this ad tapped a sensitive nerve in many viewers. One respondent listed "the little boy touching the names on the monument" as the first initial association. Their secondary associations were:

> I was wondering who died that was related to him. How was his future life going to be affected by this war or future wars. Did he understand any of this? How I want to see the names some day. What thoughts were actually going through his mind.

This respondent's secondary associations for "the baby running its fingers over the names on the wall" provide one illustration of how thoughts of war mingled with the All-American imagery: "I thought about death. The baby had blonde hair. It was wearing a cute outfit." Another respondent offered a similar ambivalence in secondary associations for the initial association: "Wall for Vietnam Memorial, nice sunny day with plenty of people":

> It pulled at my heart strings. It was a sad misguided war. This is an obvious patriotic ploy to win votes. Child fingering holes—need security for our children. Photogenic man.

In invoking Vietnam, this ad manages to activate a wealth of associations already existing in viewers' minds. One source of such associations (especially for college students) was likely to be the outpouring of popular films and television programs focusing on Vietnam at that time. There is in fact some direct evidence that viewers related "Never Again" specifically to Vietnam-genre motion pictures. One respondent provided these secondary associations for the initial association "Vietnam War Memorial":

> Huge number of needless deaths. People making crayon rubbings on the memorial to take home their losts name. The entire scar and fear in the nation by those graduating from high school—fearful they may be drafted. War movies—*Full Metal Jacket, Platoon.*

Another respondent described the music in the ad this way: "It kind of sounded like the theme to *Top Gun* in a slowed-down version." Another listed "Vietnam" as their initial association and offered the following secondary associations: "Death. Protests. *Born on the Fourth of July* (a Vietnam movie). Asians."

Aufderheide suggests that beginning in the late 1980s, a subgenre of the war film centered on Vietnam emerged, featuring as its theme what she calls the "noble-grunt."

> Films as different as *Platoon* (1986), *Full Metal Jacket* (1987), *Good Morning, Vietnam* (1987), *Hamburger Hill* (1987), *Gardens of Stone* (1987), *84 Charlie MoPic* (1989), *Off Limits* (1988), *Dear America* (1988), *Casualties of War* (1989), and TV series like *Tour of Duty* and *China Beach* have carried into film what author C. D. B. Bryan described for literature as "the Generic Vietnam War Narrative." This generic narrative features combat units in tales that chart "the gradual deterioration of order, the disintegration of idealism, the breakdown of character, the alienation from those at home, and finally, the loss of all sensibility save the will to survive." There is something terribly sad and embattled about these films and TV shows, even in their lighter and warmer moments. They celebrate survival as a form of heroism, and cynicism as a form of self-preservation. (Aufderheide 1990:83–84)

These same themes appeared throughout viewer responses to "Never Again." Twenty out of thirty-four viewers of "Never Again" mentioned either the Vietnam War or the Vietnam Memorial in their responses, more than the number who included "patriotism" in their responses. Consistent with the "Generic Vietnam War Narrative," viewers' associations with Vietnam featured sadness, uncertainty, appreciation for the veterans, disillusionment, a sense of betrayal and anger.

Figure 2.5 shows how the median response levels for various terms consistent with the Vietnam genre compare for viewers of the satire

"Levin of Arabia" and viewers of the Vietnam-based "Never Again." Consistent with the "Generic Vietnam War Narrative," viewers of "Never Again" indicated high levels of sadness. The median value for "sad" for viewers of "Never Again" (93) was better than three times higher than it was for viewers of "Levin of Arabia" (30). The median value for "fearful" was nearly three times higher for viewers of "Never Again" compared to viewers of "Levin of Arabia" (72 to 26) and the median values for the terms "angry," "anxious," and "horror" were at least twice as large or better for viewers of the Vietnam-based "Never Again."

Further indication of the role of genre in shaping viewer response to "Never Again" can be gleaned from the open-ended parts of the response document. One respondent's secondary associations for "Vietnam Memorial" were: "Sad for the lives lost in the war. The lack of respect that was given to the veterans. A war that should not have taken place." For another, the "Vietnam War" generated the following secondary associations: "Imperialism. Debacle. Failure. Retreat. Suffering." Another's secondary associations for "the Vietnam War" were: "The unwanted war. Lost lives. Disturbed soldiers. Disturbed veterans. The war we couldn't win." Yet another echoed those sentiments in these secondary associations for "Vietnam": "Lost war (failure). Bad treatment of troops. Resentment by non middle-aged

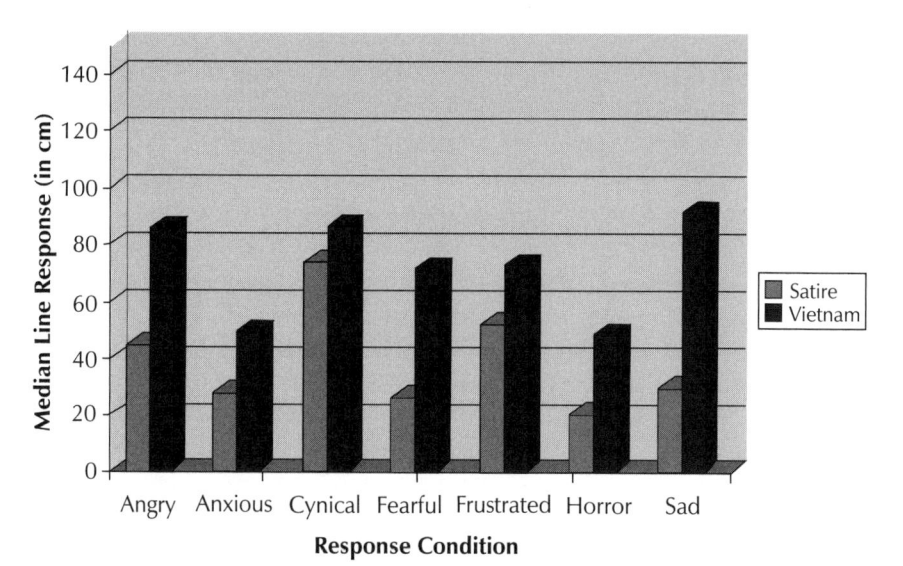

Figure 2.5. Viewer Response to Satire and Vietnam Compared

Americans. Problem w/bureaucracy." These widely held reactions also can be found in the secondary associations of another respondent for "Vietnam and not fighting for a cause":

> No backing by the public. Communism has fallen so did they die in vain? Red tape wouldn't let them do their job. Jungle warfare. Shouldn't have been there in the first place.

Another respondent listed both "Vietnam" and "senseless killing" as initial associations and offered the following secondary associations:

> Worthless. Inexperienced. Killing of youth. Hippies. Boots made for walking. Experimental weapons. Released information. Hidden news. Real war. Conditions of combat.

Viewer reactions to "Never Again" were fully consistent with the "Generic Vietnam War Narrative" evoked by the mention of Vietnam, the picture of the Vietnam Memorial, and the somber militaristic soundtrack. While some (Gronbeck 1994) would see this as a comparative ad, to do so would miss much of the substance of the way viewers actually processed the spot.

The evidence discussed here supports the contention that the audio-visual evocation of popular genres influences the way viewers process political advertising. This evidence is exploratory and not definitive; nevertheless, the consistency of this support is noteworthy. In some ways, it is striking that political ads with as many similarities as the ones we have discussed could generate such different responses.

These ads would probably be viewed by many as "negative" ads. Yet, to leave it at this would be to miss much of what makes these ads "tick." In the next chapter, we will consider how productive viewing campaign ads through the lens of negativity really is.

NOTES

1. Gina M. Garramone has applied schema theory to political advertising specifically (see Garramone 1984, 1986; Garramone, Steele, and Pinkleton 1991); see also Lau 1986.

2. Among political scientists, G. R. Boynton, Milton Lodge, and Kathleen McGraw have been at the forefront of a movement to develop research techniques that measure such representational structures (Boynton 1995; Lodge 1995; McGraw and Steenbergen 1995).

3. See also Lodge, McGraw, Conover, Feldman, and Miller 1991 for a response to the Kuklinski et al. critique.

4. See for example Lau 1986; Conover and Feldman 1984, 1986; Miller 1986.

5. For another example using free recall, see McGraw, Pinney, and Neumann 1991.

6. The use of undergraduates here is defensible on several grounds, especially in an exploratory context. Perhaps most importantly, the use of a population subgroup (students) is exactly how actual campaigns test-market their appeals, often using small focus groups. Additionally, the primary use of this data here is to illustrate a *range* of viewer uses of negativity, rather than claims about central tendency, which would be more suspect to sample bias. Further, an analysis of fifty-two studies of negative advertising concluded that the use of student samples did not significantly affect the effect size (Lau, Sigelman, Heldman and Babbitt, 1999: 859). Last and not least, are issues of cost and feasibility. For a rigorous defense of student samples in experimental designs, see Kinder and Palfrey (1993:27–28) and Campbell (1969).

7. Witness the effectiveness of early radio productions of horror; see also Nelson and Boynton 1997:133–42 on the role of music in horror.

8. See for example Devlin 1986.

9. The terms were drawn in part from the "wheel of emotions," a graphic representation of several emotional states that commercial advertisers seek to manipulate that was developed in 1984 by Stuart J. Agres of the New York advertising firm Lowe-Marschalk (Kern 1989:30–32). Additional terms were included, which, although not technically a part of the "wheel of emotions" concerned similar emotional conditions.

10. The small size of the experimental sample and the wide range of viewer response resulted in estimates with standard errors large enough to pose substantial difficulties for conventional tests of statistical significance.

Chapter Three

The Attack on Attack Politics: Why "Negative" Advertising Is Good for Democracy

If there is a single concept that is most closely associated with political advertising, both in the minds of the public and in the work of scholarly researchers, it is negativity. Over and over and over again, we hear how negative campaign ads are and how bad that is for politicians, for politics, for debate, and for democracy itself. Yet, "poison politics," writes Victor Kamber, "is as old as politics itself." The great Roman statesman and orator Marcus Tullius Cicero, he notes, "was a negative campaigner of the first rank" (Kamber 1997:6). Political attack has been a staple of American civic life at least since the nation's first truly contested presidential campaign in 1796, and today's assaults have much in common with their predecessors of two hundred years ago (Jamieson 1984, 1992a; Smith 1963). Recently, however, the argument that negativity is as a pox on the body politic has reached a tumultuous roar. Six weeks after the bombing of the Alfred P. Murrah Federal Building in Oklahoma City sparked a renewed focus on inflammatory and socially destructive speech, the late Pulitzer Prize-winning *Washington Post* columnist Meg Greenfield (1995) sounded these notes on incivility in public discourse, singling out campaign spots:

> These are assault ads, conveying the simple message, over and over, that Brand X, the rival, is a cheesy piece of goods, won't hold up, has to be cranked by hand.... This is the model for not just our commercial product sales but, rather more viciously, for our political campaigns as well.... We have gradually just gotten used to them. It's not so much that I am wonder-

ful, the candidate explains, as that the opponent is a lying, cowardly, two-faced cheat and con artist.

Greenfield is far from alone in her concern. Noting the ways in which patriotism and prejudice in televised political advertising drive a visceral rather than a rational response in viewers, Kathleen Hall Jamieson asks, "Is warranted engagement possible in such times on such terms?" (Jamieson 1992a:64).

Negative or attack advertising has become one of the most pervasive themes of American political discourse. Journalists, academics, and voters freely (and frequently) denounce negative campaigning. Negative campaign advertising has been linked to a more polarized electorate and decreased voter turnout (Ansolabehere and Iyengar 1995), erosion of the deliberative ethos in Congress (Clinger 1987:731–32; Diamond and Bates 1988:385), an alienated citizenry (Johnson-Cartee and Copeland 1991:275–76), and the bombing in Oklahoma City (Greenfield 1995). When the American National Election Study asked voters in 1992 if they remembered anything about the campaign ads they saw on TV, the single biggest response category among those who didn't ignore ads was "negative campaigning." In fact, the use of "negative" to describe political advertising may have become so commonplace, even among scholars, that it has become an umbrella under which a gaggle of quite distinguishable attributes have been gathered. To the extent that it is meaningful to distinguish between positive comments about one's self and negative remarks about one's opponent, the latter are clearly among democracy's most precious expressive freedoms. Campaign consultants and some researchers have attempted to draw a distinction between legitimate comparison and injurious assault. This chapter presents exploratory evidence suggesting that not only does this reasonable refinement prove unhelpful in assessing viewer responses to campaign spots, it is also inconsistent with free and unfettered electoral competition. If we are to diagnose the ailments plaguing campaign communication or determine whether such ailments are real or imagined, we must move beyond the positive/negative taxonomy. The following is a step in that direction.

More specifically, our task unfolds on two levels. The first challenge is to better understand political advertising, and to unpack the components of "negative" campaigns and reassemble them into a more coherent whole. This may provide the basis for a more informed and less benighted public discourse on campaign spots. Briefly, negativity has been defined in ways that are too broad (encompassing elements of campaign spots that are importantly independent of each other), insufficiently wholistic, too hostile to legitimate campaign grievances, and ultimately irrelevant in a constitutional framework grounded on free speech and retrospective accountability. We can do much more to recognize that negativity is a contestable, complex, and multidimensional concept.

The second challenge, even more important, is to place our contemporary disdain for negative campaigning into a meaningful theoretical and historical context. The ills we now focus on, such as decreased voter turnout, are more chronic than acute and can be dated back at least as far as the turn of the twentieth century. Since that time, we have seen a century-long war by political reformers on politics—which is seen as base and insufficiently responsive to the public interest—and especially on political parties which are seen as corrupt. One of the key fronts in this war has been devoted to severing the emotional, and, it is argued, irrational underpinnings of political action. As early as 1880, reformers were denouncing a politics based on reasons why a voter "should *not* vote with 'his party,' whereas the party ought to show why he *should* vote with it" (Bowker 1880). In the late nineteenth and early twentieth centuries, the mugwumps (earnest, elitist, upper-class political reformers who held conservative economic views) sought to fashion a politics derived from reason, which they saw threatened by the ever-expanding right to vote. The new voters were the unwashed masses who fueled what the reformers saw as corrupt partisan machines. While the reformers did succeed in weakening political parties, they failed to replace the passionate attachments that voters had to politics and their party, attachments often sustained in part by fierce political attack. It is not surprising that voter turnout declined as citizens had fewer reasons to get excited about politics. Emotion lies at the heart of both the assault on "negative" advertising and larger important issues of electoral democracy.

In the sections that follow, we will explore common approaches to analyzing "negative" advertising, then move to consider actual viewers' use of the term "negative" in their assessment of campaign ads. The next section examines the history of campaigning and notes the threads common to both the independent reform movement and the approaches to negative advertising. Finally, we will begin to consider ways that the theoretical underpinnings of electoral democracy can shape our analysis of campaign communication, and conclude with some potentially productive alternative avenues for future study.

NEGATIVE ADVERTISING: INCOMPLETE APPROACHES

Approaches to negative advertising come from several perspectives, each of which grasps at a part of the larger whole. Three shortcomings characterize these approaches. First, some have defined negativity narrowly, strictly in terms of an ad's verbal tone, ignoring other elements of political commercials (in particular audiovisuals) that might influence viewer response and perceptions of "negativity."[1] A second approach has been to implicitly recognize audiovisual and narrative elements, but to fuse them with all other potential sources of perceived negativity rather than treating them as importantly distinct. Finally, some separate audiovisual elements from negativity but fail to fully appreciate the wholistic ways ads are processed by viewers. Although the visual images and musical scoring of ads may be independent of an ad's "negativity," they are not independent of each other. That is, words, pictures, and music work together. Analysts who neglect such wholistic functioning may fail to find significant effects from audiovisual production elements (because they are being treated separately while they function wholistically) or to mistakenly attribute effects to particular elements rather than to the interaction of several elements. Let us consider each of these three approaches in turn.

Negative Ads as Attacking One's Opponent

One approach looks at negativity strictly in terms of an ad's "tone" (Ansolabehere and Iyengar 1995:23–24). With this view an ad becomes negative when a statement like "John Seymour *proposed* new government ethics rules," is replaced with "Bill Dannemeyer *opposed* new government ethics rules," or when "California *needs* John Seymour in the U.S. Senate" is replaced by "California *can't afford a politician* like Bill Dannemeyer in the U.S. Senate." An ad's visuals, voice-over, and musical background do not factor into "negativity." Other variations of this approach have also sought to characterize political ads largely along a simple positive/negative continuum (Skaperdas and Grofman 1995), sometimes in combination with an issue/image dimension (see Biocca 1991a).

This is surely the most straightforward definition of negativity, for which it can be praised. Approaches such as this, however, are largely silent about emotion, the affective cornerstone of negative advertising. Indeed, the tone of an ad is but a sliver of the information processed by the brain when viewing audiovisual content. By holding an ad's "production values" constant, moreover, this approach restricts one's ability to gauge the subterranean meaning political spots often evoke, meaning that surely must be counted if we are to fully explore how political advertising works. An ad's verbal tone is inextricably linked to its audio and visual components. The very same verbal statements may have manifestly different impacts when combined with different background music and visual imagery (Richardson 1998a). While some analysts recognize the salience of the emotional tone of a political spot, they treat it separately from the ad's verbal tone (Just et al. 1996). This does little to clarify the effect of political advertising in the minds of viewers who do not ordinarily make such analytical distinctions.

Bruce Gronbeck (1994) suggests that not all "negative" ads have unsavory effects on political process and culture, and argues that it is therefore necessary to distinguish among different types of negative ads, where "negative" is broadly defined as when one "creates unattractive or undesirable images of one's political opponents." He offers a three-category typology of argumentatively structured negative ads: *implicative* (attacks on the opponent are not explicit; the ad focuses on the sponsoring candidate, not the opponent), *comparative* (explicit comparison between the candidate and his or her opponent) and *assault* (the ad's single focus is an explicit attack on his or her opponent's character, motives, associates, or actions). Others have adopted essentially this same demarcation (Newhagen and Reeves 1991; Lang 1991; Johnson-Cartee and Copeland 1991). While making an important distinction that acknowledges the legitimacy of candidate comparisons (which may reflect negatively on the opposition), the Gronbeck typology is also largely silent on the question of the impact of nonargumentative ad content such as audiovisuals on viewer response.

Negative Ads as "You Know 'em When You See 'em"

Another prominent research strategy has been to code actual candidate ads as negative or positive and then use particular negative ads as a stimuli in viewer response experiments.[2] Kahn and Kenney (1999) surveyed political consultants to identify the main themes of their opponent's campaigns, coding certain responses as indicative of races characterized by "mudslinging." Campaign managers' depictions of their opponents' campaigns as "harsh," "strident," "relentless attacks" point to races that have gone beyond the boundaries of democratic civility. The consultants' language evokes emotion, though the authors' framework leaves affective response in a black box. We can know that some campaigns crossed the line, but we cannot discern exactly what they did to do so.

One might distinguish policy attacks from personal ones. Policy attacks may be seen as legitimate and relevant, but personal ones not. Yet candidates often make personal character a key element of their campaign appeals. Should their opponents be denied the opportunity to challenge such claims without fear of being attacked for engaging in negative tactics? Even when candidates don't explicitly emphasize "character," it may be a readily accessible heuristic or cognitive shortcut for many potential voters (Popkin 1994). That is, given the complexity of policy questions and the relatively low priority politics has for many voters, attempting to judge a candidate on the basis of their character may be an appealing way for citizens to make a difficult choice without exerting great effort. Even exceptionally well-informed voters might wish to weigh character in the evaluation of presidential contenders. James David Barber argued that the performance of presidents in office was a function of their personalities (Barber 1972). Should office seekers be condemned or even prohibited from anticipating such developments and attempting to respond to them?

Even if one answers "yes," and personal criticisms are not prohibited, the complexity of campaign advertising means that certain offensive elements of ads would surely still persist. Political ads are more than claims and counterclaims. They are textured audiovisual packages rich with evocative associations that may be important aspects of the emotional impact of campaign communications.

Typically, when ads are categorized by viewers or consultants as negative, audiovisual content may or may not contribute to that classification, but no effort is made to assess the relative contribution of the ad's components in provoking viewer response. We can know that viewers saw an ad as negative (or as assaultive or comparative), but studies such as these are not designed to tell us why.

Negative Ads as the By-Product of Isolated Audiovisual Production Values

Montague Kern's *30-Second Politics* (1989) does begin to suggest to us why some voters see some ads as negative. She offers a distinction between "hard-sell" and "soft-sell" negative advertising. For her, hard-sell negative advertising "utilizes dark colors and threatening voices" to create a sense of "harsh reality." Soft-sell negative advertising employs "humor, self deprecation, storytelling, or the unexpected turn of events." She goes on to offer five subcategories of negative advertising, based on the emotions evoked: guilt, fear (strong form), fear (mild form), anger, and uncertainty. Each of the five categories theoretically could occur in either hard- or soft-sell negative advertising (95).

By and large, however, Kern's approach, as well as that of others who have sought to probe the effects of audiovisual production (Kepplinger 1991; Thorson, Christ, and Caywood 1991), is to view such techniques in isolation, and not as integrated parts of a coherent whole. Separately, the audiovisual conventions of a horror story (a frequent motif for political spots) would fail to produce the same response that they do when working in tandem. For example, black-and-white images can be used to convey a "sinister" impression (West 1997:7). Then again, these images often also appear in positive ads (especially candidate biographies) without such negative implications. More recently, candidates (such as Malcom S. "Steve" Forbes in his 2000 presidential bid) and product advertisers have used black-and-white imagery simply to draw viewer attention by departing from the color norm. The key is the combination of black-and-white imagery, a "slasher" soundtrack and an appropriately compelling narrative.

VIEWERS AND "NEGATIVE" ADVERTISING: EVIDENCE FROM THE 1992 AMERICAN NATIONAL ELECTION STUDY

Researchers are not the only ones to view political advertising principally through the lens of negativity. Voters do so as well. Consider the results from the American National Election Study (ANES), the most significant academic survey of American voters, conducted during every presidential election since the 1950s. In 1992, interviewers for the ANES asked their sample of voters, "Do you recall seeing any presidential campaign advertisements on television?" and "Please tell me, what do you remember about any of these ads? (Do you remember any others?)" Up to five mentions were coded for each respondent. Each mention was placed into one of nearly two hundred possible categories. Three categories are consistent with negative campaigning ("negative campaigning," "dishonest/misleading," and "negative effect"). Each of these categories could be associated with any of the three major candidates (Bush, Clinton, or Perot) or with a "general" category for mentions lacking reference to a specific candidate, so the total number of negative categories is twelve. There were three positive categories corresponding to each of the three negative ones, again, totaling twelve when applied to each of the candidates and "general." Additionally, specific mentions of each candidate's ads were coded.[3]

Table 3.1 summarizes the "positive" and "negative" first mentions of respondents to the ANES advertising probe.[4] Each cell of the table represents the proportion of the total sample (excluding those who didn't answer or said they didn't pay attention to campaign ads), according to the nature of that recollection. The single largest response category was a general reference to negative campaigning, reported by 17 percent of respondents. Adding the two other response categories consistent with negativity (dishonest/misleading and negative effect), better than 20 percent of the respondents offered general references to negativity. Including all the references specifically tied to one of the three candidates, the proportion of negative comments rises to 28 percent. By contrast, only 2 percent of respondents offered positive recollections of the ads, either in general or in terms of a specific candidate. The imbalance in respondents' first mentions of 1992 campaign ads is clear. Negative comments outnumber positive ones by a factor of *fourteen*. This is despite the fact that the most frequently nationally aired ad by the Bush campaign, "Agenda" (Just et al. 1996:72) was not negative, but offered a summary of the president's economic plan. When they looked at the average "emotional tone" of ads in the 1992 campaign, moreover, Just et al. (1996:84) found both Clinton and Perot ads to average on the positive side of neutral (3.2 and 3.5 out of 5), and Bush ads just slightly more negative (2.7) than the neutral score (3). Why then were the ANES respondents so eager to label what they remember of the 1992 ads as "negative"?

Consider the Bush ad "Arkansas," which painted a bleak picture of Clinton's record as governor. ANES respondents mentioned this ad more often than any other spot. While it is a one-sided attack (Bush is not mentioned), it also features the audiovisual conventions of horror or dystopia, portraying a foreboding, windswept, barren wasteland representing Bill Clinton's Arkansas. It does not, however, attack Clinton personally; it focuses on his record as governor. Just et al. (1996:64) discuss the difficulty posed by such appeals, noting that in extreme

Table 3.1. Evaluations of Candidate Advertising in the 1992 ANES (first mention)

	Negative				Positive			
	Negative Campaigning	Dishonest/ Misleading	Negative Effect	TOTAL	Positive Campaigning	Honest/ Straightforward	Positive Effect	TOTAL
Reference								
General	17.0%	2.0%	1.5%	20.5%	.3%	0%	.3%	.6%
Bush	5.2	.2	.5	5.9	.1	0	.3	.4
Clinton	1.1	.2	.1	1.4	0	.1	.2	.3
Perot	.2	0	0	.1	.1	.2	.4	.7
TOTAL	23.5%	2.4%	2.1%	27.9%	.5%	.3%	1.2%	2.0%

N = 1,326 (Excludes those who didn't answer or said they didn't pay attention to campaign ads).

form, an attack on one's record can be seen as suggesting a lack of moral character and unfitness for office. They also note, however, that "candidates, viewers and even analysts have difficulty discerning when such a line is crossed."

The difficulty with these and so many other findings regarding "negative" ads is that they can tell us *that* negative ads are more easily recalled, cause lower turnout and so on, but not *why* this is so. We would need to know more about how ads work to do this, and focusing on negativity alone cannot provide that leverage. We need to know, in more specific terms, what it is about these ads that distinguishes them from other spots. This point is crucial to the growing public debate about negative ads and their consequences for the political system as a whole.

VIEWER RESPONSE TO NEGATIVE ADVERTISING: SOME EXPERIMENTAL EVIDENCE

A major strength of the ANES data is the size and representativeness of its sample. Because of this, we can be fairly confident that the predominance of references to negative campaigning found in the ANES responses reflect sentiments widely held among American voters. If one wants to dig deeper, however, into exactly what viewers mean when they use the term "negative" or what kinds of ads generate such responses, the ANES data were simply not designed for this task. Voters were not asked to respond to specific ads, nor were they asked questions that could help illuminate what they meant when they described an ad as "negative." The total number of respondents who did name a specific ad, moreover, is a small fraction of the sample. "Arkansas" was the ad most frequently cited in first mentions, but less than 3 percent of those who didn't ignore ads, or just thirty-six respondents, mentioned it. Those responses, in turn, were grouped according to the categories such as those listed above, providing precious little analytical leverage in exploring the meaning of negativity.

To further investigate the range of viewers' use of "negative" to describe campaign ads, we can turn to the small group experiment exploratory data discussed in chapter 2. Here, a limited sample size is advantageous, since it facilitates a depth of analysis that would be very difficult in a larger-scale investigation.

Experimental Design

The two ads produced for the 1990 Michigan U.S. Senate campaign of Republican Bill Schuette provide a basis for comparison. Both ads pointed out that opponent Carl Levin opposed the Maverick anti-tank missile and the battleship USS *Wisconsin*. One ("Never Again") featured Schuette in front of the Vietnam Memorial in Washington, D.C., and offered an explicitly comparative framework ("I voted for it, Carl Levin opposed it"). The other ("Levin of Arabia") featured a disheveled Levin, satirically ridiculed for his trip to the *Wisconsin* for a photo shoot at taxpayers' expense. It attacks the opponent without even mentioning the sponsor's position. According to the Gronbeck typology, the first of these ads is comparative, the second assaultive (ad scripts in chapter 2). It bears repeating that the data presented here are *exploratory*, which befits the embryonic nature of the effort to "unpack" the components of "negativity" in campaign advertising. These data do not resolve these issues conclusively, but they do provide sufficient support to pursue the larger project of moving beyond "negativity" in studying political advertising.

Viewer Responses

Negative Advertising as Comparison

Gronbeck and others argue for distinguishing comparative from assaultive negative advertising, but such distinctions may not be as easy in practice as they are in principle. Consider the range of responses offered by one viewer of Bill Schuette's ad "Never Again." When asked "how would you describe the ad to a friend?" one respondent wrote:

> This advertisement involved a Republican candidate in a short speech (soundspot) to enhance his election efforts. He talked in short sentences w/ regard to 2 or 3 weapons systems he supported that he said his opponent did not support. He made statements of support for the US pres.

This retelling casts the ad largely in comparative terms, yet this statement barely scratches the surface of the way in which the respondent processed the ad. Asked "what do you remember hearing?" the same viewer wrote:

His voice was strong & forceful. Sentences were short w/o much elaboration. Thoughts expressed weren't necessarily related. Outdoor scene, mother, America and Fourth of July flavor. Attractive scenery—no hint of poverty.

And when asked to "describe your feelings" upon viewing the ad: "I don't like to feel manipulated or be used, so my reaction was a feeling of disregard with a smile." Among the first five associations this viewer offered to the ad were: "He is using patriotism to his only personal advantage. There are enough real issues that he should be debating w/o need to manipulate votes through fear." So while this respondent fully and explicitly recognized the comparative structure of "Never Again," the range of reactions was much broader. It was the generic evocation of patriotism that seemed to generate the cynical attitude that some might see as one of the unsavory consequences of "negative" advertising. This effectively overwhelmed the ad's overt comparison of the two candidates.

In fact, most of the respondents who used the language of comparison did so in ways that offer little encouragement for those craving more enlightened political discourse. On the surface, viewer response to "Never Again" indicates that the comparison between the two candidates was something that many people picked up on. A majority of respondents (eighteen out of thirty-four) made some reference to what can be at least loosely construed as comparison. This stands in stark contrast to the infrequency of references to comparison offered by viewers of the satirical ad, "Levin of Arabia," which included the same charge about Levin's opposition to two weapons but did not make the explicit comparison with candidate Schuette's position.

The exploratory data, however, allow for a deeper exploration of what viewers took from the ad, and the responses suggest that comparison was not necessarily the dominant feature of "Never Again." Rather, many viewers' references to comparison seemed almost ritualistic in nature. One of the initial five associations with "Never Again" offered by a respondent was "specifically naming his opponent." This person offered only one secondary association for this: "Him vs. other guy. He's good. Opponent's bad." Similarly, another respondent listed "somebody voted for something the opponent didn't" as an initial association, and also offered only one secondary association for that: "Does it matter that the other guy didn't?" A third respondent included the following initial association: "He didn't, I did statement—stuck with me even after the commercial was over." In response to the probe seeking secondary associations, for "he didn't, I did," this viewer wrote: "Stuck w/ me. Made other guy look bad. All politicians say it. Good way to attack." For this respondent, comparison was actually a technique of *attack*. Very little (if any) of this type of response can be categorized as the healthy comparison of issue stands that provides the justification for elevating or even distinguishing "comparative" advertising over other forms of "negative" appeals.

This respondent, moreover, was quite atypical in actually mentioning the specific policy positions presented in the ad (even though they wrongly stated that support for a plane was at issue; the battleship USS *Wisconsin* was the other weapon mentioned in the ad). Most of the respondents who offered the language of comparison did so in terms of more global concepts such as a "strong defense" or support for the troops. For example, one put it this way: "Two candidates are running for the same political office. One supports a strong defense and the importance of it while the other does not."

It is noteworthy that the "assaultive" ad "Levin of Arabia" actually generated *more* focus, both positive and negative, on the narrow policy issue at hand—support for specific weapons and the military in general—than the "comparative" ad "Never Again." Perhaps the ad's visuals of the ship reinforced the ad's substantive charges, while the visuals of the Vietnam Memorial overrode that ad's references to the weapons. It is possible to conclude that if the goal is to foster discussion of "issues," one-sided assaultive ads can, at least on occasion, be even *more* effective than explicit comparisons.

Negative Advertising as Assaultive

Additional evidence of the cloudiness surrounding extant understandings of negativity can be found in Figure 3.1, which presents the mean line responses for the two ads studied to four conditions that might be associated with "negative" advertising: cynicism, anger, sadness and frustration. For these conditions, the satirical, assaultive "Levin of Arabia" scores *lower* than the comparative "Never Again."

Again the responses run somewhat counter to the expectations that one might have based on the nature of the negativity among these ads. "Levin of Arabia" scored lower on measures of responses related to negativity—despite being the more one-sided, assaultive ad. This points to something campaign consultants have long known, something that further challenges the conventional ways of categorizing

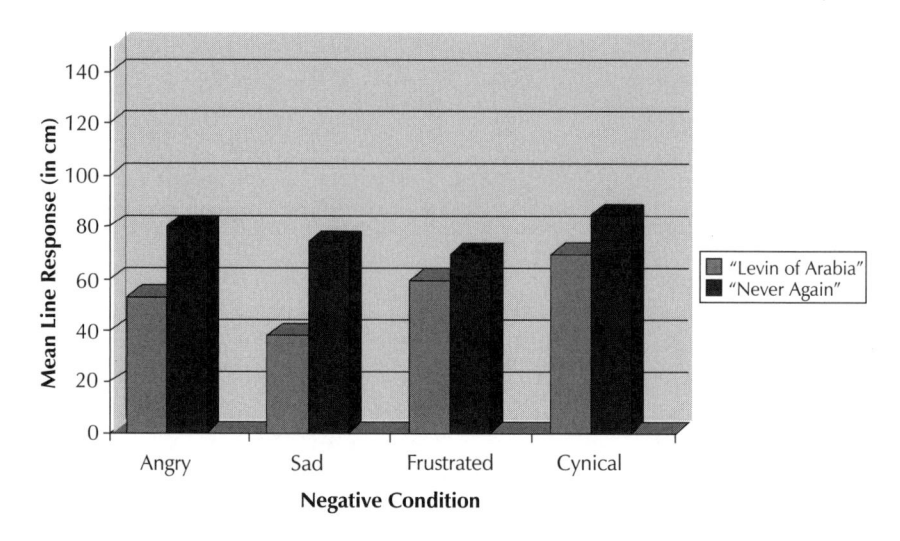

Figure 3.1. Negative Response by Ad

ads: many of the most damning indictments are effectively smuggled under the guise of humor.[5] In short, there appears to be little support for separating comparative from assaultive commercials, at least at the level of viewer response.

So what exactly do viewers mean when they describe ads as negative? The sections that follow are an effort to "unpack" the meaning of negativity in viewers' minds. The exploratory response data reveal four different uses or connotations of negativity: unbalanced, misleading, cutthroat, and emotional. Each use stands alone as at least somewhat coherent. Some might appear to bear kinship with existing academic typologies. Yet, taken as a whole, these four conceptualizations show how "negative" is not a particularly coherent term, especially when coupled with the lack of connection between the content of ads and their being labeled "negative." Ultimately, the use of "negative" by viewers is infused with such disparate meanings that it is difficult to pin down exactly what one might learn from the study of "negative" advertising.

Negative Ads as Unbalanced

Perhaps the most pervasive sense of negativity among the respondents saw the ads as offering only an attack on the opponent with no statement of the ad sponsor's position. This reaction echoed Gronbeck's assaultive category, but it was also used to describe the explicitly comparative spot. "Never Again" was included in this study specifically because of its explicit comparative nature. It named both candidates and stated both of their positions. Perhaps if that was all that was in the ad, viewer response would have been more benign, providing evidence for Gronbeck's contention that comparative ads need not wound the body politic. As with most ads, however, the visual, aural, and mythic aspects of "Never Again" (with the Vietnam Memorial as its backdrop) went far beyond mere comparison. Despite the fact that the ad says "I voted for it, Carl Levin opposed it," some viewers saw the ad as one-sided. One offered the following "retelling": "He was using the success of the war to play upon people's emotions of pride. It was one-sided, noninformative, slanted." Another wrote in response to the "feelings" probe: "I want to know the other side/refute his stance. How much is it going to cost US? What is being cut while you support the defense program?" This perception of the ad as being negative because it was one-sided suggests that for some viewers, a slender comparison is essentially no comparison. Given the limited nature of the thirty-second spot, it is not surprising that some viewers found the ad's policy comparison unfulfilling. The tone of these "negative/unbalanced" responses, however, was generally moderate compared to the other more vociferous conceptions of negativity.

Negative Ads as Misleading or Distorted

One prominent way in which viewers saw the ads as negative was the suggestion that they employed "half-truths" or "distortion." A respondent provided this retelling of "Levin of Arabia":

> I would explain the advertisement as a challenge to an incumbent Democrat (sic) Senator by a Republican. It was a negative campaign ad, that probably lacked in complete accuracy and could very well be the beginning of a vicious round of mudslinging.

Although viewers often wove more than one description of why they considered the ad to be negative through their responses, the notion that the ad was negative because it literally tried to make Carl Levin "look bad" was particularly common. Given the role that physical depictions play in satire, this might have been expected. One respondent's initial associations included: "Looked negative toward the candidate—like someone else made it (opponent). Showed the politician w/ his hair messed up and blowing. . . . Negative advertising—in a way cheating." This person elaborated with these secondary associations: "Showed bad and unpleasant pictures of him. All negative points. Hair blowing and messed up. . . . Very negative pictures."

The videotaped image of Carl Levin onboard the USS *Wisconsin* to which "Levin of Arabia" repeatedly returned presented its own damning indictment of the incumbent Senator. In this it is reminiscent of the 1988 Bush campaign's "Tank Ride" spot featuring Massachusetts Governor Michael Dukakis cruising a General Dynamics factory parking lot in an M-1 tank. Long after viewers of that ad had forgotten the specific policy charges that scrawled down the screen, they remembered the satirical imagery of the presidential hopeful awkwardly "driving" the tank. Some on the Dukakis team (and many in the punditry) felt that ultimately it was the military helmet the governor donned that made this episode so visually debilitating. In "Levin of Arabia," the candidate's windswept and disheveled hair performed a similar function, all outside the narrow boundaries of negativity as typically defined.

Negative Ads as Politics "By Any Means Necessary" in a Debased Political System

One common reading of "negative" advertising was based on an assessment of campaign *tactics*. What these responses had in common was a profoundly loathsome view of the political process. If one looks beyond the immediate references to negative advertising in these responses, one finds a good deal of cynicism about the character and truthfulness of politicians. These viewers evidently perceive politicians and their modus operandi as generally despicable. One respondent offered a succinct response to the "feelings" probe: "I don't have too much emotion. I just felt like he was making a scam."

The assaultive ad "Levin of Arabia" did prompt many viewers to describe the ad as "negative." Yet in doing so, most did not rely primarily on what defines it as assaultive in the Gronbeck typology, its one-sided accusations. Instead viewers found the ad's visual depictions negative and also saw it as negative in the way it reflected their generic notions of a debased contemporary political discourse, one characterized by falsehoods, half-truths, hypocrisy, and "bashing" one's opponents. This was in part due to the ad's successful ridicule of its target, yet it also "boomeranged" back onto the ad's sponsor.[6]

Negative Ads as Emotional (Not Substantive)

The final sense of negativity involved viewers who focused on the ads' use of emotional appeals. Typically, it is the use of fear and graphic imagery that is seen by viewers and analysts alike as supplanting rational discussion of "issues." Indeed, for some viewers, the comparative ad "Never Again" was seen as negative because it sought to play upon a combination of emotions, in this case fear and patriotism. One viewer responded to the "feelings" probe this way: "Disappointed that that ad was targeting people's fears in order to compel them to vote for someone who's pro-arms spending." They underscored this sentiment in retelling the story of the ad: "This candidate is pro-military and preys upon public's fears and hostility to try and get into office."

Of course, while an ad can be seen as "negative" because of the way it manipulates emotion, "positive" ads can be quite emotional too. In sum, upon unpacking, the attributes that lead viewers to describe ads as negative are, in fact, untethered to attack per se. Distortion, emotional appeals, and one-sidedness invite academic attention and may even warrant condemnation. But they can easily be found in positive ads as well, and can be effectively cleaved from "negativity."

A BRIEF HISTORY OF "NEGATIVE" CAMPAIGNING

Negativity, it would seem, is at once everywhere and yet nowhere. We can know it when we see it, yet we struggle to accurately and meaningfully define it. Scholars tell us that it decreases voter turnout (Ansolabehere and Iyengar 1995; Ansolabehere, Iyengar, and Simon 1999), that it increases voter turnout (Wattenberg and Brians 1999; Freedman and Goldstein 1999), or that it just depends on the specific nature of the attack (Kahn and Kenney 1999). For all that and more, however, a meta-analysis of fifty-two studies of the effects of negative advertising failed to support *any* of the major claims associated with negative ads (Lau, Sigelman, Heldman, and Babbitt 1999). It is reasonable to ask, then, how did we come to such a point?

In a narrow sense, the focus on negativity is of relatively recent vintage. For the better part of the twentieth century, including the first two decades of the television era, the major concern regarding political advertising was that candidates were using the techniques of soap-selling to beguile voters into supporting them—i.e., a fear of *positive* advertising. Theodore Roosevelt, commenting on Mark Hanna's campaign on behalf of William McKinley, exclaimed, "He has advertised McKinley as if he were a patent medicine!" (Beer 1929:165). TR himself was to become one of the great practitioners of the new-style campaign. Nearly three-quarters of a century later, Joe McGinniss wrote a best-selling expose on the Madison Avenue tactics behind the marketing of the "'new' new Nixon" in 1968 (McGinniss 1969).

At the same time, political attack was an enduring feature of the American political landscape. The nation's first truly contested presidential campaign, between John Adams and Thomas Jefferson in 1796, was marked by "lies ... innuendo, distortion and falsehood" (Felknor, 1966:18–19). While the vitriol directed at Jefferson would sustain a level of animosity later observed toward Franklin Roosevelt (Coyle 1960) and, in our times, toward Bill Clinton, Felknor argues that the first "spectacularly dirty" campaign occurred in 1828 (1966:40). That campaign was also the first "big money" presidential campaign in U.S. history, with the populist Jacksonian Democrats bankrolled by monied interests seeking to rid the nation's capital of John Quincy Adams and his cronies (Sher 1997:33–34). Handbills directed against Jackson, some of which featured coffins representing those unjustly killed at his hand, charged him with murder, ordering executions of his own men, massacring Indians, back-stabbing (literally), and hanging three Indians (Jamieson 1984; see also Sher 1997:35). When Abraham Lincoln stood for reelection in 1864, Felknor (1966:27) writes,

> (While) none of the slanderous smear words ... began with the letters Q, X, Y or Z ... a fragmentary but representative list of epithet includes: Ape, Buffoon, Coward, Drunkard, Execrable, Fiend, Ghoul, Hopeless, Ignoramus, Jokester (in the face of war tragedies), Knave, Lunatic, Murderer, Negro, Outlaw, Perjurer, Robber, Savage, Traitor, Usurper, Vulgar, Weakling.

In 1884, a Protestant clergyman sharing a platform with GOP presidential nominee James G. Blaine attacked the Democrats and their Irish supporters, claiming that the party's "antecedents have been rum, Romanism and rebellion," while twelve years later, William Jennings Bryan claimed that Republican policies were crucifying farmers and laborers on a "cross of gold."

Attack campaigning continued in the twentieth century. Anti-Semitism was not uncommon. Franklin D. Roosevelt was assaulted relentlessly, in election years and nonelection years alike. The Cold War fueled McCarthyism and the "red scare." In 1960, John F. Kennedy summed up some of the attacks that had been launched over the years by his opponent, Richard M. Nixon, during a November 3 campaign speech in Wichita Falls, Texas. Nixon, according to Kennedy,

> in 1952 said Acheson had graduated from the College of Cowardly Communist Containment, in 1951 called Truman a traitor, in 1960 called me a liar, and in 1960 called Lyndon an ignoramus. Lyndon said he called me one. I said he called him one. He called me rash, inexperienced, reckless, and uninformed. But he called *Lyndon* an ignoramus. (Kennedy 1960)

And 1960 was the *least* negative campaign of the second half of the twentieth century (Jamieson, Waldman, and Sherr 2000).

Yet, by the 1990s, academics were pointing to an apparent upward trend in negativity beginning with the early TV campaigns of the 1950s (Kaid and Johnston 1991; West 1997). Others, however, found the trend nonexistent when contrast ads were distinguished from pure attacks (Jamieson, Waldman, and Sherr 2000). What is clear is that academic interest in negative advertising specifically began with a trickle in the 1970s (Stewart 1975; Surlin and Gordon 1977) and became a veritable torrent in the 1990s. In their bibliography of research on campaign communication during the period from 1973 to 1982, Kaid and Wadsworth (1985) list 75 entries in the index under "political advertising," none of which includes the words "negative" or "attack" in the title. A cursory reading of their 2,461 total citations indicates only three include references to negativity in the title. Researchers were not oblivious to less than positive appeals. Article titles did include words such as lying, assault, bigotry, dishonesty, deception, scapegoating, mudslinging, McCarthyism, and the effects of "vindicated criminal charges." They did not, however, embrace the global use of "negativity" in probing how campaign ads work. The situation had begun to change dramatically over the following decade. After attempting to "access every relevant study" on negative advertising, and concluding that they had located "the great majority of them," Lau et al. (1999) included 52 studies in their meta-analysis, only five of which appeared before 1990. If attack politics is as old as the Republic, what prompted this profusion of published work over the last decade?

At least four factors seem particularly relevant. First, an impressive literature spanning the disciplines of communications, psychology, and political science focused on the evaluative power of negative *information*.[7] Second, several vivid examples of seemingly effective negative advertising captured the attention of researchers during the 1980s, including the National Conservative Political Action Committee

(NCPAC) campaigns of 1978 and 1980, Mitch McConnell's reversal of a substantial deficit in the polls en route to upsetting incumbent Senator Walter "Dee" Huddleston in Kentucky in 1984, and perhaps most prominently, the 1988 Bush campaign's troika of spots attacking Michael Dukakis, "Tank Ride," "Harbor," and "Revolving Door."[8] This was not simply an overreaction to a few striking cases. While Jamieson et al. found no trend toward negativity from 1952 through 1992, they and the other two studies they chart all point to a marked upswing in negativity beginning after 1976, which was the second least negative campaign of the television era (Jamieson, Waldman, and Sherr 2000; West 1997; Kaid and Johnston 1991).[9] Third, television itself was seen as magnifying the emotional impact of political attack, short-circuiting more reasoned deliberation and seemingly threatening the very foundations of democracy (see Jamieson 1992a:50–54). Finally, perhaps the most recognizable form of negative advertising that has emerged employs the stark and ominous audiovisual conventions of the horror story or "slasher" film, literally terrifying viewers and ratcheting up the emotional resonance of attacks considerably (Nelson and Boynton 1997; Richardson 1998a). Such elements, however, are precisely those overlooked in extant conceptions of negativity, and of how political advertising works more broadly.

"NEGATIVITY" AND THE POLITICAL REFORM MOVEMENT

Yet, if the turn toward negativity is a relatively recent phenomenon, it has its roots in the deeper currents of reformist thinking that have dominated debates over democracy for more than a century. The fundamental weakness of nineteenth-century mugwump reformism and the twentieth-century political science that has grown in its image is a thin or arguably nonexistent theory of electoral democracy, especially in terms of the unease directed at the political role of emotion. Then, as now, reformers have sought to elevate rationality and reasoned discourse, and to eradicate the emotional underpinnings of political appeal. Especially in recent years, these have been the emotions evoked through negativity. The century-long decline in voter turnout, however, is far less likely the result of negative advertising than of the century-long attempt of reformers to delegitimize political parties. Parties had served the function of providing citizens a complex of emotional attachment, intellectual substance, and cognitive shortcuts (often through attacking the opposition) that supported popular politics during the nineteenth century, especially between the Civil War and 1896 when voter participation was at its zenith.[10] In short, it's no surprise that people are less engaged politically when they have less to be *excited* about.

Even more importantly, no theory of electoral democracy actually underpins the disdain for negative campaigning. In short, *so what* if negative advertising is more powerful or more persuasive than positive advertising? The notion of negativity may carry considerable psychological currency, but it is not a concept particularly useful in political terms. Even if the case against negative campaigning was warranted, no remedy is available consistent with the First Amendment to the Constitution, and no theory of campaigns and representation is offered to make such a claim sensible. This may be because representation through electoral democracy has been, by and large, the result of political struggle and is not in fact well grounded in any theoretical framework (on electoral democracy, see Natchez 1985:35–39; on representation, see Pitkin 1969, especially 1–6). The Constitution of the United States actively sought to limit popular participation. The right to vote was extended not because of new insights into the values of democracy or the enhanced capability of the citizenry, but because of political efforts to expand the scope of conflict by admitting new voters.

Higher voter turnout carries little intrinsic value of its own. In defense of higher turnout, one can point to Condorcet's jury theorem, indicating the larger the size of the "jury," the greater the likelihood of a "correct" decision, but such an argument depends precisely on the assumption of objective facts and values that politics must contest. Nor is higher voter turnout necessary or sufficient to sustain the benefits of stronger participatory theories of democracy (Pateman 1970; Barber 1984). Indeed, rather than seeing higher turnout as a benefit, independent reformers at the turn of the last century saw it as a threat that needed to be responded to.

Facing an expanded electorate fueled by "irrational" passion, the mugwump answer has been to build a better voter, which may be to say, to remake humankind. The parties, while not necessarily the creatures of any well-formed theory themselves, performed the seemingly desirable functions of facilitating mass participation and legitimation while maintaining some level of elite responsibility. At least the original mugwumps were consistent. They said they wanted *less* participation on the part of the unwashed masses. Twenty-first-century mugwumpery proclaims an interest in expanding participation while prescribing the very remedies that discourage it, at least among the nonelite, by depleting politics of its passions. Nor is it clear exactly which contemporary institutions can help reformers build the better voter. None of the usual suspects (parties, the media, or organized interests) have the credibility or popular support to fashion a reformed campaign style.

For the constitutional framers, literal or pure democracy was undesirable. To the extent that citizen participation in government was seen in any role beyond consent (essentially in retrospective judgement of governmental performance), it was to be nurtured through republican institutions—the schools, town councils, and other aspects of small-town agrarian life celebrated by Thomas Jefferson. Yet republicanism was usurped by the nation's development and its political struggles, including the expansion of the right to vote and the rise of urban industrial society. No theory of mass electoral democracy accounts for these changes or supports a critical assessment of them. Yet reformers persist in pursuit of an idealized, hyperrational electorate where campaigns are governed by strict norms of democratic civility and reasoned discourse.

In part, this understanding has been seeded and nurtured by candidates themselves who readily denounce their opponents' ads as negative or attack advertising, perhaps hoping to generate a backlash. Such self-serving motives find ready support in a populace predisposed to view most advertising in an unfavorable light. So it was that during the 2008 presidential nomination battle, New York Senator Hillary Rodham Clinton's campaign responded to even the slightest criticism from rival Barack Obama as betraying the Illinois' Senator's promise of a "new" kind of politics.

"NEGATIVITY" AND POLITICAL COMPETITION

The attention given to political ads by candidates, the media, and academic researchers may have significantly shaped the perceptions voters have about negative advertising. Certainly, enhanced journalistic and academic scrutiny of ads is desirable. But it seems to have led to an incessant drumbeat of evaluation that often has focused on minutiae to the neglect of larger, more salient concerns and left viewers with the impression that all political ads are fraudulent and hopelessly "biased."

Regardless of the origin of the viewers' evident desire for balance in political ads, it is a curious vision of how campaigns work. Why shouldn't candidates stress their opponents' failings? History tells us this is as American as apple pie. The nation survived decades, indeed centuries, of such appeals with little notice or objection, as candidates were left to fend for themselves in the competition for public support. College football coach Bobby Bowden put it this way responding to opposing coach and personal friend Lou Holtz's charge that Bowden's team had run up the score against Holtz's team in a game early in their coaching careers: "You can only coach one football team out there. It's not my job to keep the score close. That's your job." It was the job of victorious North Carolina Senate candidate John Edwards, whose 1998 campaign spot "False" is a vivid exemplar of a successful response ad, replete with a narrator forcefully intoning "Bull!" in reference to charges from opponent Lauch Faircloth's attack ads. Where ads are false or misleading, accurate information can be offered. As needed, emotion can be met with emotion, as Edwards's ad did. Jamieson notes that even more challenging emotional appeals, such as those based on race, can also be defused as Harold Washington did with TV ads during the 1983 Chicago mayoral campaign (1992a:109–11). Reformers would seemingly condemn emotional appeals altogether in campaigns, especially those with negative connotations. That, however, may be about as sensible as limiting emotional appeals in the proverbial coach's halftime "pep talk."

BEYOND "NEGATIVE" ADVERTISING: SUGGESTIONS FOR THE FUTURE

None of what has been written so far should be taken as an unequivocal endorsement of the current state of political campaigning or as implying that there is nothing that can be done or that needs to be done. Indeed, those who seek to improve the ways campaigns function have several potentially useful options open to them. All involve moving beyond negativity as the centerpiece of the discourse on political campaigning. Let me briefly suggest three possibilities.

Focus on Specific Pathological Elements of Ads

The most pressing weakness in the research of negative advertising is that it has been overly broad in ascribing its causal claims. Making sense of the wide range of plausible—even persuasive—yet contradictory findings requires researchers to more carefully delimit the aspects of the campaign spots they are investigating and the phenomena they wish to link them to. Coding some ads as negative and others as not is too simplistic, ignores too much of the audiovisual content of political communication, and leaves too much uninvestigated to produce a more coherent understanding of how political ads work. Nor is it easy to imagine what can be done about "negative" advertising that wouldn't trample upon constitutional guarantees of free and unfettered debate. For those intent upon addressing the ills attributed to "negative" ads, at the very least the challenge is to focus on specific aspects of campaign commercials that can be legitimately criticized in ways that simple negativity cannot. As demonstrated above, these specific elements may include distorted and misleading claims, emotional and other simplistic appeals that serve to override reason and evidence, and the deliberate use of stereotypes. While such elements are often present in negative ads, *positive* ads can also be distorted, emotional, stereotypical, and one-sided. Even in "negative" ads, many of these tactics are not deployed against candidates themselves. Rather, they are aimed at policy positions, "suspect" groups and others. In this way, they may evade detection under extant formulations of negativity. The same is true of ostensibly "positive" ads that tout one candidate's "character" or "roots in the community" in ways that subtly or not so subtly impugn the opposition on these same grounds.

Refine a Critical Audiovisual Grammar

Additionally, scholars and journalists can follow up Jamieson's (1992a) pioneering work in developing an audiovisual grammar to more effectively challenge ad claims without reinforcing suspect messages, a subject we will return to in chapter 4. The primary limitation of the "visual" grammar that Jamieson has developed and that has been widely adopted by ad analysts around the country is that it is essentially a visual way of confronting the *narrative* claims in ads. It is not designed to confront the way *audiovisual* elements of ads "make" their points. Elsewhere, Jamieson has written that visual communications lack a logic and grammar for argument (1988:11–13, 59–61, 66). This is true in a narrow sense, but in a broader sense it can scarcely be denied that visuals persuade, which is to say, they argue. We know less about persuasive aesthetics than we do about persuasive rhetorics, narrowly conceived, but clearly we must learn more if we are to engage contemporary political communication.

Here, too, we can glean insight from history. Visual images, particularly political "cartoons" and drawings, only became a part of daily newspapers with technological advancements during the 1880s. Cartoonists of the era, drawing upon a centuries old repertoire of visual satire, used hyperbole to lend moral conviction to complex political issues. They did this in large measure by appealing to the familiar caricatures and symbols (some drawn from classic literature, art, and mythology) readily recognized by a diverse audience (Robertson 1995:181–210). Today's political communication also traffics in popular culture, which suggests a third focus for future work.

View Ads Wholistically, in the Context of Popular Culture

To view ads as positive or negative is to view them wholistically, but it is a narrow wholism devoid of substantive meaning. As we saw in chapter 2, there is reason to believe that viewers use additional wholistic frames in processing political ads, specifically by recognizing the generic audiovisual conventions of popular culture (see also Nelson and Boynton 1997; Richardson 1998a). A spot like the 1988 Bush campaign's "Revolving Door" is not merely "negative." Through evocative use of the motifs of a Hollywood horror story (a genre widely recognized by all sorts of viewers), the ad literally places Michael Dukakis and the hordes of felons he allegedly unleashed in the starring role of a mini-"slasher" film. The ad "Levin of Arabia" embodied the same generic evocation of satire as 1988's "Tank Ride." In 2004, Bush–Cheney ads invoking the look and feel of the action-thriller genre invited viewers to picture Mr. Bush as Jack Bauer, the antiterrorist hero of the popular Fox TV series 24, while implying his opponent would not do "whatever it takes" to keep America safe. We may be able to learn more of what viewers glean from campaign ads by acknowledging the substantive meaning imparted by the synergistic use of the audiovisual conventions of popular culture that most viewers readily recognize, than by pursuing the tidy but inadequate positive/negative demarcation. Combined with a critical perspective focusing on patterns of behavior rather than the minutiae of competing policy claims, efforts to address the audiovisual evocation of conventional packages of meaning drawn from popular culture may contribute to improving the ad watch journalism that has arisen as an independent check on political advertising (Richardson 1998b).

All of these efforts will ultimately bear sweeter fruit if they more effectively place campaigns in the broader democratic process. To do this, researchers will have to do more than they have so far to explicate the theories of electoral democracy to which they subscribe. The functional role of the voter, after all, appears to be essentially limited. The choices citizens face are shaped by the broad brush strokes of patterns of policy and performance, not the nuanced etchings of particular incidents that provide the controversy typically surrounding evaluation of campaign ads. The voter must decide simply whether the record of the incumbent (candidate, party, or point of view) warrants reelection. Claims that it does not (i.e., "negative" ads) are a critical part of that process.

Those seeking greater levels of participation must also confront the role that emotion (negative as well as positive) plays in motivating voters, and consider the way political parties have historically provided the institutional pillars of participation—if only to facilitate promising alternative visions for the future. We live in televisual times, and our communications will inevitably be comprised of audio, visual, and narrative elements—and will be richer because of that. That richness can work in ways both attractive and repulsive, but a balanced view of human nature and its politics would expect nothing less. In the broad scheme of things, political ads are essential manifestations of our political world. A polity that turns its collective back on politics because of disdain for campaign advertising is one which, in essence, is turning its back on its own rich, complex, and sometimes flawed humanity.

Given the accumulated weight resting upon the concept of negativity, probing the meaning and usefulness of the term is an endeavor of some urgency. So too, is consideration of promising alternative approaches to understanding political advertising. It is possible that in some ways, the very product of academic and journalistic attention to negative campaign tactics may have served to increase citizen cynicism with politics. If this is so, and if we can develop new ways of thinking about ads that don't so readily and unnecessarily lead to apathy or disdain, the quest for a new agenda in political advertising research is clearly warranted.

It might also be advisable for scholars, journalists, and citizens to reconsider their embrace of terms such as "negative" to describe political advertising. Few would argue that comparison is not a legitimate, indeed an essential, aspect of political campaigns. The evidence presented here, albeit limited by its exploratory nature, suggests, however, that virtually any unfavorable mention of one's opponent appears to trigger charges of negativity—regardless of the specific credibility of that mention, while the truly debilitating aspects of ads go underappreciated. While it is unlikely that any such linguistic revolution is imminent, there is much that can be done to avoid unnecessarily contributing to the cynicism and disdain for politics that has been the legacy of reformism and that has been further propelled by viewing political advertising primarily through the lens of negativity. One logical point of departure for this endeavor is to examine the "ad watch" journalism that emerged during the 1980s and 1990s to police the content of campaign ads, and more broadly, to engage citizens and candidates in the campaign process. That subject is the focus of our next chapter.

NOTES

1. Indeed, in a forum on negative advertising published in the *American Political Science Review*, none of the three pieces of original research addressed audiovisual elements at all, with the exception of one which held them constant (Ansolabehere, Iyengar, and Simon 1999; Kahn and Kenney 1999; Wattenberg and Brians 1999).

2. Newhagen and Reeves 1991; Lang 1991; Basil, Schooler, and Reeves 1991; Freedman and Goldstein 1999.

3. Warren E. Miller, Donald R. Kinder, Steven J. Rosenstone, and the National Election Studies. *American National Election Study, 1992: Pre- and Post-Election Survey [Enhanced with 1990 and 1991 Data]* [Computer file]. Conducted by University of Michigan, Center for Political Studies. ICPSR ed. Ann Arbor: University of Michigan, Center for Political Studies, and Inter-university Consortium for Political and Social Research [producers], 1993. Ann Arbor: Interuniversity Consortium for Political and Social Research [distributor], 1993.

4. Additional "mentions" in response to the ANES probe were not included in this analysis because they are far fewer in number than first mentions and they are hard to separate from or combine with first mentions (because the same respondent may essentially repeat their previous mention—which should not be counted as additional evidence of negativity or its absence).

5. See also Richardson and Jasperson 2001.

6. Jasperson and Fan 2002; see also Garamone 1984 and Shapiro and Rieger 1992; for an opposing argument, see Johnson-Cartee and Copeland 1997.

7. See for example Hamilton and Zanna 1972; Kernell 1977; Lau 1982, 1985; Kellerman 1984; Reeves, Thorson, and Schlueder 1986.

8. "Revolving Door" is often described as "the Willie Horton ad," though

Horton did not appear in this Bush spot but rather in a similar ad produced by a nominally independent group.

9. Early Cold War–era campaigns were particularly nasty. In 1950, the *New York Times* editorialized, "So complete is the character assassination in some cases that those who reach public office will have lost the confidence of the voters who put them there. . . . When almost everyone is calling everybody else a liar and thief, the result becomes a standoff. There is, then, no black and white of reputation in the public mind, only a muddy gray." Congressional committees addressed unfair campaigning, and by 1954 announced a new campaign code, only to have the announcement ceremony degenerate with charges over which party would violate it first (Felknor 1966:11–12).

10. McGerr 1986; see also Schattschneider 1960, especially chapter 5; Burnham 1965; and Converse 1972.

Chapter Four

The Ad Patrol: Campaign Advertising and Ad Watch Journalism

As the view that campaign advertising was increasingly characterized by strident, negative, and often false attacks became more widespread, journalists and academics sought to subject political ads to objective standards of truthfulness. This seemingly straightforward task, however, would prove far more daunting than imagined. In this chapter, we will explore the origins and evolution of "ad watch" journalism, examine both its print and broadcast variants, consider some of its limitations, and explore some possible ways that journalists and other analysts might more effectively engage audiovisual campaign communication, including recognition of the ways ads draw upon the genres of popular culture to communicate their messages.

The 1988 presidential campaign was widely seen as a landmark in shallow, negative campaigning. The ads were often based on half-truths or outright falsehoods. The news media in particular felt used, as it began to recognize its own role, often unwitting, in reinforcing some of the ads' more questionable elements. Kathleen Jamieson's *Dirty Politics*, for example, documented how journalists adopted the very language of the Bush campaign's assaults in their descriptions of the "Willie Horton" story, weaving a narrative that while compelling, veered sharply from the facts (Jamieson 1992a:15–42, 128–35). Jamieson and others (Broder 1990; West 1992) urged the media to take a more active role in evaluating the veracity of claims made in campaign spots. By 1992, ad watch journalism had become a staple of election coverage.

Soon, however, the ad watches themselves drew the attention of scholarly researchers. Did these segments effectively counteract the advertisements they analyzed? Were journalists any less likely to reinforce the claims of the ads they were attempting to critique? One prominent study suggested that ad watches were ineffective, that viewers were actually more inclined to support candidates whose ads were being criticized, and that ad watches turned off voters, at least those who lacked strong attachments to either of the major political parties (Ansolabehere and Iyengar 1995:137–41). Other researchers presented evidence that ad watches did in fact work as intended (Capella and Jamieson 1994). While the two sides differed in their interpretation of the content of ad watches (and therefore in their expectations regarding what effects they should have), the basic orientation of ad watches, scrutinizing the factual validity of candidate advertising, was not questioned. Both sides, it seemed, shared the fundamental vision of campaign advertising as consisting of a series of claims, each of which could be subject to appropriate standards of truth. What may have eluded them, however, was the sum of all those claims: the broad patterns of conduct and philosophy that are the true basis of the persuasive appeal of political commercials.

More specifically, many ad watches focus their attention on specific factual claims or statements found in campaign ads, but fail to examine the larger arguments those narrow claims support. When this happens, journalists may effectively be chopping the puzzle into smaller and smaller pieces, rather than helping voters by putting the pieces together into a meaningful whole. Focusing on the truthfulness of isolated claims, rather than on broad patterns of behavior and record may contribute to the alienation among voters that some scholars have attributed to ad watch journalism. As voters are deluged with endless demonstrations of politicians' technically questionable statements, their level of disdain for all politicians and for politics itself rises. The more appropriate question, therefore, may be less whether candidate X voted to raise taxes fourteen times or forty-two times (as her opponent suggested), but instead, has X voted for a pattern of policy, and if so, what have the outcomes of that policy been, as best as we can tell?

It is not simply that citizens lack the capacity for sustained involvement with the technical details of public policy—though many citizens clearly are uninterested in them. Rather, even when citizens do grasp the finer points of policy, they are limited to expressing their preferences at the ballot box by casting their votes for one of a limited number of candidates or parties, none of which are likely to perfectly express their views. Voters lack a meaningful mechanism for bringing their detailed policy preferences to bear on government through elections. Even when ad watches inform citizens that candidate X only voted for tax hikes fourteen times instead of forty-two as candidate Y's ads charged, voters are still left with the choice between X and Y—and not a full array of candidates whose support for tax increases (or any other policy position) varies across the full range of possibilities.

Consider the claims and counterclaims surrounding Medicare (the federal program that provides health care to senior citizens) during the 1996 campaign. Journalists pointed out that Democratic charges that Republicans wanted to "cut" Medicare were false or misleading, because GOP plans would still involve increases in Medicare spending, though at slower rates than provided for under the current law. Democrats responded that with more Medicare beneficiaries each year and higher health care costs, slowing the rate of growth in Medicare spending would mean reductions in benefits from current levels. One side or the other may want to frame this as a debate about when a cut is a cut, but the questions most relevant to voters are not so narrow. Ultimately, what difference does it make if the Republicans are proposing cuts in Medicare or merely cuts in the rate of Medicare growth, if citizens cannot communicate such nuanced indications of their preferences through the ballot, and if the actual policy outcomes are in any event extremely uncertain?

Voters would probably be better served by examination of each candidate's or party's past record of performance, in broad terms, than by detailed examination of their current proposals or of the charges and countercharges they hurl at each other through their campaign ads. This is, after all, what the ads themselves are getting at: that the opponent's record is a good indicator of what we can expect if that person is elected. Too often, ad watches become mired in the detailed analysis of the component elements of the record, while neglecting to draw conclusions about the larger pattern the record as a whole suggests. This is not the only information voters might find useful, and we would not wish the parties to become captives of their pasts. Yet, the governing and policy patterns of candidates and parties are perhaps the single most relevant bits of information needed to make the voting decisions that constitute the essence of democratic governance. And while on Medicare and other issues ad watches did occasionally venture to provide such a context, they were more likely to treat claims in isolated fashion, placing single votes alongside career-long voting patterns in ways that left readers to wonder where the candidates really stood.

For example, a 1996 ad for Robert G. Torricelli, Democratic candidate for the U.S. Senate in New Jersey, framed opponent Richard A. Zimmer's votes on Medicare as part of a pattern:

> For millions of older Americans, Medicare is a lifeline. But just last year, Dick Zimmer voted to cut Medicare twenty-five times. Zimmer voted to cut Medicare benefits. To raise Medicare premiums. To limit your choice of doctor. To deny coverage for mammograms. To deny coverage for colon-cancer screening. To deny coverage for diabetes blood tests. Even against restoring safety standards in nursing homes. Dick Zimmer. Too extreme for New Jersey.

Zimmer's votes are painted as a pattern of behavior, a record of repeated opposition to Medicare spending.

By contrast, Jennifer Preston's ad analysis in the *New York Times* avoids assessing the issue in terms of a consistent record, and treats the claims in isolated fashion:

> It is true that Mr. Zimmer voted to cut the growth in Medicare spending by $270 billion last year and against proposals that would have provided Medicare coverage for an annual mammogram for women over 49 and eligible for Medicare. He voted against amendments that would have provided Medicare coverage for some colon-cancer tests, and payment for blood-testing strips for diabetics. He contends that it made no sense to expand and extend Medicare coverage when the entire program faces financial problems.
>
> Mr. Zimmer voted against an amendment that would have reinstated Federal nursing-home safety standards. He says he supports giving states greater control over nursing homes. (Preston 1996)

Preston avoids judgment on the candidate's overall record in favor of a recitation of particular votes. No mention is made of Zimmer's circular reasoning: a vote to deny funding is based on the funding problems the program already has (from previous votes to deny funding). The reader is left to wonder what it all means. Are these votes representative? Are they significant? Where *do* the candidates stand on this issue? Preston concludes her analysis noting that

> The advertisement succeeds in fanning fears among the elderly about higher premiums. That will help Mr. Torricelli's efforts to portray himself as the candidate who can be trusted to trim, not gut Medicare. But the advertisement may not resonate with voters who are familiar with Medicare's huge financial problems.

Why does the ad succeed in fanning fears among the elderly? Why does it help Torricelli's efforts to be trusted on the issue? Why wouldn't it resonate with voters aware of Medicare's huge financial problems? It's almost as if journalists feel incapable of making such judgments explicitly, on the basis of record, and are compelled to leave it to the reader to connect the dots, however convoluted the array of dots may be.

To some degree, this may reflect the nature of exposition rather than reporter motivations. Even if one sought to address patterns of behavior or record, one might do so by aggregating isolated events. There is, however, reason to believe there is more going on than that.

The fragmentation of news coverage (Bennett 1988:44–51) has been widely noted and frequently denounced. Yet it remains buried deep in the wellsprings of the conventions of daily journalism. In part, the failure of ad watches to address broad patterns of behavior and record, even when the ads themselves center on such claims, can be seen as an inevitable result of the "Jack Webb" values of the newsroom ("just the facts, ma'am"). The ad watch merely reenacts the larger dance of political (and much other) reporting in America, where a reticence to engage too deeply the meaning of the facts overshadows the quest for an analytical, pattern-oriented mode of journalism.

It need not be so. Consider how Howard Kurtz, who covers the media for the *Washington Post* and is one of the leading practitioners of ad watch journalism, described the criteria for ad analyses:

> The guidelines were very straightforward: What was the candidate trying to accomplish with the ad? How did the claims stack up against his record and his opponent's record? What was left out? Were facts used selectively, leaving a false or misleading impression? Those are the basic questions we tried to answer. (Kurtz 1997)

To assess the degree to which ad watches did in fact emphasize isolated claims and avoid broader patterns of behavior, I collected twenty-six ad watches from three different newspapers, the *Washington Post*, *New York Times*, and *Charlotte Observer*, during the 1996 campaign. The *Post* and *Times* were selected as exemplars of nationally oriented reporting with a critical elite audience, while the *Observer* was chosen as a leading practitioner of civic journalism in a locally oriented paper.[1] Four different races were covered: President, U.S. Senate (NJ), U.S. Senate (VA), and Governor (NC). The sample focuses on the month of October (though a few stories from other months are included as well) and consists of all the ad watches I could obtain, either through subscription or courtesy of reporters. I have no reason to believe there is anything unrepresentative about this collection of stories.

In a normal news story, each paragraph contains roughly one major theme, making the paragraph an attractive unit of analysis (Covington et al. 1993). In ad watch stories, however, paragraphs tend to be longer and fewer (and in some cases paragraph organization was absent altogether). This made the individual sentence a more attractive unit of analysis for the present study, a decision reinforced by the conventions of ads themselves, which also pack essential claims into single sentences. The alternative, coding either by paragraph or even by story, would leave the task of weighing a number of conflicting themes and tones in coverage, losing valuable data in the process.

A total of 524 sentences were coded. The primary variable of interest addressed whether a sentence focused on a claim as an isolated event or as part of a pattern or larger issue.[2] Table 4.1 presents the coding results for this variable. The data indicate a rough balance between sentences focusing on patterns, which I argue are more useful to voters, and those focusing on isolated issues which are less useful. Table 4.2 takes the source of each sentence into account. It shows that the statements about patterns are concentrated in those sentences that restate the ads' claims, where the statements treating claims as isolated issues are concentrated in journalists' evaluation of the claims.

These data suggest that while a majority of the sentences in candidate advertisements focus on broad patterns, a majority of journalists' own sentences focus on isolated issues. Howard Kurtz articulated exactly the kind of emphasis on stacking ad claims against the candidates' records I would advocate, and it is manifest in the ad watches he authored that I studied. In Kurtz's work, 72.5 percent of sentences addressed patterns, while 23.7 percent focused on isolated incidents.

Table 4.1. Pattern versus Isolated Issue (by Sentence)

Focus	Percentage
Pattern	47.5
Isolated issue	42.2
Background	4.6
Other/none	5.7
N = 524	

Table 4.2. Pattern versus Isolated Issue by Restatement versus Evaluation

Pattern/Isolated Issue	Sentence Restates Ad's Claims (%)	Evaluative/Other (%)
Pattern	60.2	35.6
Isolated issue	25.6	57.8
Background	5.9	3.3
Other/none	8.3	3.3
N	254	270

But when looking at all the other authors included in this study, the percentage of sentences that focused on patterns was only 39.2, with 48.3 percent focusing on isolated incidents. The percentage of sentences addressing patterns is only 28.1 among all other reporters when restatements of ads' verbal or visual claims are not included. (For Kurtz, 61.7 percent of sentences address patterns, even after excluding restatements of candidate claims.) Broken down by newspaper, the focus on patterns is greatest in the *Washington Post* (53.3 percent) when Kurtz is included, but higher in the *New York Times* (41.5 percent) than the *Post* (36.7 percent) when Kurtz's stories are not included; 22.3 percent of sentences in the *Charlotte Observer* focused on patterns.

A few brief examples from Kurtz's work can illustrate how ad watch journalists can focus on important patterns of behavior and record. In discussing a Clinton–Gore ad counterattacking Republicans on the issue of foreign campaign contributions, Kurtz wrote:

> This is a hastily assembled attempt to shift the public focus from questionable contributions to the Democrats from Indonesians and other foreign interests. To say that Clinton fought for campaign finance reform is an exaggeration, since it has never been a top White House priority. (1996a)

Consider also Kurtz's analysis of a Dole–Kemp spot charging the president with backing wasteful government spending:

> While figures in the ad are in dispute, its political message is unmistakable: that Clinton is a spend-and-tax liberal who favors bigger government. . . . The Dole campaign did not spell out the $432 billion in bigger government. But the notion that the administration is costing us an extra $432 billion is at odds with the record. Federal spending as a share of gross domestic product has declined under Clinton from 23.3 percent to 21.7 percent, the lowest share since 1979. (Kurtz 1996b)

The latter analysis was part of a story longer than most ad watch features. It contained thirty-nine sentences, while the average ad watch in this study's sample was only twenty sentences long. Perhaps increasing the space available would increase the quality of print ad watches. Either way, it is clear that ad watch journalism can address broad patterns of behavior and record when journalists are motivated to do so.

Ad watch journalism is of course not limited to the print media. Indeed, perhaps the most significant animating force in the evolution of the ad watch was the work of Kathleen Hall Jamieson and a team of graduate student researchers at the Annenberg School of Communication at the University of Pennsylvania in designing a visual grammar for broadcast ad watches. The Annenberg team began with the recognition that many television ad watches actually served to reinforce the very claims reporters were attempting to critique in their analysis. When journalists did stories on ads back in 1988, they would typically freeze a frame from the ad on the screen while using voice-over narration to make their points about the accuracy of what was being shown. For viewers, however, the power of the visuals they were seeing overwhelmed the impact of the analysis they were hearing. In analyzing "Tank Ride," for example, reporters were quick to note that the ad falsely charged Dukakis with opposing weapons that he actually supported. They also complained that the ad attacked Dukakis for supporting positions consistent with arms treaties which Bush, too, was on record as supporting. Thus the news coverage of the moment was quick to point out the ad's plain distortions and misrepresentations of "fact." As Germond and Witcover (1989) concede in their campaign postmortem, however, "the operative element was that devastating picture of Alfred E. Neuman (the nerdish character from *Mad* magazine) in the tank." The ad's visual images and satirical genre rode roughshod, not only over the ad's own "message," but also over commentators' criticisms. It took the Annenberg team the better part of two years and numerous experimental manipulations to develop a visual grammar or framework that allowed reporters to clearly communicate their analysis without visually reinforcing an ad's questionable claims (Jamieson 1992a, 1992c; Jamieson and Campbell 2001).

In the visual grammar the Annenberg team devised for broadcast ad watches, ad clips were relegated to display inside a canted, graphic representation of a TV screen. This served to communicate to viewers that it was an ad they were seeing, not a part of the news. Jamieson's focus groups had indicated that many viewers were confused by the early ad watches, mistaking the ad images as actual news content. The similarities in the visual design of ads and news no doubt contributed to the confusion. Additionally, graphic labels containing the analysts' critical assessments were superimposed over the canted screen showing the ad. This served to visually underscore the claims reporters were making verbally. Additional labeling clearly identified the video as coming from a campaign ad, and a final label featured the network's copyrighted corporate logo, an attempt to discourage the makers of political ads from mimicking the look and feel of the ad watch for their own purposes (see figure 4.1).

The Annenberg team's recommendations were adopted on a widespread basis during the 1992 campaign. A videotape illustrating the recommended format for television ad watch segments was distributed during the annual convention of the National Association of Broadcasters in the spring of 1992, and CNN, ABC, CBS, and NBC all used a variant of the grammar in their campaign coverage. The results were impressive. Howard Kaplan, an admaker for the Bush–Quayle campaign, told a postcampaign conference at the Annenberg School that "it was a terrible feeling when I used to open the (*New York*) *Times* and they used to take my commercial apart, or watch CNN and watch

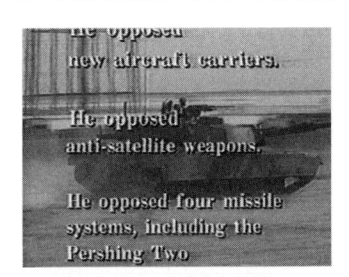

Ad Watch 1.0 (1988)
In 1988, ABC News Correspondent Richard Threlkeld sought to counter the false claims of the Bush ad, "Tank Ride." Jamieson's focus group research revealed that the effect of Threlkeld's voice-over narration and the full screen image drawn from the ad was to reinforce, not counteract, the ad's claims.

Ad Watch 2.0 (1992)
Jamieson's team designed a visual grammar to disclaim and displace questionable assertions in ads, by visually distancing the ad from the reporter's analysis of it. The ad is no longer shown full screen, but appears in a canted graphic representation of a TV screen. Jamieson anticipated admakers would rush to copy the grammar for use in their work.

Figure 4.1. The Visual Grammar of Ad Watch Journalism

them take it apart. . . . I think these reality checks made our commercials less effective" (Jamieson and Campbell 2001:322).

By 1994, however, reporters were once again airing ads full screen and focusing their reports on strategy and process rather than accuracy. The ad watch grammar had not been institutionalized. New reporters were now on the beat, and they had not shared the experiences of the 1988 and 1992 campaigns (Jamieson and Campbell 2001). Furthermore, the ad watches themselves soon drew detractors. Pfau and Louden (1994) found mixed evidence on the efficacy of ad watches in the 1992 North Carolina gubernatorial campaign. Ansolabehere and Iyengar (1995:139–42; 1996) found ad watches to backfire, amplifying the ad's message rather than displacing it. They found that the primary effect of ad watches was to turn voters away from the political process and decrease voter turnout.

But these findings, too, have been challenged. Jamieson has argued that the ad watches Ansolabehere and Iyengar used in their study were not representative since they found little to challenge in the ads while most ad watches target major distortions. Their ad watches did effectively communicate information to viewers; viewers did not reject the ad's sponsor, but the ad watch didn't urge them to (Jamieson 1996). Indeed, Capella and Jamieson (1994:355) found that ad watches appear to do precisely what they are designed to accomplish, namely put the claims of the ad in context so that the ad is judged less fair and less important than is the case in the absence of the ad watch.

This debate illustrates a fundamental flaw in the way many view the purposes of ad watch journalism. Ansolabehere and Iyengar no doubt speak for many when they describe those purposes thusly: if ad watches work as intended, the audience receives information to rebut or discount the claims made in campaign advertisements (1996:73). Is it inconceivable that ad watches might actually find merit in candidate claims? It is no wonder that ad watches contribute to voter alienation if they are envisioned as only a means to bash lying politicians. Close examination of the experimental results reported by Ansolabehere and Iyengar gives further cause to resist the rush to abandon the ad watch as fundamentally flawed. Consider the content of the ad watches themselves. The ad watch with the largest effect on viewers, causing a 27-percent pro-Bush shift in the gap between the two candidates, targeted a Bush ad attacking Clinton for raising spending and taxes in Arkansas. CNN's Brooks Jackson pointed out in his ad watch that Bush, too, had raised taxes and increased government spending (Ansolabehere and Iyengar 1996:76). While perfectly reasonable to report, this can scarcely be expected to effectively counter the claims of a well-crafted political spot, especially when the audiovisual and narrative dimensions of the ad go unchallenged.

In this case, those dimensions were substantial. The ad in question (of which large portions were included in the Jackson ad watch) featured an up-tempo, stylized bluegrass/country music fiddle and banjo duet and a series of satirical pictures of Clinton interspersed with images suggesting the impact on everyday Arkansans of Clinton's tax hikes. The ad begins with a picture of the kind of sign found on interstate highways as one crosses state lines, reading "Arkansas." The state slogan "the natural state" beneath the word Arkansas appears to have been brushed out of the image. The narrator says, "To pay for his increased state spending in Arkansas Bill Clinton raised state taxes." Then the image cuts to speeded-up, grainy, and unflattering video of Clinton at what appears to be a legislative signing event where the applause of the gathered politicians is exaggerated by the fast motion. The narration continues, "And not just on the rich." On the words "the rich," the video cuts to a scene of a wooded trailer park—conveying both the poverty of rural Arkansas and the cruelty of Clinton's tax policies. The narrator continues: "He increased the sales tax by 33 percent." The video cuts from the trailer park to a cash register's digital readout, "hosiery $6.00," and then quickly back to the furiously applauding politicians. "Imposed a mobile home tax" (video of a recreational vehicle trailer, door open, on a bright sunny day with colorful lawn chairs arrayed around what appears to be a small table in front of it; a barking dog can be heard in the background). "Increased the beer tax" (video of beer being poured into a glass, soundtrack courtesy of Anheuser-Busch or Joseph Coors). "He assessed a tourism tax" (video of a roadside motel, cut to profile views of a tourist couple, cameras pressed to their eyes). "Created a cable TV tax" (extremely snowy video with a horizontal roll—standard imagery of a tube on the fritz—of Clinton playing the saxophone on what one might guess to be late-night television; three wild saxophone squawks, unlikely to be the handiwork of a former first-chair all-state band member, add to the tone of ridicule). "Supported a tax on groceries" (video of grocery store manager bagging at the checkout counter). "And now if elected president Bill Clinton has promised to increase government spending 220 billion dollars" (back to the signing video, which zooms in on a smiling Clinton; the phrase "$220 billion" is superimposed on the screen as the narrator reads the amount, and the politicians resume their furious applause). "Guess where he'll get the money?"

(video of that phrase in white on black background). The fiddle/banjo duet winds up to audience applause and whistles as the screen fades to black.

Brooks Jackson's ad watch mentions neither visuals nor music or sound effects. Here, they combine to shape a biting, satirical portrayal of the Arkansas governor, one whose sharpest political jabs (such as that Clinton taxes the poor) are coated in the ad watch radar evading stealth technology of humor and ridicule. To even begin to address how this ad might be working, serious attention to the details described above would be in order. Jackson also frequently discusses the ad's claims in isolation and fails to adequately elaborate on context or pattern. Consider the sales tax charge. Jackson's response: "True. Sales taxes increased by 50 percent, actually, from 3 cents for each dollar of sales to $4^1/_2$ cents. All to pay for education." Fair enough, but is Clinton a big taxer as Bush suggests or not? How much did education need the additional spending? What about the subterranean charge that Clinton's taxes will hurt the poor? Jackson does go on to note, after discussing several more Bush charges on taxes, that "the total Arkansas tax burden is still low. In fact, it ranks 46 out of 50, taking just $93 in state and local taxes for every $1,000 of personal income," but he never directly addresses the broader Bush claim.

The ambiguity of Jackson's analysis is aptly captured in his closing line: "Nothing really false here and the ad does deal with the vital issues of taxing and spending but the ad does take some liberties." Nothing in this ad watch is likely to persuade viewers to reject or even question the Bush ad, which is why Jamieson argues that it is unsurprising that viewers of the piece would actually increase their support of Bush even though his ad was being scrutinized. If viewers were exposed to the ad watch only, this might not be the case. But in the competition between the largely unfiltered Bush ad shown as part of the ad watch and the ad watch itself, the Bush ad wins.

Apart from the shortcomings already discussed, the fact that an attack against Clinton would prove most effective in moving voters is still not surprising, and for reasons that have little to do with the ultimate utility of the ad watch as journalism. As a relative newcomer to the national political stage, Clinton's image in the public was far more malleable than Bush's. This was also the key to the successful demonization of Michael Dukakis in 1988. Given the relative paucity of information on Clinton, Bush's charges have room to operate. As Jamieson (1992a) points out, researchers suggest such negative attacks (1) carry more weight in evaluative thinking than "positive" information (Lau

1982, 1985), (2) better alter existing impressions than positive information (Kellerman 1984), and (3) are easier to recall (Reeves et al. 1986; Newhagen and Reeves 1989). So the ineffectiveness of the ad watch in question may be more a function of the political dynamics involving unknown candidates and addressable shortcomings in ad watch journalism, rather than inherent flaws in the project. At the least, the failure of this ad watch lay more in what it didn't do—but could have—rather than in what it did do.

There is also reason to believe that the proliferation of the ad police has had a restraining effect on some of the more outrageous claims made in campaign spots, and candidates now routinely provide specific documentation to journalists to support their ads. They also often use excerpts from ad watches in responding to their opponent's charges. It is far too soon to abandon journalists' efforts to more deeply engage the discourse of campaign advertising.

Still, while Jamieson may be correct—ad watches may place the claims of campaign spots in context—Ansolabehere and Iyengar's claim that ad watches contribute to voter alienation may also be true. As Jamieson notes, most ad watches point to major distortions. As a consequence, the image of politicians emerging from ad watch journalism may be a negative one, more negative than circumstances require. In particular, the focus of ad watch analyses on the truth of the political claims contained in a candidate's advertising may put too fine a point on the broader political issues at stake. Perhaps more important, ad watches have actually failed to examine key parts of the claims ads make because journalists have been unwilling to explore the audiovisual and narrative components of spots with sufficient rigor. In the ad watches I studied, only 10 percent of the sentences addressed ads' visuals, and that less than 1 percent involved critical analysis of ad visuals. Addressing such shortcomings may be one way to provide citizens with more meaningful campaign information.

The "visual" grammar developed by the Annenberg team was a visual way of communicating reporters' views about the *verbal* claims of campaign ads. It was not designed to address the audiovisual elements of ads. If journalists were slow to engage the claims made in campaign advertising, they have been even slower in engaging audiovisuals. The conventions of reporting have been the bedrock for generations of print and broadcast journalists, and becoming more engaged in audiovisual production would not obviously seem consistent with the highest callings of the civic purposes of the press. As we noted in chapter 2, there is a long running current of thought that views audiovisual communications as essentially aesthetic in their persuasive appeal, and as such far less reliable than the logically grounded argumentation of the printed or pure text. These tendencies must be overcome if the ad watch is to fulfill its potential contribution to a more enlightened campaign conversation.

The 1992 campaign produced a particularly telling example of a simplistic focus on message and argumentative content, narrowly construed, centering on an advertisement produced by Patrick Buchanan's campaign attacking George Bush for funding "obscene art" through the National Endowment for the Arts (NEA). The critics seemed to miss most of what viewers were likely to have experienced in watching the Buchanan ad. The ad featured clips from a film about black gay life, entitled *Tongues Untied,* funded in part by the NEA. The ad cops attacked the spot for "inaccuracy," because the film received its NEA funding during the Reagan, not the Bush, administration. This "inaccuracy" earned bright red labels of "false" adorning the screen (and obscuring the ad's images of sadomasochistic sex), while the critics fussed over the ad's allegedly "misleading" details (Jamieson 1992a). Critics also pointed out the minuscule percentage of federal spending attributable to the NEA: If you care about how your tax dollars are spent, they implied, then you should not give a second thought to NEA programs, because they are too small.

However meritorious such criticisms might have been in their own terms, they missed how the ad was likely to work for most viewers and assumed viewer conventions for receiving the visual-and-verbal arguments of the ad that probably differed radically from the ways in which most viewers experienced the spot. If nothing else, the ad's "issues," "positions," and "arguments" lay less in the verbal details than in the visual form, cultural genre, and political context. Buchanan's admaker could have rebutted the criticisms by pointing out that Bush had not altered the course of the NEA from its Reagan days, and conservatives had been attacking public funds for "obscene art" for years. To such viewers, Buchanan's appeal was to reject a general climate of libertine conduct and "anti-American" values that Buchanan wanted to suggest had found no great foe in President Bush. The ad targeted philosophical differences more than policy details. And in that connection, the ad evoked the genre of pornography, associating it with a "permissive" climate that had been opposed for the most part unsuccessfully, when at all, by the Bush administration. Viewed in this way, the Buchanan ad made appeals and invoked "truths" in ways scarcely touched by the criticisms of the ad cops.

In 1996 things were much the same. A Dole–Kemp ad assailed President Clinton's truthfulness, juxtaposing what he said ("the era of big government is over") with descriptions of what he did ("proposed a massive government takeover of health care"). Ad cops quickly noted the time order of the two points had been reversed—in proper order they could imply he had learned his lesson—as well as documenting other frailties in the veracity of the ad's claims. What none of them did, however, was even to comment on the wholistic impression of the ad, that Clinton was a slick liar, vividly underscored by the zooming focus on a TV screen image exaggerated to heighten the contrast between image and "reality." For many, subsequent events may have borne out this charge. My point is that, rightly or wrongly, it completely evaded analysts' radar screens. In chapter 5, we will see that there was little improvement in coverage of the 2000 campaign. In chapter 6, we will note the crucial role the media played in 2004 in amplifying the attacks on Democratic presidential nominee John Kerry by the "Swift Boat Veterans for Truth." Those attacks would eventually be largely discredited, but not until after a small paid ad buy became a major "free" media sensation.

BUILDING A BETTER AD WATCH: FROM AD WATCHING TO CRITICAL AD READING

I would like to suggest a handful of guideposts with which ad analysts might improve the quality of their craft. First, ad watch journalists should address *patterns* of behavior and record. Do not hesitate to render judgment—or at least take competing arguments to their logical conclusion. Second, take ads' audiovisual and narrative elements seriously, and be aware of the wholistic way in which conventional associations may be evoked in viewers' minds. Third, work to develop an audiovisual grammar capable of matching the subterranean claims and evocations of political spots blow-for-blow. Fourth, use the reactions of actual viewers to inform ad watch reporting. Fifth, allow reporters the time and space necessary to produce comprehensive ad analyses. Taken together, these guideposts imply that the ad analyst must define a point of view and take a stand—though not necessarily a partisan one. Still, a defense of the progressive, reformist ideals that have motivated journalism over the last century is probably more useful than the mere assertion of blind or transcendent objectivity. Let me briefly elaborate on each of these guideposts in turn.

Focus on Patterns: The ad analyst should seek to avoid missing the forest (of major issues of political performance and record) for the trees (the scores of individual votes and claims bandied about by campaigns at election time). This does not preclude presenting more than one side to an argument, nor does it mandate placing issues in a rigid ideological framework, more versus less government, for example. Instead, analysts can find guidance by asking first whether an issue is a major matter of public policy—How much does it cost? How many people are affected? What is the likelihood of policy making an impact?—and then asking whether the competitors have developed a pattern or record of behavior on this or similar issues. To some extent, such an approach may clash with the norms of contemporary journalism, especially where an issue makes for good copy even if it is not a major matter of public policy. Consider the infamous prison furlough debate in 1988. The story of Willie Horton, widely reported throughout the media, made for good copy but was a poor vehicle for analyzing public policy. The furlough policy had actually been started under Dukakis's predecessor as governor, a Republican, and had actually been eliminated by Dukakis, so the whole issue scarcely reflected on his record (see Jamieson 1992a). To truly focus on patterns, ad watch analysts must resist and actively counter the power of the compelling but unrepresentative or even irrelevant case. Finally, ad watchers need not stop with focusing on patterns of policy and performance. Reporters can and should call out candidates and parties who have demonstrated a repeated pattern of questionable attacks in their advertising.

Take Audiovisual and Narrative Seriously: Analysts can begin by paying greater attention to audiovisual and narrative elements in ads. It is also necessary to take them seriously, and to engage their implicit arguments. To say, for example, that an ad uses black-and-white imagery to portray the sinister nature of crime without addressing the actual nature of the criminal threat and public policy impact on it is to magnify rather than analyze an ad's subterranean claims.

Reporters may also be uncomfortable with engaging the audiovisual and narrative details of campaign spots because it is not the kind of thing they have been trained for or are used to doing, and they might even be criticized for trying. Here, analysts can do at least two things: rely on actual viewers for insights and broaden their own analytical repertoire. Familiarity with the audiovisual conventions of the genres of popular culture is one important tool in understanding how political ads work. Knowledge of pop culture, including rap artists such as Ice-T and Sister Souljah and sitcom characters like Murphy

Brown, proved to be relevant political knowledge during the 1992 presidential campaign (Delli Carpini and Keeter 1996:12) and may serve as the type of heuristic device that Popkin (1994) argues characterizes much voter information processing. The increasing migration of print news content to the Internet, the expectations of an audience much more attuned to visual communication, and the emergence of a cadre of journalists who themselves are more comfortable with audiovisual critique may all contribute to ad watch journalism that more forcefully engages the audiovisual content of ads.

Develop a Comprehensive Audiovisual and Narrative Critical Grammar: To succeed as antidotes to misleading campaign claims, ad watches must develop an audiovisual grammar capable of responding to the ways ads use popular genres to evoke associations and emotions described in chapters 1 and 2. The development of multimedia computer programs offers the potential for major advancements in critical analysis of campaign spots, especially in addressing the way ads invoke the audiovisual conventions of popular genres of film, music, and fiction. Let me offer a few illustrative possibilities. Newspaper and television station websites are perhaps the single best location for enhanced ad watch journalism. A website could present multimedia ad watches combining detailed "factual" background of the kind featured in most ad watches (such as voting records, independent analyses, and so forth) with analysis of the audiovisual intertextualities of campaign advertising. Print and broadcast ad analysts can also work to use symbols and graphics to better convey the points of their commentary (Richardson 2002). It may be that a satirical ad could be analyzed using the very conventions of satire. If a candidate's ad is making use of sound effects and carefully selected visuals, an ad watch can do the same. Sound is notably absent from Jamieson's ad watch grammar, and its development is one field of potential value for ad watch practitioners.

Development of a critical grammar for ad watches is perhaps the most crucial task facing analysts because of the tendency for the repetition of an ad during an ad watch to overpower the analyst's critique, as was the case in the CNN ad watch discussed above. Without presenting at least a part of the ad being scrutinized, an ad watch might not even resonate with voters who view the ad. Yet even a single image from an ad can serve to evoke the whole spot in a viewer's mind, making it difficult to avoid repeating the claims of a suspect ad (Jamieson 1992b). Rigorous deconstruction of ads is one of the few tools available. How rigorous is largely a function of the analyst's tolerance level for what may be seen as advocacy rather than reporting. An extreme deconstruction could subject the sponsor of an ad to the same audiovisual and/or argumentative challenges that faced the candidate targeted by the ad. For example, faced with a bleak and horrific ad indicting a candidate for leniency on prison furloughs using a single prominent case to great impact, an ad watch might use the very same techniques to indict the sponsor. This would mean if the suspect ad used unflattering images or a scary soundtrack in depicting the opponent, the ad watch could do likewise in depicting the sponsor. This is the fight fire with fire deterrence theory of ad watch journalism. It can level the playing field now tilted to ad sponsors, whose audiovisual production values easily overwhelm analysts' verbal retorts. This approach is also likely to meet much resistance among mainstream journalists reticent to appear biased against one side or another. Less dramatic deconstruction could unpack the components of an ad, isolating the soundtrack or special effects and decoupling an ad's charges from their audiovisual reinforcements. This can even be done with a trace of humor. Horror music could precede the actual analysis of claims rather than accompanying them. The same could be done with visual effects including the use of black-and-white images, blurry or unflattering images and so on. For example, an ad watch could begin with scary music and the analysts' voice-over (Candidate X has begun airing a frightening indictment of Candidate Y . . .) but when the actual ad appears the music will stop and the ad's own soundtrack will be edited out, leaving the images without their powerful resonance. Alternatively, icons could be used to signify things like sound effects or unflattering images. In this case, rather than replaying the actual ad, the ad watch would reconstruct the ad—for example, substituting a generic unflattering image of a politician or a logo standing for scary sound effects or clever graphics.

Edward Tufte has written extensively about graphic and visual communication. Contemplating how to combat manipulated visual imagery, he wrote:

> One way to enforce some standard of truth-telling is to insist that the innocent, unprocessed natural image be shown along with the manipulated image, and, further, that the manipulators and their methods be identified. If images are to be credible, their source and history must be documented. And, if an image is to serve as serious evidence, a more rigorous accounting should reveal the overall pool of images from which the displayed image was selected. (1997:25)

One intriguing possibility for applying this approach to political advertising would be to combat the use of unflattering slow-motion video by playing the video at normal speed. Then, the audio track, containing the attacking candidate's message, would sound speeded up and distorted. The effect could be quite powerful.

Another common distortion found in campaign ads occurs when the sequence of visual images in an ad are different than the sequence of the events the visuals depict. Analysts could place the video sequences in their proper chronological order, provide the suppressed context, and offer evidence to counter the ad's false implications.

In terms of the visual elements of campaign coverage more broadly, and visual reporting in general, journalists might be well advised to consider Tufte's observation that "information displays should serve the analytic purpose at hand; if the substantive matter is a possible cause-effect relationship, the graphs should organize data so as to illuminate such a link. Not a complicated idea, but a profound one" (1997:49).

Use Actual Viewer Responses to Inform the Ad Watch: Surveys or focus groups of citizens designed specifically to gauge what viewers are seeing, hearing, and thinking about political ads may provide clues to the way an ad is working that might otherwise elude analysts. Such investigations would be well advised to collect a range of pertinent data (such as those discussed in chapter 2), including things such as viewer's free-recall associations, their perceptions of sights and sounds and the way they might reconstruct the ad for a friend if asked to do so. While this tactic might not be appropriate for all ads aired during a campaign, it could be particularly useful for dealing with those spots that have been most frequently broadcast.

Provide Sufficient Time and Space for Comprehensive Ad Watches: It will take column inches in print and minutes of precious air time in broadcast journalism to implement many of these suggestions. Editors should not shrink from this task. Typically television ads account for the single biggest category of spending by the major party presidential candidates. The enormous resources devoted to campaign commercials by candidates and parties, and the primacy of audiovisual information in shaping political learning and thought (Graber 1997, 2001) indicate that resources devoted to ad watch journalism will not be misspent.

An important related concern is the issue of selecting which ads should be featured. Typically, attack ads or those with some controversy are more likely to be reported. Indeed, some ads, such as the

Republican National Committee's 1996 spot attacking the suggestion made by President Clinton's lawyers that Paula Jones's lawsuit be postponed because the president was covered under the Soldiers and Sailors Act, are reported even though the ads never actually aired.

The issue of selection turns on journalists' news judgment and the intended audience for an ad watch. Analysts must ask, "Will my audience want to know about this?" This may mean that a controversial ad produced but not aired is covered while a noncontroversial ad that was aired wouldn't be covered. This may not be as much a problem if the ad watch coverage is successful at deconstructing the ad message and placing its claims in the proper context. Fortunately, in most cases, reporters will not have to make such selection decisions. It is often obvious during the course of a campaign which ads are receiving major airplay. During the 2000 campaign, the Brennan Center for Justice provided frequent press releases based on data from the Campaign Media Analysis Group (CMAG) tracking ad buys by candidates in media markets across the country. Ads with major air time deserve attention. Analysts could do worse than to simply videotape the nightly local news broadcasts each week where ads are often run either immediately adjacent to the program or during commercial breaks and report on the top two or three ads being run by each candidate. More precise data on ad buys can also be obtained from actual station logs. One other criteria which might inform coverage decisions is the potential dovetailing of ads with candidates' other campaign communications including stump speeches. Many voters in 1988 reported seeing the "Willie Horton" ad when in fact they had heard about Horton from news coverage and were reading into the Bush campaign's "Revolving Door" ad's specific mention of Horton. Even if such ads didn't receive major airplay, they become relevant by their link, often emotional, to prominent campaign themes.

No doubt the entire project outlined above must answer questions of bias, objectivity, and advocacy. Two responses immediately suggest themselves. First, as Howard Kurtz has suggested, journalists do their audience a disservice by hiding behind the convenient "he said, she said" formulas of conventional objectivity. He urges reporters to break the shackles of mindless objectivity (Kurtz 1993:109). Second, for those for whom such a departure would seem inappropriate of a news reporter, ad watches can be labeled as editorial and placed accordingly. This may be easier said than done, but it is one straightforward way to address this concern. Finally, candidates can be offered the opportunity to respond to ad watch analyses, something many analysts already do.

Much of what has been said in this chapter, however, points to the limits and liabilities of the mainstream media as a vehicle for the critical analysis of campaign communication. If Graber's optimism about the enlightening potential of visual communication is to be realized, it will require the efforts of many voices and visions. The role the Internet can play in this endeavor is readily apparent. The challenge lies in cultivating the cadres of visual analysts necessary to fulfill the task. No doubt they will have to be drawn from far and wide, and while "alternative" media outlets (perhaps even MTV) may rise to the occasion, it may be that a new generation of students and faculty in fields such as communications, design, journalism, political science, and related disciplines can ultimately best carry the effort forward. Perhaps the story of a group of journalism and law students at Northwestern University who helped exonerate four men wrongly convicted of murder (Protess and Warden 1998) can serve to inspire the public-spirited political communication projects that could finally realize the liberating potential of visual communication. At the very least, news organizations and others with their own websites could offer interactive features allowing citizens the ability to edit and critique the ads themselves (Richardson 2006). In a sense, YouTube is already serving such a function.

As we have worked our way outward from campaign advertising's foundations in the audiovisual conventions of popular culture to the ways that researchers and journalists have engaged political advertising, we have considered some directions in which these efforts might be more productively pursued. In this chapter I have tried to show how an ad watch journalism focused on patterns of record and behavior is most useful to citizens in American elections, where as political scientist V. O. Key argued, the role of the voters is to pass retrospective judgment on party performance and not to send forth nuanced signals of policy preference. Most of the ad watches studied, however, treated ad claims in an isolated manner and avoided judgment of record and pattern. Journalists who were motivated to address issues of pattern and record did so, and the percentage of their analyses devoted to treating claims in an isolated manner was substantially lower than other authors. I would advocate that journalists adopt the pattern approach as a means of making a more meaningful contribution to the American electoral process.

I have also suggested that ad watches would benefit from a greater attention to the audiovisual details of political commercials, and the way in which such details can be combined to evoke conventional patterns of associations in the minds of viewers. In the following chapter, we will pay close attention to the state-of-the-art in political advertising by analyzing some of the audiovisual techniques used in the 2000 presidential campaign.

NOTES

1. "Civic" or "public" journalism emerged after the 1988 campaign as an attempt to steer campaign coverage toward citizen concerns and away from campaign strategy and process; see Schudson 1998.

2. Sentences that made overt claims of patterns and those that mentioned only an isolated incident but which were part of a litany or claim of a pattern of behavior were coded as focusing on a pattern.

Chapter Five

Visual Political Communication in Campaign 2000

The Bush–Cheney advertising campaign against Vice President Al Gore during the 2000 campaign provides an illuminating glimpse at how audiovisual, narrative, and emotional elements combined to effectively communicate what the Voter News Service exit poll suggested was one of the Republicans' most relentless, effective, and damning indictments of Campaign 2000: "Al Gore will say anything."

As the election neared, the U.S. economy seemed to soar on the wings of record growth, the nation was essentially at peace, and President Clinton's job approval rating was at or near historic heights. Clinton would leave office with the highest final job approval of any president since such polling began. Largely based on these elements, many academic election forecasters predicted Gore to win the vote in the fall, and, for the most part, with a rather comfortable margin of advantage. When Gore's victory failed to rise to expectations, analysts focused on a range of explanations, including suggestions that the Gore campaign was particularly weak or ineffective. Indeed, after the election, one Bush campaign operative recalled worrying during the debates that Gore would ask, "Which part of peace and prosperity don't you like?"

In fact, the nation's economic condition was more complicated than the GDP growth rate most forecasters relied upon suggested. The growth in real disposable income (RDI) per capita in 2000 was actually slightly lower than the postwar average during presidential election years; combining a wide range of election models, a pair of researchers found that the 2000 election actually fell remarkably close to the consensus forecast (Bartels and Zaller 2001).

Yet exit poll data suggests other forces were at play as well. While Clinton's job approval was high, though lower among those who turned out to vote on Election Day than among the American people as a whole, nearly two-thirds of voters surveyed had a negative view of Clinton personally. After all, as a GOP consultant remarked about press attention to various and sundry scandals, Clinton had been subjected to what amounted to the "longest running negative advertisement in history." By the fall of 2000, Clinton's conduct had become the major unarticulated premise of the campaign. Because the narrative, audiovisual, and emotional elements of the discourse had become so well known and so well fused together, merely evoking one prominent element could evoke the entire complex of cognition and affect. And so it was that George Walker Bush ended each campaign appearance with his pledge to restore honor and dignity to the White House, a transparent attack at the incumbents, and his line was usually met with the most vociferous response of any he delivered. And so it was that while Republican ads rarely mentioned Clinton in a disparaging fashion, in visual terms they relentlessly linked Gore with the deep and sticky webs of unfavorable associations viewers held toward the Clinton–Gore administration.

We have already noted the wholistic way narrative and audiovisual elements of campaign ads draw upon widely recognized networks of conventional understanding to provide the form or structure that viewers often use to reconstruct the meaning of political communication. When a narrative and audiovisual package becomes widely recognizable, it provides an especially effective cognitive "shorthand" for communicating emotionally powerful messages. The wholistic functioning of the elements of the package (the way they work and fit together), allows those familiar with the package to fill in details (about related objects such as candidates) consistent with it, even if they in fact are not present in that candidate to the degree the package would suggest.

The media's incessant all-Monica, all-the-time bender, and to a lesser degree focus on other Clinton "scandals"[1] served to indelibly mark upon the public's memory a series of audiovisual, emotional, and narrative linkages. With the passage of time, the most scandalous behavior may prove to have been not the unfaithful and deceitful president's, bad as that was, but that of investigative journalists (Kalb 2001) and the president's various and sundry accusers (Conason and Lyons 2000). But for an extended period of time, televised images of tense White House press briefings, and alternatively scandalous, embarrassing, and revolting reports and revelations flickered across TV screens around the country. What the Bush–Cheney campaign was able to do in their ads was to visually graft this sordid and long running national soap opera firmly onto viewers' associations with Al Gore. In cognitive terms, the Bush ads primed viewers to activate elements negative to Gore, rather than other available but less negative webs of associations they might possess regarding the vice president.

The key visual component of this strategy was to show Gore, when he appeared in Bush ads,[2] always on a canted television screen: Gore on a TV set on a kitchen countertop, or with the silhouette of a canted TV screen superimposed over images of Gore, and so on (see figure 5.1). Computer graphics simulating fuzzy static punctuated images of Gore to further emphasize that he was on TV, presumably suggesting the untrustworthiness of both the man and the medium. The very visual grammar that allowed ad watch journalists to more forcefully convey their critique of campaign spots powerfully invites viewers of the Bush ad to activate unfavorable networks of associations with Gore. Indeed, the explicit use of a canted television within a visual frame in ad watches (which more than likely criticize rather than praise) signals the kind of distortions and transgressions that warrant action by the ad patrol.

The power in the Bush approach is that it relies on a widely recognized package of audiovisual, narrative, and emotional information. The impact of the pieces together is greater than their separate elements. How the images and the narrative fit together is significant. Gore, for instance, could have tried to use the same visual strategy Bush used. And while the image of any politician "on TV" might invite certain levels of distrust, such sentiments would not be as emotionally vivid as the specific links with the Clinton–Gore scandals that defined not only politics but popular culture as well for an extended period of time. Clinton's conduct had become a staple of late-night television shows like the *Tonight Show with Jay Leno* on NBC, the *Late Show with David Letterman* on CBS, and ABC's *Politically Incorrect* with Bill Maher. Such programs are actually important sources of political "news" for many Americans. Half the respondents in a January 2000 Pew Research Center survey said they regularly (16 percent) or sometimes (35 percent) glean information about the candidates from comedy programs such as *Saturday Night Live* and nontraditional outlets like MTV. These figures rise to 24 percent and 55 percent, respectively, for those under age thirty.[3] During the final months of 2000, Letterman even began recycling Clinton humor with a "classic Clin-

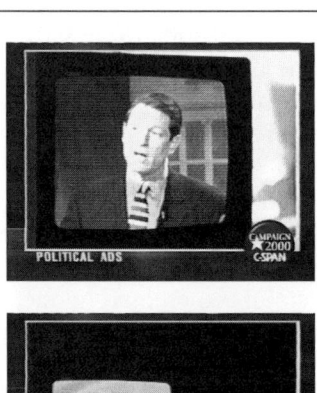

Gore on canted television

Gore inside TV silhouette

Gore on kitchen countertop TV

Gore on TV with fuzzy static

Figure 5.1. Gore Shown "on TV" in Bush Ads

ton joke" feature where he revisited jokes from years gone by. The standards for "truth," or at least what becomes popular wisdom, are much lower than even those of journalism, let alone those of the courtroom. The Bush ads were able to draw upon these widely held "understandings."

In any event, Gore's ads did not attempt to always depict Bush as "on TV." Some Gore ads, for example, did feature video of Bush speaking. Bush was even relegated to a box in a portion of the screen. But the box was not recognizably a TV. In one Gore ad, Bush was shown on a TV. In that ad, however, the TV itself was placed in the context of a graphic representation of an issue paper (criticizing the Texas governor's claim to having improved the test scores of his state's students), and against the backdrop of an empty classroom. In the Gore ads, the package of elements that worked so well in the Bush ad is lacking. The simple politician on TV has become the more ambiguous politician on a TV in an empty schoolroom. Gore's ad team needn't be faulted for this. They're trying to tell a different story. As the name of the website that appears at the end of the ad (1800thefacts.com) suggests, the Gore message is that the facts are on our side. The classroom setting is consistent with that appeal, and Bush on a TV does work in that context. But it is part of a different whole (see figure 5.2).

Visually, the Gore ads might even appear to be Bush ads if you don't read the text and discount the slightly less than flattering images of the Texas governor. It is hard, however, to imagine the Bush ads' visuals appearing in a Gore ad.

By contrast, in the Bush ads, familiar backdrops such as the White House briefing room combine with the unflattering slow-motion images of a defensive politician. The visual image alone evokes the narrative of a defensive Clinton or Gore and all the accompanying baggage they carried. The backdrop at the White House briefing room is familiar, and the use of hyper-close-ups primes viewers to draw upon more negative associations than might otherwise be the case. When I've shown several of the Bush ads to students in the classroom and then asked where they remember Gore as being when he was shown in the ads, some invariably remember "the White House." When asked what else that reminds them of, some volunteer "Clinton." This is not surprising, given the saturation level coverage of the scandal-prone president. While college students in 2000 might have only Clinton's presidency as a frame of reference, Clinton had been president for eight years. Given the way recent information is easier to recall, even those who had experienced many other presidents

116   Chapter 5

The Gore ads where Bush appears lack the graphic evocation of "TV" found in Bush ads. Bush is in moving video in the top two frames, but is not shown as "on TV." In the bottom frame, Bush *is* shown on TV, but the graphic of an issue paper and the schoolroom context do not wholistically activate associations with scandalous lying as the Bush ads featuring Gore did.

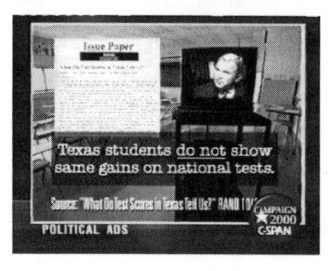

Figure 5.2. **Bush Appearing in Gore Ads**

might still associate such imagery with Clinton. This then becomes a tempting vehicle the Bush campaign can use in its ads, effectively melding press coverage of Clinton's serial indecencies and deceptions to media reports of Gore's "exaggerations." Even those who are inclined toward less upsetting associations regarding President Clinton, will probably find the slow-motion video clips of Gore waving his finger, evocative of Clinton's own now infamous finger-waving denial. If, in fact, viewers draw such associations between Gore and Clinton's worst qualities, it would mark a particularly effective communication of one of the GOP's main campaign appeals (see figure 5.3).

In some Bush ads, Gore appears on a TV set in a spacious, moderately upscale kitchen. This framing keenly evokes the emotional dis-

Gore shown "on TV" in Bush ads at the White House briefing room (left) and striking a pose made infamous by Bill Clinton's denial of a "sexual relationship with that woman . . ." (right)

Figure 5.3. Gore Placed in Clintonesque Settings in Bush Ads

tress caused by the worst of the Clinton administration's scandals, reminding viewers of the particular discomfort of having the family dinner punctuated by journalists and politicians probing the intimate details of the president's affair with an intern. But now, it is Gore "lying on TV," not Clinton. Memories tagged with such emotionally riveting content are more easily stored in our brains, and more readily recalled even if they are not "rehearsed" or recalled frequently (Graber 2001). Try as we might, we cannot prevent the Bush ads from dredging up these affective responses and cognitive associations. The political power of the ads lies in transferring onto Gore that which originated with Clinton.

Gore's own "problems with the truth" took on a life of their own. Consider the rap on Gore as serial exaggerator which found great currency in the press, despite lacking substantial basis in fact. Gore's "claim" to having "invented the Internet," for example, rested on a misquote of Gore's remarks and a carefully choreographed public relations campaign orchestrated by Republican Party operatives (Parry 2000). Gore never said "I invented the Internet." On March 9, 1999, he told CNN's Wolf Blitzer, "During my service in the United States Congress, I took the initiative in creating the Internet" (Parry 2000). Gore was in fact an early advocate of efforts to create the Internet as we now know it; and he is widely credited with popularizing the phrase "information superhighway" through his tireless crusade to promote cyber communications. As one observer put it,

"Behind every major invention and inventor stands a patron. Behind the Internet stands Gore" (Coopersmith 2000).

But far fewer Americans were aware of this than would have been familiar with the endless parade of jokes from TV's late-night comics about Gore inventing stuff. Ultimately, the image of Gore as a liar/exaggerator could stand on its own, and be deployed by the Bush campaign to devalue Gore's position on completely unrelated issues, such as education and prescription drugs.

In the final frames of a Bush ad on prescription drugs, a slow-motion video clip of Al Gore appears, on a TV, with a "website" address (prescriptionfordisaster.com) superimposed over Gore's image. As the additional superimposed text "Gore's Rx Plan?" flies in from the left, accompanied by the sound of typing on a computer keyboard, the narration concludes ". . . A prescription for disaster. . . ." Viewers can read Gore's lips as he "finishes" the narrator's sentence: "For you!" The same technique is used at the end of another Bush ad; where the narration concludes, "Just more politics from Al Gore," "for you" say the vice president's lips. These Bush ads use audiovisual production techniques to essentially turn what was one of Gore's most authentic and effective refrains in his acceptance speech ("I want to fight for you") into its virtual opposite.

Al Gore's remarks about prescription drug costs drew widespread media scrutiny and were the basis for a Bush attack ad run during the closing days of the campaign in key media markets across the country. Gore chose to kick off his health care message in a town-hall meeting with two hundred retirees on August 28 in Tallahassee, Florida. After hearing several complaints about prescription drug costs, he suggested the pharmaceutical industry should lower prices. According to the *Tampa Tribune,* Gore offered as an example his mother-in-law, Margaret Ann Aitcheson, whom he suggested paid more (108 dollars per month) for her arthritis medication (the prescription drug Lodine) than it cost to fill his fourteen-year-old black Labrador retriever Shilo's prescription for the same drug (less than 39 dollars per month). "Don't you think that ought to be changed?" he asked (Wasson 2000). Three weeks later, the *Boston Globe* reported that Gore had "mangled the facts," relying not on personal experience but on a House Democratic study which in turn relied on wholesale rather than retail costs, assuming that the dosages were the same and ignoring the fact that a generic equivalent was available (Robinson 2000). Governor Bush seized on his rival's remarks as further evidence that Gore had a tendency to "make up facts to make his case," and that "he'll say anything to be the president" (Seelye 2000). Gore's aides suggested that the vice president's overall point was valid; indeed, the *New York Times* reported that a check of "several pharmacies and veterinary clinics in Washington found a price disparity between Lodine and Etogesic (the dog version) capsules roughly similar to that given by Mr. Gore," though the capsules were of different sizes (Seelye 2000); moreover, overall drug costs had risen by 13 percent or more every year since 1996 (Associated Press 2001). But for the press, pundits, late-night comics, and Republican loyalists, it was yet another example of Gore's fabrications. Gore's remarks were featured prominently in a Bush ad aired during the closing weeks of the campaign. It is a particularly telling example of the way audiovisual communication can distort and mislead. In doing so, the Bush ad draws upon strategies of visual manipulation that Tufte found in classic texts of magic: *suppressing context* and *preventing reflexive analysis* (emphasis in original; Tufte 1997:68).

The ad starts with a video clip of Gore inside the silhouette of a TV, appearing to be talking and gesturing to a pharmacist. The narration begins, "Remember when Al Gore said his mother-in-law's prescription cost more than his dog's? His own aides said the story was made up." A newspaper clipping from the *Washington Times* appears on the screen; the image fades into a white screen with black lettering that reads "Now Al Gore is bending the truth again," as the narrator says the same thing. Gore reappears, again in the silhouette of a TV, waving his finger à la Clinton. Above him read the words "*Wall Street Journal*, October 26, 2000" as the narrator continues, "The press calls Gore's social security attacks nonsense." The word "nonsense" is superimposed, just as in an ad watch, over Gore. (Of course, more accurate would be "the editorial board of the *Wall Street Journal* calls Gore's social security attacks nonsense.") The ad shifts to a video clip of George Walker Bush (notably *not* inside the silhouette of a TV) wearing a suit and a hard hat, with the words "Governor Bush: $2.4 Trillion to Strengthen Social Security & Pay All Benefits" superimposed on the screen as the narrator says, "Governor Bush sets aside $2.4 trillion to strengthen social security and pay all benefits." The ad then shifts back to the TV silhouette, with an animated and perhaps slightly agitated Gore at the podium during a debate. He says, "There has never been a time in this campaign when I have said something that I know to be untrue. There has never been a time when I've said something untrue." The TV silhouette and Gore in it fade, revealing the word "Really?" in black text on a white background as the announcer asks somewhat incredulously, "Really?" Viewers I've shown the ad to often assume the footage of Gore is taken from his October debates with Bush. This is consistent with the wholistic, top-down processing of visual information. The presidential debates were second in audience only to the August conventions, and clips from the debates were replayed with frequency on TV news. So when an image of Gore in a debate is shown (a detail), it is not surprising viewers might assume it was from Gore's debates with Bush (a familiar form). Only upon closer examination does it become clear that it's not the Texas governor at the opposing podium, but rather former New Jersey Senator Bill Bradley, debating Gore in January, before the Iowa precinct caucuses. The sequence of images in this Bush ad suppresses context by suggesting that Al Gore made up a story about the cost of his family's prescription drug costs, then launched "nonsense" attacks against Governor Bush, and then denied ever having said anything "untrue" during the campaign. In fact, Gore's denial, shown at the end of the ad, occurred half a year before he made his comments about his family's drug costs.

There are many plausible ways to read Gore's "exaggerations." The media certainly has a right to focus on whatever issues it thinks are important, to press candidates to respond in detail, and to take such detailed indications and explore their significance in depth. The Bush campaign, too, has a right to push its own interpretations of the vice president. The Internet address gorewillsayanything.com featured at the end of some of the ads succinctly captures the Bush–Cheney perspective. The danger for those in the press inclined to draw attention to Gore's exaggerations is that they will be swept up in the vortex of the partisan perspective. The stories about Gore's exaggerations readily meld with the Bush campaign spin that Gore will say anything. Indeed, the VNS exit poll found that 74 percent of voters agreed with the statement that "Gore will say anything." Only 58 percent agreed that "Bush will say anything."

A Bush ad visually invites precisely this interpretation. Headlines torn from the pages of the nation's newspapers are emblazoned, ad watch style, over the familiar images of Gore on TV. In the visual meltdown that frequently represents memories and thoughts, the charge that "Gore exaggerates" (the press) morphs into "Gore lies like Clinton" (the Bush ad), reinforced by the independent credibility of the press. Many will confuse where they saw it, heard it, or read it, but will nonetheless accept the depiction of Gore as truth-challenged (see figure 5.4).

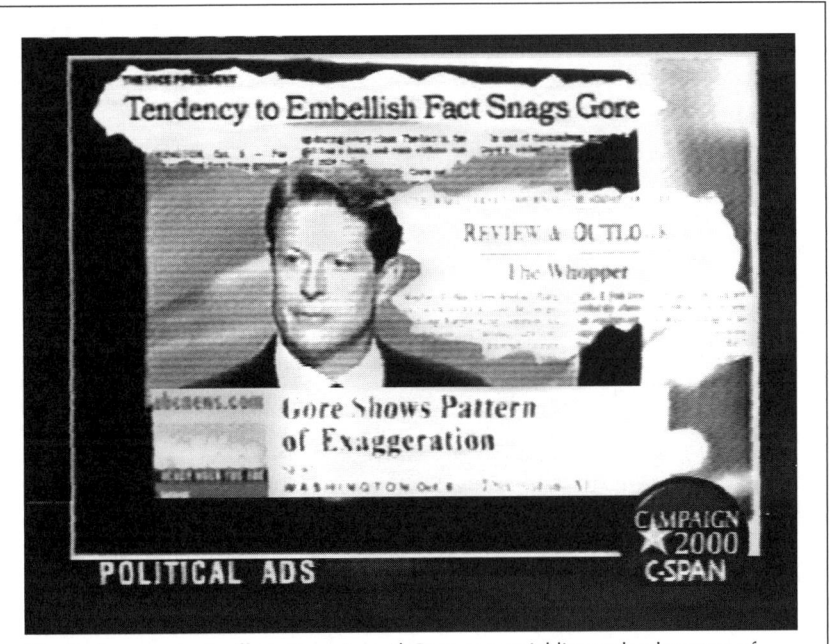

The Bush campaign's efforts to portray Al Gore as a serial liar took advantage of extensive press coverage of Gore's exaggerations. Ads beginning with the narrator asking, "Why does Al Gore say one thing when the truth is another?" effectively fuse the stronger Bush charge with the press coverage.

Figure 5.4. The Meltdown of Gore as Exaggerator and Gore as Liar

By the spring of 2002, ten governors, Republican and Democratic alike, "tired of high prescription drug costs burdening states' Medicaid budgets," were calling upon Congress to block patent extensions for lucrative brand-name drugs. Said William Janklow, Republican governor of South Dakota, the drug companies are "gouging people" (Adams and Harris 2002). But during the 2000 campaign, journalists, following the same line of inquiry as the Bush ads, focused substantial attention on the accuracy of Gore's remarks, attention that might have been better directed at the broader, more significant underlying issue. Imagine what would have happened if reporters had learned then that in fact Grandma Gore was getting her prescriptions filled for free by the White House physician! (Shrum 2007).

One of the key elements of the Bush ads, and of campaign ads generally, is their ability to draw graphic linkages between candidates (either themselves or their opposition) and other people, things or emotions. Graphic information can be less linear than text. It can also be powerful in shaping pattern recognition. Both elements may be of use to analysts. To more fully do so, however, reporters may wish to consider how much more often campaign ads use graphics than does TV news.

One technique for visualizing comparison is "adjacency," or sequential presentation of images: first one candidate is shown, then the other. As Tufte notes,

> Connections are built among images by position, orientation, overlap, synchronization, and similarities in content. Parallelism grows from a common viewpoint that relates like to like. Congruity of structure across multiple images gives the eye a context for assessing data variation. Parallelism is not simply a matter of design arrangements, for the perceiving mind itself actively works to detect and indeed to generate links, clusters, and matches among assorted visual elements. (1997: 82)

Adjacency (or temporal parallelism) is a common way of visualizing linkage in both ads and news.

The communication of comparison through sequential imagery can be amplified by visual punctuation of adjacent images. In one Bush ad, for example, an image of the Texas governor sitting with schoolchildren becomes visibly brighter through a starburst-like visual effect, providing stark contrast with the darkened images representing Al Gore's plans. Barry (1997:134–35) suggests darkness and light can exert "profound effects on emotional states," noting humans' primitive fear of darkness (see figure 5.5).

Throughout this book, we have seen how visual elements are central to understanding the meaning of campaign advertising. Visual communication is both detailed and wholistic. Forms provide the structure for interpretation, and in some cases, reconstruction or even generation of details. To neglect the audiovisual elements of campaigns and especially campaign advertising is to neglect a part of their essence.

Yet, as Messaris (1997) notes, visual communication lacks a defining propositional syntax, or the grammar by which images can be related to one another in terms of analogy, contrast, causality, or other propositions. It is not that visual conventions for conveying contrast and causality are completely nonexistent, but rather that the same visual syntax can be interpreted differently by different viewers. This also

In the first frame (top left), the image of Governor Bush and schoolchildren (with the text "Governor Bush Tests and Holds Schools Accountable for Results" superimposed on the screen) is normally bright. Visual effects in the second image (bottom left) make it much brighter, as a "starburst" of light briefly brightens the screen before yielding to a darkened image (top right) with superimposed text reading "Al Gore Tax Plan Leaves Out Half of All Taxpayers." Subsequent images representing Gore's plans (bottom right) are also visually darker than the Bush images.

Figure 5.5. Visually Punctuated Adjacency in Comparison by Sequential Imagery

allows political admakers to advance claims visually while maintaining "plausible deniability" in regards to specific elements of the message, which, after all, are subject to conflicting interpretations. This may make analysis of campaign advertising highly subjective, but that is not something that we can avoid. As much as various analysts and reformers would like to see a politics of pure reason, that is simply not possible. In its stead, we are left with a subjective, often emotional political dialogue in which the stories political advertising tells about American politics are a central element. We will consider what this means for American democracy in our final chapter.

NOTES

1. In the ten years following the first reports of the "Whitewater" story, the *New York Times* alone printed 364 stories with the word "Whitewater" in the headline and a total of 1,841 stories with "Whitewater" in the headline or lead paragraph, according to a Lexis-Nexis search. In March 2002, Robert W. Ray, the last occupant of the office of independent counsel on Whitewater matters, issued his final, 2,090-page report finding "insufficient" evidence to "sustain a criminal prosecution beyond a reasonable doubt" that either of the Clintons had committed any crimes. Responding to the implication that there might have been evidence of wrongdoing but that it was "insufficient," the Clintons' attorney, David E. Kendall remarked that one could say with "equal justification" that there was insufficient evidence that "the Clintons had pilfered Powerball tickets, trapped fur-bearing mammals out of season or sold nuclear secrets to Liechtenstein" (Lewis 2002:A30).

2. While I do not have access to all the ads run by the Bush campaign, I have seen many of them and I am not aware of any Bush ads where Gore wasn't "on TV." I believe the ads discussed here to be reasonably representative of the Bush ad campaign; many were run in the Philadelphia market, which at one point was the most targeted market in the campaign (Marks 2000).

3. Pew Research Center for the People and the Press (2000).

Chapter Six

Terror TV: Political Advertising during the Bush Years

As the twenty-first century unfolds, the political communication landscape is being torn asunder. Audiovisual political communication is more prevalent than ever. Today, candidates, parties, and organized interests are joined by individual users of YouTube, MySpace, the "blogosphere," WiFi, and cellphones, as well as conventional broadcast, cable, satellite, and wireless providers, in producing multimedia political "content."

At the same time, traditional journalism, its institutions, and its values, face unprecedented challenge. The sale of the *Wall Street Journal* in 2007 to conservative Australian media mogul Rupert Murdoch signals the twilight hour of the independent journalism that, for more than one hundred years, sought first and foremost to serve the public interest.[1] The pillars of that era were family-owned major metropolitan newspapers whose owners were largely able to resist the most egregious cost-cutting, quality-cutting demands of Wall Street and the investment community. Only two remain largely free from corporate control today: the *Washington Post* and the *New York Times*. They, too, may find it impossible to resist the relentless profit-push that has led to less staff and less news (not only are page sizes shrinking, but traditional "news" content is increasingly being replaced by coverage of entertainment, business, and "feature" stories). Bennett et al. argue that current market conditions represent the worst conditions for the survival of an independent press: "extreme concentration of media ownership, a generally withdrawn public, and an avowedly timid professional press" (Bennett et al. 2007:185; see also Baker 2002; McChesney 2004; and Cook 2005). America now appears poised to enter a brave new world of campaign communication where the various filtering roles of the traditional mass media, to shape and constrain campaign discourse no longer function, just as the potential sources and channels of political communication are expanding exponentially.

THE AUDIOVISUAL POLITICS OF TERROR

Along with the communications revolution, the nation's political environment has also changed, the result of the terrorist attacks of September 11, 2001, and the subsequent declaration of a "global war on terror" by the Bush administration. The psychology of terror would have profound consequences for the behavior of American voters. Political psychologists Sheldon Solomon, Jeff Greenberg, and Tom Pyszczynski have advanced a "terror management theory" of social behavior suggesting that when a person confronts their own mortality at an unconscious level, they engage in a process of "worldview defense" (Greenberg, Pyszczynski, and Solomon 1986; Solomon, Greenberg, and Pyszczynski 1991; Rosenblatt et al. 1989). They note that merely confronting mortality invokes typical defense mechanisms (that won't happen to me). It is only after conscious concern with death has subsided that people subconsciously begin to defend their worldview, and become more hostile to those with different beliefs and values, moral transgressors, and critics of their worldview. In post-9/11 America, an entire nation confronted its mortality. A global war on terror would be a constant reminder of that mortality, which in turn would evoke a set of psychological responses that could be used to rally support for precisely the politics the Bush–Rove GOP had to offer.

2002: 9/11 AND THE TURN TOWARD WAR IN IRAQ

The 2002 congressional "midterm" elections would mark the first post-9/11 political campaigns, and while some proclaimed "everything changed," one of the first major indicators that some things had not changed was the resurgence of fierce partisan political conflict. It would take some time, but America's newfound political unity would be over before the nation's voters would cast their ballots in November.

Public opinion polls, especially in the first months after the attack, registered strong bi-partisan support for a military response in Afghanistan, and remarkable approval of President Bush's handling of his job, even among Democratic voters. On October 7, 2001, U.S. and coalition forces from all over the world launched military strikes in Afghanistan. By mid-November, the coalition-supported Northern Alliance had routed the ruling Taliban government. Operation Enduring Freedom, as the campaign had been named, was seen as one of the CIA's "finest hours" (Schroen 2005; but see also Berntsen and Pezullo 2006). The early military success, however, did not capture or kill Osama bin Laden, Al Qaeda's spiritual leader and sponsor of the 9/11 attacks. Indeed, by mid-December of 2001, the hunt for Bin Laden intensified in the Battle of Tora Bora. A CIA operative stationed there at the time argues that the United States could have captured Bin Laden if administration officials had provided the troops he requested (Berntsen and Pezzullo 2006). A final March 2002 push, "Operation Anaconda," involved the most intense fighting of the Afghan War, but in the end, Osama and other "high-value targets" had escaped.

The focus of the Bush administration's "Global War on Terror" was about to shift westward, to Iraq. That shift in focus would eventually tear apart America's post-9/11 unity, and if Karl Rove had his way, Republican congressional candidates would make it so. Mr. Rove, a longtime Bush aide and the "architect" of Mr. Bush's election campaigns, signaled in a January 2002 speech at the winter meeting of the Republican National Committee (RNC) that GOP candidates should run on war and argue that they would keep the nation safer than Democratic candidates. Yet, only four days before Rove's speech, President Bush had publicly noted the "spirit of unity that had been prevalent when it comes to fighting the war" (Berke 2002). In June, copies of a White House strategy presentation for Republicans became public, revealing Rove's advice that the Republicans should "focus on war" (and the economy) and challenge Democratic candidates as weak on national security.[2] Described by *Wall Street Journal* editorialist Paul Gigot (2007) as "arguably the most influential White House aide of modern times," Rove's signature contribution to Republican campaign strategy was his relentless focus on his party's core base of supporters (Halperin and Harris 2006). In a country where core conservatives outnumber core liberals, Rove reasoned, playing to the base works. Trying to sway low-information, undecided voters in the political "center" is inefficient, ineffective, and likely to sap the motivation of the base. Sharp attacks that divide Democrats while reinforcing Republican campaign themes are much more effective as they allow an energized base to in turn mobilize enough other voters to prevail. The social psychology of terror would give such a strategy a fertile environment in which to flourish.

By June 2002, President Bush's job approval rating, while still quite high, was dropping at a rate of 2 percent each month. Despite the president's opposition, Democratic calls for a new federal agency to coordinate domestic security were gaining traction, while reports of unheeded warnings within the government before the September 11 attacks were appearing on a daily basis. In May it was reported that on August 6, 2001, President Bush had received an urgent briefing by the CIA entitled "Bin Laden Determined to Strike in U.S.," which mentioned the World Trade Center, Washington, D.C., and plans to hijack airplanes. Bush's then National Security Adviser, Condoleezza Rice, later stated at a press briefing that no one "could have predicted" that Al Qaeda "would try to use an airplane as a missile," even though both government and press reports dating back to the mid-1990s documented Al Qaeda plans to crash airliners into strategic targets (Woodward and Eggen 2002). On June 6, FBI Agent Colleen Rowley testified on Capitol Hill about the agency's failure to process potentially critical clues to the attack before it happened. That night, the President would make a nationally televised address announcing his support for a cabinet department on domestic security (Bumiller and Mitchell 2002). By fall, Democratic senators who voted to protect the collective bargaining rights of most employees of the new agency would face charges that they were "opposed" (to the agency they were first to argue for) and "soft" on terrorists.

Perhaps more than any other congressional contest, the battle between incumbent Senator Max Cleland (D-GA) and his GOP challenger Saxby Chambliss would come to embody the narrative and audiovisual manifestation of the politics of terror. Early in the race, Cleland ran ads touting his support of President Bush on education and taxes. Georgia was one of five states with Democratic senators that Republicans strongly felt they could pick up in 2002, according to that leaked White House strategic analysis. The National Republican Seantorial Committee (NRSC) made the unusual decision to spend perhaps a million dollars during the first week of June on behalf of Chambliss, who had been recruited by the White House and was facing an underfunded challenger in the GOP primary (WSB-TV 2002). The ads argued he would work with President Bush to keep America safe in the face of the terror threat.

The specter of September 11 hung over the midterm campaign. Many candidates would not air any ads on the actual first-year anniversary of the event. On September 9, 2002, the Cleland campaign released a sixty-second spot entitled "One America," directly addressing the terror attacks:

> September the Eleventh changed America, our enemies actually believed our freedom and diversity were our weakness, instead they awoke a sleeping giant. I believe this poem reflects the true strength and character of our country. As the soot and dirt and ash rained down, we became one color. As we carried each other down the stairs of the burning building, we became one class. As we fell to our knees in prayer, we became one faith. As we mourned together our great loss, we became one family. As we retell the sacrifice of our heroes, we become one people. We are one color, one class, one faith, one family, one people, we are the power of one, we are united, we are America. (*The Hotline* 2002)

Cleland's ad reflected the emotional bonds of solidarity wrought by the worst terrorist attack in U.S. history. It was a spirit that would prove fleeting. Within a week, the focus of the campaign would increasingly shift toward Iraq. Growing political pressure would lead many Democratic incumbents, especially those who favored war against Iraq, including Cleland, to call for a congressional vote on the war, and sooner rather than later. In early October, Cleland would become the first candidate in 2002 to specifically mention Iraq in his advertising as he trumpeted his support for President Bush.

The Chambliss campaign would turn to the legislative battle over the proposed Homeland Security department to attack Cleland, accusing him in a press release of "bending to union bosses and endangering the American public" through his opposition to Republican plans for the agency (Tharpe 2002). The Chambliss campaign went further when it released an ad that began with a montage of images of Osama Bin Laden and Saddam Hussein, visually linking them with Cleland; the ad's announcer states that Cleland "voted against the president's vital homeland security efforts eleven times" (Wilfong 2002a). Democratic and Republican legislators split on the question of granting employees of the new agency collective bargaining rights; Cleland favored a compromise that would allow President Bush to loosen civil service rules and to decertify the union in the interest of national security (Tharpe 2002). In fact, Cleland supported the creation of the agency before President Bush did, and voted for a Democratic plan to create the agency that had cleared committee (Espo 2002). Cleland's votes "against" the agency were largely votes over various Republican-sponsored amendments introduced in committee (Espo 2002; Wilfong 2002a). After nearly a week of intense criticism from the

Cleland camp, the ad was reworked, with the same charges in the script but with the Bin Laden and Hussein images removed (Wilfong 2002b).

While preprimary polls showed Cleland with a 60 percent favorable rating among Georgia voters, his lead over Chambliss narrowed over the course of the campaign, inviting observers to speculate that the attacks were taking their toll. The race would be the most expensive in Georgia history, with the two candidates spending more than $16 million combined. The campaign also saw last-minute visits by President Bush.

While the broadcasting of Chambliss's attacks on Cleland appeared to weaken the Democratic incumbent, an exercise in "narrowcasting" may also have been critical influencing the election's outcome. White House political adviser Karl Rove identified the decision of Georgia's Democratic Governor, Roy Barnes, to remove the confederate battle flag from the Georgia state flag as one that could motivate previously apathetic rural, white, male voters. By narrowly targeting that message to that group, Republicans were able to avoid generating a backlash among other voters that such a racially charged appeal might generate. The experiment proved remarkably successful as Republicans swept the incumbent Georgia Democrats from office (Frontline 2002).

Max Cleland voted with President Bush on the Iraq War. He served in Vietnam where he lost three limbs in a grenade explosion and earned the Silver Star for valor in the face of the enemy. His opponent, Saxby Chambliss, who never served in the military (avoiding Vietnam through deferments), would, in the end, win election by attacking Cleland as soft on national security.

It is hard to comprehend that outcome without understanding the vast power of audiovisual political communication. One crude measure of how effective the Republican strategy was in shaping the campaign discourse about Cleland can be taken from news stories in the Lexis-Nexis database of U.S. newspapers and wires. Between June 1 and September 11, 2002, 36 stories included the words "Max Cleland" and "Saddam" or "Osama" out of a total of 695 stories mentioning "Max Cleland," or 5 percent. Between September 12 and November 4 (the last day before Election Day), 132 stories linked Cleland and Saddam or Osama out of a total of 578 stories mentioning "Max Cleland" (or 23 percent).

Georgia's U.S. Senate race reflected broader national trends. The Wisconsin Advertising Project compiled data on ad buys in the nation's one hundred largest media markets during the 2002 campaign. Following Karl Rove's strategic advice, one in every five Republican U.S. Senate ads mentioned "foreign policy, defense, and terrorism," three times more often than Democratic candidates did in their ads (Goldstein and Rivlin 2003:52). Nationwide, as in Georgia, the tone of campaign spots turned markedly more negative after the middle of September; in general, more competitive races were also more negative (Goldstein and Rivlin 2003:28, 30).

In the end, the president's party gained seats in both the House and Senate in a first midterm election, the first time that had happened since FDR in 1934. Not surprisingly, the lessons of 2002 would bear directly on the 2004 campaign, when once again Republicans would field a candidate who avoided serving in Vietnam in opposition to a Vietnam war hero, played out against the backdrop of the Iraq War.

2004: THE POLITICS OF TERROR: ANOTHER VIETNAM, ANOTHER "MELTDOWN"

The October 2002 congressional vote to authorize the use of military force in Iraq would come to wreak havoc on Democratic Party presidential politics. Democratic campaign consultant Robert Shrum described how both foreign policy and political advisers warned that those who voted against the resolution would not be seen as "serious" presidential contenders in the first post-9/11 battle for the White House (Shrum 2007:388). The legacy of the 1991 Persian Gulf War loomed large. Then, coalition forces quickly routed the Iraqis from occupied Kuwait, proving false fears of the United States becoming bogged down in "another Vietnam." Expectations in 2002 were that the military campaign in Iraq would be quick and decisive, and prospective presidents did not want to be on the wrong side of history.

Days before the war began, Vice President Cheney, appearing on CBS's *Face the Nation*, stated that the fight in Iraq would be "weeks rather than months," and that American troops would be "greeted as liberators" (Milbank 2003). Such thinking had led the administration to resist calls from within the military establishment that significantly more troops would be necessary, especially to keep the peace after the invasion. Nearly three weeks before Cheney's remarks, Army Chief of Staff Eric K. Shinseki, echoing long-standing Army doctrine, told the Senate Armed Services Committee that "several hundred thousand soldiers" would be required to secure a postwar Iraq (Slevin 2003).

The war appeared destined for overwhelming success in its early hours, but the emergence of widespread looting within days of the invasion would presage the disorder that would follow. While President Bush infamously appeared on the aircraft carrier USS *Abraham Lincoln* beneath a banner declaring "Mission Accomplished" and pronounced major combat operations in Iraq over on May 1, 2003, the situation on the ground in Iraq would continue to deteriorate (Ricks 2006; Chandrasekaran 2006). As the Democratic presidential primary season began, the expectations of the political and foreign policy elite would be turned on their head. The early front-runner was former Vermont governor Howard Dean, who made opposition to the war the centerpiece of his campaign.

Massachusetts Senator John Kerry would soon face a dilemma. Once the front-runner himself, Kerry had to decide whether or not to "go negative" and directly attack Dean. His campaign team feared a backlash, especially in Iowa, where the state's precinct caucuses would be the first official battle in the nomination contest. Iowans were less comfortable with attack politics than residents of many other states, and might punish candidates who turned on other Democrats. In a strategy meeting of campaign advisers, Kerry's pollster, Mark Mellman, presented data showing little effect from the various lines of attack against Dean. Media adviser Shrum argued that in his experience, even with far more damning indictments against the opponent, in a multi-candidate field, both the attacker and the attacked would be hurt, and the benefits would flow to a third choice (in this case likely to be John Edwards). Perhaps, Shrum suggested, another campaign would take the lead in launching attacks on Dean. Kerry reluctantly signed on to the strategy despite his personal animosity toward Dean (Shrum 2007:415). In the end, it was Richard Gephardt, who faced high expectations for Iowa after having won there in 1988, who would mount the assault on Dean. Edwards would benefit, but in the end so did Kerry.

Recognizing that national security loomed large in voters' minds, the Kerry campaign sought to draw upon the candidate's Vietnam experiences. They began airing an ad in Iowa featuring Del Sandusky, a swift boat veteran and crewmate of Kerry's, speaking directly to the camera about how, when their boat was under fire, Kerry "saved our lives." While that ad was running, another swift boat veteran (not part of Kerry's crew) who had been pulled out of the water by Kerry after he had been knocked off his boat during a gunfight, would contact the campaign after reading historian Douglas Brinkley's book *Tour of Duty* (about Kerry) and ask if there was anything he could do to help. Jim Rassman, a Republican, would be flown to Iowa by the campaign to appear with Kerry. He had not seen Kerry since the incident thirty-five years earlier. When the two met they shared an emotional embrace and their story received widespread coverage in the media. Rassman's appearance juxtaposed with the "Del Ad" (as the Kerry team would later refer to the spot featuring Sandusky) was a stroke of incredible good fortune for the campaign. Shrum would write that the spot had more impact in Iowa than any other (Shrum 2007:425). Kerry's swift boat heroics would prove, however, to be a mixed blessing as the campaign wore on.

Kerry's success in Iowa was also in part due to the campaign's own use of "narrowcasting." Kerry consultant Kenneth Strasma noted that in the run-up to the caucuses, Iowans were being deluged with wall-to-wall political ads. He described for PBS's *Frontline* how the campaign used detailed demographic data to compile a profile of the typical Kerry voter, and then targeted exactly those kinds of people. To generate such profiles, campaigns rely on the vast collection of data on private citizens maintained by companies such as the Acxiom Corporation, headquartered in Little Rock, Arkansas. Acxiom collects data on individual consumers (including you and me), based on product surveys, information provided by merchants and credit card companies, public databases, and more. What political consultants soon learned was that information that might not seem political, like whether a person owned a cat as opposed to a dog, or chose to block caller ID, could be used to predict political preferences (*Frontline* 2002).

After Kerry followed his victory in Iowa with another in the New Hampshire primary, he would essentially cruise to the nomination, carrying all but three of the fifty-four states and territories. There would be, however, one notable bump in the road. During a campaign appearance before a veteran's group in West Virginia, Kerry responded to a question from a veteran suggesting that his vote against an $87 billion supplemental spending request to fund the Iraq War meant he would abandon troops in the field. Kerry denied that, explaining that he "actually did vote for the $87 billion" before he "voted against it" (Shrum 2007:451). Kerry was referring to his support for a Democratic version of the bill that would have required paying for the supplemental spending with revenue offsets rather than borrowing, but his remarks would prove among the most memorable and damaging of the campaign, and would be endlessly aired in Bush ads throughout the campaign.

The Democratic National Convention in Boston would emphasize Kerry's military credentials and Vietnam experience. It had proven a winning formula before, and Kerry was doing surprisingly well among veterans, a group not previously known for supporting liberal Democrats from Massachusetts. That would make the subsequent attacks on Kerry's service all the more powerful. The convention had barely adjourned when a group calling itself the "Swift Boat Veterans for Truth" (SBVT) began airing ads in a small number of states attacking Kerry's Vietnam service and challenging the merit of the Bronze Star he had won for valor. The ads' allegations would receive extensive coverage on cable, especially on Fox News. Kerry, angered that his honor and good name were being attacked, wanted to strike back, but the campaign was told by pollster Mellman that the ads were not having a noticeable effect on voters. The story would continue to spread, albeit largely beneath the radar of the mainstream media, propelled by the currents of right-wing talk radio, TV, and the Internet. Finally, after two weeks, the effect of the attacks began to show up in Mellman's polls (Shrum 2007:469).

Kerry's ability to respond was also constrained by the campaign's decision to accept federal funding for the general election. Doing so guaranteed Kerry would receive $75 million from the government to run his campaign; in exchange, Kerry would have to agree not to raise and spend additional monies on his own. The problem was that while Kerry would have to spread the $75 million over the thirteen weeks between his nominating convention and the election, because the Republican Convention would be held at the beginning of September, Bush would have only eight weeks to fund. That meant that Kerry faced a strategic conundrum in responding to the SBVT attacks. Not responding was damaging the campaign now, but responding now would leave them with less money to combat Bush attacks later in the race.

In a race as close as the 2004 presidential contest, it can be difficult to ferret out the effect of discrete campaign events. Right after the convention, Kerry had moved out to a lead of several points over Bush. August, however, would witness not just the SBVT attacks, but also an elevation of the terrorist threat level to code orange. Additionally, there was a backlash against Kerry's criticism of President Bush for having continued to read the children's book *The Pet Goat* in a Florida classroom for several minutes after having been told of the attack on the World Trade Center. The combined effects would erase Kerry's gains in the public opinion polls by the end of August (Shrum 2007:464).

It would be at least two weeks after the SBVT ads began airing before major news organizations would begin to investigate the truthfulness of the ads' claims. When they did, the charges were found to be largely baseless (FactCheck.org 2004a; Zernike and Rutenberg 2004; Dobbs 2004a, 2004b; Dionne 2004). By the time those stories appeared, however, the attacks had taken on a life of their own. Indeed, during the critical month of August 2004, more news stories appeared mentioning Kerry and Vietnam than mentioning Kerry and Iraq; in fact, in August, more stories mentioned Kerry and Vietnam than mentioned Kerry and Massachusetts. It was if Kerry had become the senator from Vietnam. By mid-month, reporting on Kerry's Vietnam record in the 1960s was dominating coverage of candidate Kerry in 2004 (Richardson 2007). Another Vietnam, indeed.

The SBVT trolled the murky waters of campaign finance. Coordination between independent groups like the SBVT and partisan organizations like the White House political shop would be illegal under federal campaign finance law. Nominally "independent," records indicated most of the group's funding came from two men with longstanding ties to George W. Bush, one a political associate of Karl Rove, the other a trustee for the Bush presidential library. The ad itself was produced by the same team that had produced ads for George H. Bush attacking Michael Dukakis in 1988 (Zernike and Rutenberg 2004). In late August, the national counsel for President Bush's reelection campaign, Benjamin Ginsberg, would step down after it was revealed that he provided legal advice to SBVT (Balz and Edsall 2004).

The group's charges also benefited from the way Republican political operatives have mastered the "new media" environment, including various right-leaning websites and blogs as well as the opinion-driven reporting of Fox News (see Viguerie 2006 for a detailed insider's account of the rise of the conservative "alternative" media; but see also Brock 2004). It was as if the SBVT ads had ignited a conflagration that spread like a wildfire among conservatives yet which was, for two weeks, largely invisible to the Democrats, the Kerry campaign, and the mainstream media. By the time they realized what happened, the damage had been done. The ad patrol and the Kerry campaign would find it much harder to dislodge the storylines that had been seeded weeks before.

The most remarkable aspect of the spreading domination of the swift boat story is how small the ad buys themselves actually were. Data compiled by Nielsen-Monitor Plus and the University of Wisconsin Advertising Project indicated that the SVBT accounted for just 739 of the more than half a million spots broadcast between the start of the campaign and late August. The first wave of ads saw an average of ninety-two spots per day run in just seven media markets in three states, reaching only 6.5 million viewers (or roughly 2.1 percent of the population). So it is truly astounding that in the University of Pennsylvania National Annenberg Election Survey conducted between August 9 through 16, 2004, fully 57 percent of respondents indicated they had "seen or heard about a television ad from some Viet Nam veterans that says John Kerry did not earn his medals in the Viet Nam War but lied about his war record" (PollingReport.com 2004). The role of cable in fanning the flames of the firestorm could be seen in the Annenberg survey's finding that heavy consumers of cable news were more than twice as likely than others to have reported seeing the ads; frequent listeners to talk radio were also more likely to report exposure to the ad (Jurkowitz 2004).

It was the kind of "meltdown" that destroys campaigns. Voters are "pack rats," as Jamieson noted, in describing what had been the mother of all meltdowns, attacks on 1988 Democratic presidential candidate Michael Dukakis over Massachusetts prison furlough program and the furloughed prisoner "Willie" Horton (Jamieson 1992a). Citizens collect and store information from a range of sources but tend to forget the origin of that information. Over time, charges from ads are remembered as charges from news, giving the charges more credibility. The SBVT allegations, magnified by the media, would prove devastating. A CBS News poll found that support for Kerry among veterans, evenly split between the two candidates after the Democratic convention, had fallen to the point where Bush enjoyed an 18-point edge among that group after the charges were aired (Jurkowitz 2004). The Annenberg survey indicated that 46 percent of respondents nationwide found the SBVT ad to be "very" or "somewhat" believable; nearly one in five Americans surveyed, and nearly two in five Republicans, would respond that they thought Kerry had not earned the medals he was awarded for his service in Vietnam (Polling Report.com 2004).

While few would see the ad as an ad, one in three Americans would tell pollsters they had seen the spot (Jurkowitz 2004). This could very well be the case, given the media's intense focus on the commercial.

While some respondents may have reported seeing the ad when they had merely heard about it, those who did see the ad would encounter a persuasive production. By genre, the ad adopted the audiovisual conventions of a military documentary. It actually begins with a black-and-white group photo of sailors with Kerry in the middle, followed by video footage of a speech where Democratic vice presidential nominee John Edwards says, "and if you have any questions about what John Kerry's made of, just spend three minutes with the men who served with him thirty years ago." At that point, the soaring musical score, which had reached a crescendo with the crash of a cymbal, turns decidedly darker. Text on the screen zooms out: "Here's what those men think of John Kerry." A speaker, shown in color, appears against a backdrop of black-and-white war photos, stating that he served with John Kerry, as does the following speaker. A third speaker then charges that Kerry "has not been honest about what happened in Vietnam." The ad continues as men of military bearing speak authoritatively, charging Kerry with "lying" to get his medals, being untrustworthy, dishonoring his country, and lacking "the capacity to lead." Behind them, dark black-and-white images of waves pounding small boats signal the peril of the sea. A somber musical score provides a somewhat militaristic beat and tone. The subtitles listing the names, military rank, and military honors of the speakers evoke the bond of trust and honor between the nation and its soldiers, and give the speakers profound credibility.

How could one reconcile the seemingly compelling testimony in 2004 of presumably honorable men and the fact that many of their own earlier accounts contradicted what they were now saying? In late August, 2004, PBS journalist David Brancaccio interviewed Kathleen Hall Jamieson, among the most distinguished students of political advertising, about the ad campaign and the SBVT charges specifically. He asked, how could one find the truth, given the conflicting claims from so long ago? Jamieson responded that it was possible that Kerry's attackers were so offended by his criticism of the war after he returned from combat, something they saw as untruthful and close to if not actually treasonous, that they could not conceive of such a person acting in a heroic fashion. That is, their own values led to a cognitive dissonance so strong it would not allow them to fathom Kerry as virtuous in even the slightest way, let alone heroic: ". . . human memory requires us to create a consistent story, particularly about people we intensely dislike," Jamieson would conclude (Now 2004a). Often people use "top-down" processing to make sense of information or to re-create details of past events. In doing so, we may use the "form" or big picture, to reconstruct the details. Kerry himself appears to have been guilty of much the same thing in having said that he was patrolling inside Cambodian territory on Christmas Eve, 1968 (which would have meant participating in an illegal war), when he was in fact near the Cambodian border in late December (Kranish 2004).

Military documentary was not the only popular generic form from which the Bush team would craft their advertising. By 2004, a host of TV action dramas were portraying a world where the intelligence and law enforcement communities confronted terrorists who roamed the streets of America, among them *CSI*, *The Agency*, and *Alias*. To reinforce in voters' minds the idea that America faced a grave and imminent terrorist threat, the Bush–Cheney team would air spots that evoked the look and feel of the most popular of all the TV terror dramas, Fox's *24*.

On *24*, the terrorists operate in America, threatening the routines of daily life, particularly the family. The show's "real time" production style and simultaneous plot development (graphically telegraphed in multiple split screens, frequently juxtaposing plotting evil-doers and innocent if not unsuspecting family members) were echoed in the Bush–Cheney ad "Risk." It begins with a narrator intoning, "after September 11, our world changed. Either we fight them abroad or face them here." The ad's opening visuals consist of a series of rectangles framing elements of a common picture evoking "Ground Zero" after the 9/11 attack against a black background.

The Ground Zero imagery may prime viewers to think of September 11, 2001, when several seconds later they hear the narration about Kerry favoring cuts in intelligence "after the *first* Trade Center attack," (emphasis added) which sounds to the ear a lot like "after the *World* Trade Center attack." (The first attack on the WTC, in 1993, occurred in the immediate aftermath of the Cold War, a period when not only liberals, but the Bush–Quayle administration itself—and its Defense Secretary Dick Cheney—supported cuts in military programs. A financial scandal in the intelligence community precipitated the specific legislative response Kerry voted on.) Gradually, the "9/11" image fades into that of a black-clad rifleman, seen from behind, which in turn fades into the image of a facial close-up of a young child. The ad visualizes Americans' worst fears while juxtaposing them with the Bush mantra that Iraq was in fact the most significant front in the war on terror. The superficial appeal of the argument would be augmented by the audiovisual power of the ad. In fact, a classified

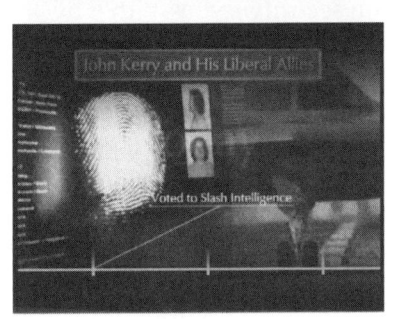

Terror TV: Political Advertising during the Bush Years 139

Visual images from the Bush–Cheney campaign's ad "Risk" depict a terror threat to the nation's home front. The ad opens with a mosaic style image with an American flag in the foreground and the ruins of the World Trade Center in the background (top).

The "tiles" of the mosaic unevenly shift to black before revealing a masked rifleman on a street. The ad's narrative reinforces claims of a threat on the streets of America. The use of tiles mimics the split screens prominently featured on *24* (middle).

The ad's images of a fingerprint, computer screens displaying mug shots and streams of data (along with high-tech beeps in the soundtrack), reflect common motifs representing law enforcement and security in action-thrillers such as *24* (bottom).

Together, the Bush ads invite viewers to see Bush as Jack Bauer, and John Kerry and the liberals in an adversarial role alongside the terrorists.

Figure 6.1. Action Thriller and 9/11 Imagery Dramatized a Threat to the Home Front

National Intelligence Estimate completed in April 2006 would report that the consensus view of the sixteen spy agencies in the U.S. government was that the Iraq War and occupation had "helped spawn a new generation of Islamic radicalism and that the overall terrorist threat has grown since the Sept. 11 attacks"; one American intelligence official succinctly stated, "the Iraq war has made the overall terrorism problem worse" (Mazzetti 2006).

Even more evocative of TV's *24* was the Bush–Cheney spot titled

"Peace and Security," which began with an image of a clock, which would reappear throughout the ad, moving ever closer to the strike of midnight. Each segment of each episode of 24 is marked by a digital clock. The ad featured images of a businessmen, mothers, and children, each going about their day, some nervously checking their watches; a ticking sound can be heard in the background, the context suggests a time bomb about to go off. The ad's narration restates the charge about Kerry voting to cut intelligence funds after the first World Trade Center attack and also charges Kerry with refusing to support body armor for the troops in Iraq. In fact Kerry never specifically voted against body armor. The ad's claim is based on Kerry's vote against the Republican backed $87 billion supplemental war spending bill. He voted for a bill to provide that funding but also to pay for it, through taxes on the wealthiest 1 percent of Americans (see also Richardson 2006).

While the specific claims of the ads were largely fraudulent or distorted, the ads' evocation of 24 would reinforce the central message (fear of another attack) driving the Bush–Cheney campaign. More precisely, Bush–Cheney sought to instill fear of John Kerry. Much of their advertising sought to discredit Kerry on security issues, either by challenging the senator's voting record or, perhaps to greater effect, by portraying Kerry as a "flip-flopper." The ad titled "Searching" would combine the twin messages that terror was imminent and that Kerry would be unreliable with literally explosive visual effect. That the only words spoken are Kerry's own contributes to the ad's eerie disquiet.

In "Searching," we see clips of Kerry's comments from various settings where he had elaborated his positioning on the war. He had voted to authorize the use of force, and is heard saying the decision to disarm Saddam was right and he supported the president on it. He also compliments the early part of the military campaign that deposed the dictator. Then we hear Kerry saying "I don't believe the president took us to war as he should have," followed by Kerry's "wrong war, in the wrong place, at the wrong time," remark. The clips of Kerry are the kind of unflattering imagery typically seen in depicting opponent candidates, but the visual transitions between images become downright thermonuclear. It might seem that such audiovisual nuance would be fairly insignificant, however researchers probing the social psychology of terror have been able to evoke a profound behavioral response (worldview defense) in experimental subjects through subliminal cues that increase the salience of one's own mortality (Green-

The Bush–Cheney ad "Peace and Security" begins with an image of a clock, albeit not a digital one as each episode of *24* does.

Throughout the ad, images of clocks appear, as do images of ordinary citizens checking their own watches. In *24*, the routines of daily life (typically personified by Special Agent Jack Bauer's family) exist in uneasy tension alongside dire terrorist threats, punctuated by the ever-present clocks that mark the beginning and end of each segment of the show. "Peace and Security" presents the same juxtaposition, inviting viewers to identify with those checking their watches. Graphics claim "John Kerry & Congressional Liberals" are "Putting Our Troops at Risk." One image shows a clock ominously ticking toward midnight. As the ad closes, viewers see a young family heading for the family minivan with the same graphic "Putting Our Troops at Risk," suggesting Kerry and the liberals are putting ordinary American families at risk of terrorism on their home front.

Figure 6.2. Like *24*, the Bush–Cheney Ad "Peace and Security" Featured Recurring Clock Images

142   Chapter 6

berg et al. 1994). In fact, subliminal exposure to 9/11 related stimuli created precisely such effects (Landau et al. 2004).

Beyond the thermonuclear transition effects, the ad concludes with Kerry commenting "I have always said we may yet find weapons of mass destruction," (another reminder of imminent death) followed by

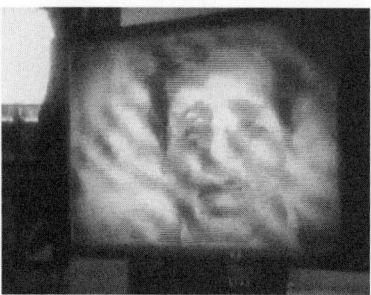

The Bush–Cheney ad "Searching" featured John Kerry saying seemingly inconsistent things about the war in Iraq. FactCheck.org would argue that the ad was "the most egregious example so far in the 2004 campaign of using edited quotes in a way that changes their meaning and misleads voters" (FactCheck.org 2004b).

The ad's visual elements are no less strident. The bottom two images (left) illustrate the ad's use of graphic transitions between clips of Kerry. The blurred image in the middle image visually reinforces the ad's attack on Kerry's shifting positions. The glowing burst of light in the lower image seems almost radioactive, as if to underscore the potentially deadly consequences of Kerry's misguided indecisiveness.

Research suggests that even incidental evocations of one's own mortality can induce "worldview defense," resulting in hostility toward those with different values and beliefs, moral transgressors and critics of one's worldview (Greenberg, Pyszczynski, and Solomon 1986; Solomon, Greenberg and Pyszczynski 1991; Rosenblatt et al. 1989). If the Bush–Cheney campaign's relentless emphasis on the death threat posed by terrorism provoked such a response, the political consequences could prove pivotal.

Figure 6.3. The Bush–Cheney Ad "Searching" Featured Thermonuclear Transition Effects

the closer: "I actually did vote for the $87 billion before I voted against it." In late September, FactCheck.org would find that the ad was "the most egregious example so far in the 2004 campaign of using edited quotes in a way that changes their meaning and misleads voters" (FactCheck.org 2004b).

The Bush–Cheney campaign's effort to define the race for the White House in terms of terror would find dramatic reinforcement in the final weekend of the campaign when a taped message from Osama Bin Laden became public. Pro-Bush elements of the media would argue that Bin Laden had sought to aid Kerry (see Now 2004b). CIA analysts would eventually conclude the opposite: the Bin Laden videotape was clearly designed to assist the president's reelection (Suskind 2006:335–36). Osama saw Bush as Al Qaeda's best recruiting tool ever. If the Osama tape made Americans think about the life and death threat posed by terrorism, it almost surely would rebound to Bush's benefit. Consider an experiment that found inducing "mortality salience" by asking respondents to contemplate their own deaths increased support for Bush over Kerry substantially (Cohen et al. 2005).

The Kerry campaign had taken flight when their advertising (the "Del Ad") converged with campaign events (the appearance after thirty-five years of Jim Rassman, the swift boater whose life was saved by Kerry). It would ultimately be grounded when the Bush–Cheney ad effort to frame the campaign in terms of terror would dovetail with the release of the Bin Laden tape and the social psychology of terror. Bob Shrum, Kerry's media adviser, would later write that a one-night election eve poll taken by the campaign would reveal Kerry's lead in the battleground states had fallen to a single percentage point, a four-point decline since the release of the Bin Laden tape seventy-two hours earlier (Shrum 2007:488).

To judge by the poll numbers, the 2004 Bush campaign was remarkably successful. In the Spring of 2004, the CBS News/*New York Times* poll found the president's job approval rating had fallen to the lowest point of his presidency (with just over 40 percent of Americans approving of how he handled his job as president). Over the course of the campaign, that number would slowly rise, peaking at 51 percent in November just after the election. It would be only the second time in U.S. history that a reelected president's party would also gain seats in both the House and Senate. A fearsome GOP voter turnout operation would increase Mr. Bush's vote by nearly 25 percent against his second-place total of 2000.

After the election, public approval of Mr. Bush would consistently drop, eventually to levels not seen since the depths of Watergate during the Nixon administration. The country was so divided that the difference between Republican and Democratic views of the president would be farther apart than at any point for any president in the history of polling. Republican approval of President Bush in July of 2007 (63 percent approval, 30 percent disapproval) was the mirror opposite of the president's approval among *independents* (who disapproved of Mr. Bush by a 61–26 margin). The Democratic Party, never known for the unity of its views, was united in one thing: nearly 9 in 10 Democratic identifiers disapproved of how Bush was handling his job as president; only 9 percent of Democrats approved of Mr. Bush's job performance (http://www.pollingreport.com/BushJob1.htm). Perhaps, as Illinois Senator Barack Obama had suggested, the 9/11 fever was finally lifting.

2006: CREEPING DESPERATION HERE AND THERE

It would be clear that the 2006 congressional midterm elections would take place in a very different political environment than that of 2002 or 2004. Public opinion on the Iraq War would continue to sour throughout the year, with a growing majority of Americans concluding that the War had not been worth fighting. Polls would also show, however, a nation split on whether to withdraw American troops (http://pollingreport.com/iraq.htm). While Democrats would sense an opportunity, the political context was complex. In the end, the party would field several candidates with military service records in Iraq in key House and Senate races.

In a typical election year, keen observers of Congressional elections count only about 5 to 10 percent of all races as competitive. The vast majority of districts have literally been computer-designed to insure incumbent and partisan success (Oppenheimer 2005). With partisan control of the House of Representatives hanging on a swing of just sixteen seats, however, enormous resources would be devoted to that handful of races that are competitive. In 2006, arguably three of the most competitive House races would take place in southeast Pennsylvania and suburban Philadelphia. In two of those races, Democrats would field Iraq War veterans as candidates. Patrick Murphy, an Iraq War vet and former Army lawyer, would challenge GOP incumbent Mike Fitzpatrick, while retired vice admiral Joe Sestak would oppose a ten-term member of Congress, Curt Weldon, who served as vice chair of the House Armed Services Committee but was also being investigated on corruption charges by the FBI (Hefling 2006). Control of the Senate would eventually hinge on the victory in Virginia of Jim Webb, a decorated Marine veteran who served in Vietnam, was Navy Secretary under Ronald Reagan, and who switched from Republican to Democratic after he became disaffected over the war in Iraq.

In races across the country, and not just those involving vets, images of the fighting in Iraq would become a staple of the campaign advertisements of both parties. In his ads, Democratic challenger Murphy would feature war footage he had shot himself on his tour of duty. In Ohio, the NRSC would air ads in support of GOP incumbent Mike DeWine that would reprise the body armor allegations made against John Kerry in the 2004 presidential campaign. Like Kerry, DeWine's challenger, U.S. Representative Sherrod Brown had voted against the Republican version of the $87 billion Iraq supplemental spending bill (also like Kerry he voted in favor a Democratic bill providing the same funding). The NRSC would spend more than $1.1 million to air the ad across the state (Koff 2006).

During 2006, total spending on campaign ads would approach $2 billion (with an additional $250 million spent on spot cable), a remarkable increase of nearly 18 percent over the amount spent in the presidential election year 2004 (Teinowitz 2006). According to FactCheck.org, ads paid for by the two parties national campaign committees, which often fund attacks candidates themselves might want to distance themselves from, were overwhelmingly negative: 81 percent for Democrats, 91 percent for Republicans (Coile 2006). One of those national committee sponsored spots would become the most talked about ad of the entire campaign.

In late October, the NRSC began airing an ad in Tennessee attacking Democratic U.S. Senate candidate Harold E. Ford Jr., an African American member of the U.S. House of Representatives. Titled "Who Hasn't?" the spot became widely known as "the *Playboy* ad." It featured a series of provocative mock person-on-the-street comments from stereotypical citizens. It begins when a black woman says "Harold Ford looks nice. Isn't that enough?" followed by a white woman stating "terrorists need their privacy." Next, an older man says "when I die, Harold Ford will let me pay taxes again." The next speaker is a hunter in camouflage and face paint who notes without irony that, "Ford's right. I do have too many guns." The next speaker to appear is an attractive blonde-haired white woman with bare shoulders (visible only from the shoulders up) who shimmies while saying "I met Harold at the *Playboy* party." Other speakers follow, referring to higher marriage taxes, North Korea, and campaign contributions to Ford from "porn movie producers." That is followed by the ad's disclaimer, read by a female narrator, and then the reappearance of the blonde woman. She whispers, "Harold, call me," while winking and holding her hand to her head as if holding a phone.

Ford, who was single at the time, had attended a 2005 Super Bowl party along with 3,000 other people in Jacksonville, Florida, sponsored by *Playboy* magazine. Said Ford, "I like football and I like girls." It was the ad's racial undertones, however, that drew controversy. Former Defense Secretary (and Republican) William S. Cohen (whose wife is African American) called the ad "a very serious appeal to racist sentiment" (Files 2006). Hilary Shelton, director of the NAACP's Washington bureau, said the spot took aim at the unease with interracial dating still present in some voters (Toner 2006). Indeed, as recently as 1998, nearly 40 percent of South Carolina voters opposed an amendment removing their state's constitutional ban on interracial marriage—thirty-one years after the U.S. Supreme Court struck down such bans as violating the Equal Protection Clause of the Fourteenth Amendment in the case *Loving v. Virginia* (1967). Political scientist John Geer, a noted expert on campaign ads who has written in defense of negative spots, described the ad as "playing to a lot of fears," adding that it "frankly makes the Willie Horton ad look like child's play" (Toner 2006). Ken Mehlman, Chairman of the Republican National Committee (RNC), did think the ad was fair. (A year before, at the annual convention of the NAACP, Mehlman had publicly apologized to black voters for the racially polarizing appeals Republicans had used for decades to court white voters in the South [Kornblut 2005].) The campaign of Ford's opponent, Bob Corker, however, sought to distance itself from the ad, describing it as "over the top, tacky, and not reflective of the kind of campaign we are running" (Files 2006).

An experimental study by researchers at the University of Michigan found that racial cues embedded in campaign ads can "prime" racial attitudes—that is increase the likelihood that such attitudes will be part of a viewer's response to the issues raised in the ad (Valentino et al. 2002). Certain language, moreover, can become racially coded, as was the case with Ronald Reagan's linkage of "big government" with "special preferences" for minority groups (Edsall and Edsall 1991:203). Scholars have also recognized, however, that blatantly racist appeals will not thrill voters (Mendelberg 2001; Valentino et al. 2002).

The "*Playboy* ad" is an interesting case in point. On the one hand, the ad's evocation of race is explicit, manifest in the audiovisual portrayal of the white woman's salaciously whispered invitation: "Harold. Call me." On the other hand, Ford himself is never shown in the ad, and the ad's script touches on some issues not normally associated with race (terrorism and North Korea). If we scratch deeper than appearances, though, the ad appears to straddle the nexus of associations drawn from popular culture and racially charged stereotypes. The *Playboy* reference signals a libertine sexuality—one that may also dovetail with popular perceptions of the sexually promiscuous behavior of black men. The ad's title, "Who Hasn't," is drawn from the statement of the last of the ad's series of speakers, a white man who tells the camera, "so he took money from porn movie producers, I mean, who hasn't?" The man ends the statement with a wide grin, which he quickly turns into a more serious frown, underscoring the stigma attached to sex films.

The Political Communication Lab at Stanford University posted a series feedback graphs that visualize the real-time response of Democratic, Republican, and Independent viewers of a series of 2006 campaign commercials (http://pcl-wp.stanford.edu/s7/). The graphs chart the moment-by-moment response of viewers to campaign ads as measured by dial meters that allow users to indicate how favorable they feel by turning a dial. Several negative ads from 2006 races around the country were charted. The response to the "*Playboy* ad" stands out even among the negative spots. It appears to have recorded the most negative response of any ad (in this case from Democratic partisans). By the end of the spot, Democrats are registering an almost completely negative response, something that does not appear to be present in the response of any category of viewers to any of the spots tested and posted on the website (though the response to a Democratic attack ad in the Tennessee race is also quite polarized). The response pattern from independents tracks that of Democrats fairly closely. Those two lines stand in stark contrast to the response line for Republicans, which hovers on the positive side of neutral throughout the ad.

While Democratic and Independent voters may have responded negatively to the ad, that doesn't mean it wasn't effective. Ansolabehere and Iyengar (1995) argued that negative advertising is more effective for Republicans. That could make the risk of backlash in "red" state Tennessee one Republicans were willing to accept. Some pundits even speculated that merely reinforcing voter awareness that the light-skinned Rep. Ford was in fact African American would be a desirable outcome of such an ad campaign and the press coverage it would generate. Such would be the signature politics of George W. Bush's and Karl Rove's Republican Party. As we noted earlier, Bush/Rove politics was "the politics of the base" (Halperin and Harris 2006). Having concluded that trying to influence undecided voters with low levels of political information was ineffective and inefficient, Rove sought to mobilize his party's core supporters. Even if it meant pursuing policies that alienated the "center."

In the closing days of the campaign, the RNC aired a spot comprised of Al Qaeda training videos, starring Osama and his top lieutenants. The only sound to be heard was a ticking bomb, before an announcer would state: "These are the stakes. Vote November 7th." Political scientist John Geer would tell a well-connected GOP friend that the ticking bomb smacked of desperation. An e-mail would come back: "John, we're desperate" (Grunwald 2006).

While the "*Playboy* ad" was paid for by the RNC, it was produced by an independent group that was supposed to keep an "arm's length relationship with the actual campaigns"; RNC Chair Mehlman said that was why he hadn't seen the ad before it was broadcast and why he lacked the power to order that it be pulled from the air (Toner 2006). When it became known that Terry Nelson, a Republican political operative who had been hired to do PR for Wal-Mart, helped create the ad, pressure from labor and civil rights groups caused the retailer to cut ties with the strategist (Barbaro 2006). Even after the ad stopped airing, it could still be seen on the website YouTube (Halicks 2006). The ad would also be shared via e-mail. Such "viral videos" and websites like YouTube would play an even large role as the 2008 presidential campaign began to unfold.

2008 AND THE FUTURE: CAMPAIGNING IN THE DIGITAL AGE

The first "campaign ad" of the 2008 presidential race to draw widespread interest would appear on YouTube on March 5, 2007. "Vote Different" was a "mash-up" of the famous "1984" spot directed by Ridley Scott (*Alien*, *Blade Runner*, *Thelma and Louise*, and *Black Hawk Down*) and aired only once by Apple Computer (during Super Bowl XVIII). The original ad was set in the dark and ominous world of George Orwell's "big brother" from the novel *1984*, perhaps the most widely recognized sci-fi dystopia of all time. Monotonous masses of grey prisoner/workers march to their tasks in dimly lit tunnels while being lectured by television images of the ever-present dictator. The scene shifts to a large darkened auditorium with the monotonous masses seated, stone-faced, looking at a huge, bright video screen. Suddenly a colorfully clad female runner appears, charges toward the massive screen and hurls a huge mallet at it. The explosive impact spectacularly smashes the image of big brother, giving way to the ad's tagline: "On January 24th, Apple Computer will introduce Macintosh. And you'll see why 1984 won't be like *1984*." (The commercial can be viewed on YouTube at http://youtube.com/watch?v=OYecfV3ubP8.)

In "Vote Different" (on YouTube at http://youtube.com/watch?v=6h3G-lMZxjo), the voice and image of big brother are replaced with that of Hillary Clinton. Mrs. Clinton's comments are taken from actual statements on the candidate's website that she made as part of the "conversation" she sought with the American people to launch her presidential campaign. The sound of her voice is altered so that it echoes somewhat eerily; at times it sounds the way phone calls sometimes sound when broadcast on TV or radio. The ad's combined effect is to portray the Clinton campaign as a cold, contrived, heartless machine—a line of criticism that draws upon some of the New York senator's better-known liabilities, at least among detractors. The ad's creator would later suggest that the ad was a response to a report in the *New York Times* about the Clinton campaign "bullying" donors and political operatives that appeared after a well-publicized spat between Clinton and David Geffen, a former Clinton supporter who held a Hollywood fund-raiser for Barack Obama (Vargas and Kurtz 2007).

The ad's brilliance, as Gaby Wood wrote in *The Observer*, is the way its form and content were beautifully intertwined" (Wood 2007). "Vote Different" was posted anonymously by a person identified as only as "ParkRidge47." (Mrs. Clinton was born in Park Ridge, Illinois, in 1947.) Wood wrote, "the anonymous posting was itself the equivalent of the girl with the mallet—a way of smashing the old order of demagoguery and spin by surreptitiously democratic digital means" (Wood 2007). Needless to say, the ad's generic evocation of dystopia, the same theme that worked so well for Apple in its battle with behemoth IBM, would help it effectively draw upon the existing web of associations already present in viewers—exactly the process that this book has repeatedly sought to call attention to.

Within days of being posted on YouTube, "Vote Different" would

150   *Chapter 6*

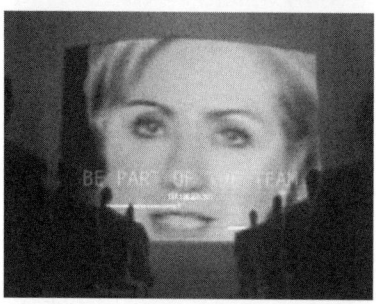

In 2007, a political operative (initially identifying himself only as "ParkRidge47") who had worked for a consulting firm hired by Democratic presidential hopeful Barack Obama, posted the ad "Vote Different" on YouTube. The ad was a "mash-up" of an ad originally aired by Apple Computer based on George Orwell's novel *1984* and images drawn from a web video produced by Hillary Clinton's campaign.

In "Vote Different," Clinton is placed in the role of "Big Brother," the omnipresent head of the party machine with ever peering eyes.

A colorfully dressed female (contrasted with the gray prisoners assembled in the auditorium) launches a mallet at the "telescreen" eventually blowing it to bits.

The ad's brilliance, as Gaby Wood wrote in *The Observer*, is the way its form and content were beautifully intertwined" (Wood 2007).

"Vote Different" signaled the emergence of citizen producers of political content and became the first "viral video" of the 2008 presidential race.

Figure 6.4. In "Vote Different," Hillary Clinton Is Depicted in the Role of the Omnipresent Totalitarian "Big Brother"

go "viral." Political blogs, advertising blogs, and eventually the mainstream media would all call attention to the spot. The spot would be covered by news organizations from Asia to New Zealand. By midsummer, "Vote Different" would record more than 3.5 million views on YouTube, more than twice as many as any other video on "Hillary Clinton" posted on YouTube and better than six times more than the most-viewed video officially provided to YouTube by the Clinton campaign. Soon, the online *Huffington Post* would reveal that Phil de Vellis, a senior strategist at Blue State Digital, a web consulting firm that had done work for the Obama campaign, was "ParkRidge47." De Vellis would resign, seeking to insulate his employer, who had no knowledge of his actions (Wood 2007).

"Vote Different" was not the first time a YouTube video would impact national politics. In 2006, a campaign worker for Virginia U.S. Senate candidate Jim Webb would post video of opponent U.S. Senator George Allen calling the worker "Maccaca" at an Allen campaign rally the worker was recording for Webb. The video would eventually receive extensive coverage in the press. Combined with other campaign mishaps (including Allen's multiple, contradictory explanations for the remark), the video would be seen as having a role in turning Allen from a frontrunner (not just for reelection to the Senate, but as a potential GOP presidential candidate), to a political has-been. The outcome of the Virginia race would eventually place partisan control of the U.S. Senate in Democratic hands for the first time in a dozen years.

"Vote Different" will certainly not be the last user-sponsored video of the 2008 campaign. In fact, news organizations, political pressure groups, and commercial websites have already begun to solicit user-created video. In 2004, the comedy website jibjab.com posted a video "This Land," a parody of Woody Guthrie's song, "This Land Is Your Land" that was one of the first viral videos. That same year, MoveOn .org sponsored an ad-making contest, "Bush in 30 seconds" (http://www.bushin30seconds.org/); the following year, the group sponsored a similar contest, "Bush in 30 years," (http://www.bushin30years.org/), seeking ads critical of the president's social security privatization plan. MSNBC's "Hardball with Chris Matthews" announced its "campaign ad challenge" (seeking the "next viral video") in July, 2007 (http://www.msnbc.msn.com/id/19862336/).

The "Hardball" ad challenge emerged after two other YouTube videos featuring political candidates went viral. "I Got a Crush on Obama," a music video featuring the curvaceous "Obama Girl" (Amber Lee Ettinger, a swimsuit model and actress), attracted nearly as many YouTube viewers as "Vote Different." A spin-off video, "Hott-4-Hill" involved a similar parody ode to candidate Clinton. Both videos seemed to be more about creative expression and generating income and exposure for the ad's creators and "stars," than about making political points. Nevertheless, despite the fact that up to this point, viral videos have largely been apolitical satire, the potential power of the medium has not been lost on political operatives.

Candidates themselves have begun to use the Internet to distribute campaign videos, including more humorous spots. Hillary Clinton's campaign posted a web video mimicking the closing scene of the HBO original series *The Sopranos* to invite viewers to help the campaign select its theme song.

If anything, the proliferation of political spots may lead to even greater uses of the existing audiovisual conventions of popular culture. The same communications advantages that candidates have recognized in the past (ready associative linkages, entertainment value, ability to attract "free media" coverage by the press) may appeal to independent producers of political video.

For candidates and campaigns, a future of user-produced video may prove more perilous. It may be harder to keep "on message," and harder to compete for media attention, especially at a time when journalism is increasingly pressured to entertain. Viral videos trafficking in the genres of popular culture may prove a particularly strong challenge to campaigns. Consider for example, the implicit associations of the "Obama Girl" video. While Ms. Ettinger's dark complexion and dark hair may not be as evocative as the blonde in the "*Playboy* ad," the ad clearly has an "urban" feel to it, which becomes tied to the ad's over-the-top sexuality. The danger to the Obama campaign is that the ad might contribute to the marginalization of the candidate as the "urban" candidate (which comes with its own set of racial connotations). Unauthorized narrowcasting could conceivably morph into precarious broadcasting. There is no reason to conclude that the ad's producers had political effects in mind, but from the candidate's perspective, anything that drives attention from the candidate's message is potentially suspect.

It remains to be seen whether user-posted video, viral and otherwise, can empower ordinary citizens. Without question, a line has been crossed and a new era is emerging. It seems, however, that we will need far greater evidence of change before abandoning the idea that the very same factors that govern the response of citizens and the media to old-fashioned campaign ads will apply to the new form. That is, ads that are entertaining, or confrontational and negative, are more likely to spark interest than positive or issue-based communications. A popular YouTube video featuring Democratic presidential candidate John Edwards combing his hair to the tune of "I Feel Pretty" is a case in point.

On the other hand, one trend that does appear likely to blossom is narrowcasting. The 2008 race is likely to see the emergence of political ads targeted to cell phones and other personal electronic devices. The potential for mischief in such top-down, partisan communications environments would appear to be enormous, especially given the way campaigns have used more narrow forums (including direct mail and radio) in the past to disseminate charges too divisive for broader audiences.

At this point, observers can only await history's verdict. Will an empowered citizenry take charge of their government through cyber-democracy? Or will campaigns fall to new lows in targeting polarizing appeals ever more narrowly (in ways ever more difficult to detect through the radar screen of the mainstream political establishment), dividing rather than uniting the nation along the way? And what, pray tell, does all of this hold for the future of the republic? What will come from this whirling vortex of polarization, microcommunication, and high finance, in a world dominated by fewer and fewer corporate interests, at the very moment when the promise of a digital democracy is more palpable and real than ever? It is to such questions that we shall turn in our final chapter.

NOTES

1. Mr. Murdoch is the owner of (among other holdings): 20th Century Fox, the Fox Broadcasting Company, DirecTV, *TV Guide*, MySpace, Americanidol.com, and more than one hundred newspapers worldwide including the *New York Post*.

2. The analysis was dropped accidentally in a Washington, D.C., park and later found by a Democratic Senate staffer (Schatz 2002). A copy of Karl Rove's Powerpoint presentation can be viewed online at: http://www.politicspa.com/mehlman-rove_files/v3_document.htm.

Chapter Seven

Conclusion: Reason, Passion and Democracy in the Digital Age

Disdain for American election campaigns, and political advertising in particular, runs wide and deep. Upon closer inspection, however, we have seen that the indictment against campaign ads is less a coherent whole than a fractured and sometimes contradictory rage. Politicians fault their opponents and the media, the media faults politicians, scholars question how well informed voters are, criticize the media's focus, and the cynicism of politicians. Many citizens find the whole process repugnant. Who's right and who's wrong? Can we ever know?

Our final chapter will attempt to place the various debates over campaign advertising into the broader context of the American political system, seeking to distinguish matters of true concern from mere annoyances, separating threats to the republic from threats to our viewing pleasure. To that end, we will summarize the bill of particulars directed at political ads, then consider the following questions: Do campaigns really matter? Do negative campaigns depress voter turnout? What is the proper role for citizens in the American republic? Do ads shortchange reason? How much reasoning is necessary in voters? How great a threat are distortions in political ads? Is there such a thing as "truth" in politics?

THE CASE AGAINST NEGATIVE POLITICAL ADVERTISING

Of all the ads singled out for their destructive effects during the 2000 campaign, perhaps none was more widely reviled than a spot produced by the NAACP National Voter Fund. The ad focused on the case of James Byrd Jr., a black man murdered by three white men who dragged his body from the back of a pickup truck in Jasper, Texas, on June 7, 1998. Byrd's daughter, Renee Mullins, says in the ad, when George W. Bush refused to sign hate crimes legislation in Texas, "It was like my father was killed all over again." The stark black-and-white visuals of a pick-up truck with a chain dragging behind it and the unnerving sound of the dragging chain give the advertisement added impact and urgency.

Pundit Andrew Sullivan called it "the Willie Horton ad of 2000" (Sullivan 2000). Editorialists from California to the New York island denounced its irrational and emotional appeal.[1] Many also noted that while the ad was a thinly veiled endorsement of Democratic presidential candidate Al Gore, it was technically an independent expenditure not limited by campaign finance laws.

Set aside for the moment the fact that some of the alarm was misguided.[2] What are we to make of the state of American electoral politics and the campaign ads that are its major manifestations? We have seen that the indictment of contemporary campaign advertising is broad and intense. Many denounce the shallowness of thirty-second spots, and find particularly objectionable those that supplant reason with emotion. Some suggest that political advertising, at least in its "negative" form, serves to deter many citizens from voting (Ansolabehere and Iyengar 1995). Others have found roughly half of all ads to be unfair, misleading, or deceptive. Some target "issue" advertising—appeals that, by not urging viewers to "vote for" or against a particular candidate, fall outside the campaign finance rules that govern ads that do advocate election of particular candidates. These issue ads, critics note, can be funded with unlimited and anonymous contributions, which they see as a threat to democratic accountability. More broadly, the cost of advertising is implicated in the incessant chase for campaign cash that preoccupies elected officials throughout their tenure in office. No sooner have they won election than they must begin soliciting funds for their next race. The result, some suggest, is an influence peddling bazaar, or, as former U.S. Senator Max Cleland once put it, a democracy "more like an auction than an election."

Virtually all of these criticisms have been given voice by Paul Taylor, a distinguished former political reporter for the *Washington Post*, who worked to establish the Alliance for Better Campaigns and the coalition Free TV for Straight Talk. In an interview with PBS, Taylor said that "the worst thing about political advertising is that it doesn't nourish over time." He articulated his desire for advertising based on more than "quick impressions . . . often formed not by reasoned arguments but by appeals to emotion . . . by tools that are fairly conducive to the false inference and the half-truth." He suggested that voting turnout had been on a "steep, steep decline," during "the same period where the thirty-second spot has become the coin of the realm." While he stopped short of asserting a causal relationship, he said, "it seems to me that there is some connection somewhere." As an alternative, he advocates minidebates and free TV time rather than thirty-second ads. Where candidates do run ads, Taylor argues that the candidates themselves should appear in the ads. He also favors stricter disclosure requirements for so-called issue ads run by parties and independent groups (Taylor 1998–2001). Taylor's calls for free TV time and greater disclosure requirements for issue ads are also supported by the Task Force on Campaign Reform, a group of fourteen scholars in the fields of electoral politics, voting behavior, and political communication (Bartels and Vavrek 2000). Let us attempt to place the reform debate in a broader political context and consider these various critiques and reform proposals in turn.

THE ROLE OF CAMPAIGNS: DO THEY REALLY MATTER?

Perhaps the first place to start is to situate campaigns and campaign advertising in terms of elections and our constitutional order. There is, in fact, a stream of academic research that suggests that campaigns themselves do not matter very much if at all. Rather, these scholars argue, elections are determined by fundamental political and economic forces: "peace, prosperity, and moderation" (Zaller 1998:186).[3] Political scientists are often able to predict the outcome of a presidential election before the campaign unfolds, since election results are so closely tied to factors such as the state of the economy and the public's approval of the president's job performance.[4] But other researchers have found that campaigns do matter.[5] They do so by helping to clarify for voters important political and economic issues, and in close elections, the nature and quality of campaigns themselves may actually prove decisive. Researchers have used detailed data on ad buys and county-level voting returns from the 1992, 1996, and 2000 presidential campaigns to estimate the effects of advertising specifically on election outcomes. They concluded that advertising itself *does* matter, though its effects are small and tend to be balanced by the responses of opponents (Althaus, Nardulli, and Shaw 2002). Of course such small effects would loom large in the minds of campaign strategists: if elections are largely determined by forces outside of the candidates' control, advertising stands out as one vehicle by which campaigns can influence election outcomes.

In an even larger sense, campaign ads matter because they tell the stories of American politics. Murray Edelman wrote that politics is more about the construction of beliefs than about the allocation of values (2001:33). That is, the significance of the political struggle is not so much about distributing values—"who gets what, when, and how" but about the beliefs that shape the allocation of values. For example, if voters believe that people are poor because they don't work hard enough, and that those who are rich are deserving of their wealth, support for policies aimed at addressing poverty will fall while those aimed at protecting the wealth of the rich will rise, regardless of how such policies might affect the overall economy. While the candidates may differ on the merits of alternative tax plans, the resolution of those differences is principally a function of the contest over beliefs, not the debate over the allocation of values or resources. Campaign advertising plays a key role in shaping and reflecting political beliefs.

Campaigns also matter because they help to shape the political agenda after the election. Consider the issue of prison furloughs, the core of the Bush campaign's attacks against Michael Dukakis's record on crime in 1988. A Lexis-Nexis search for the term "prison furloughs" in the headline and lead paragraph of U.S. news sources returned no "hits" for all of 1987, the year before that campaign. The same search for 1989, the year after the campaign, returned twenty-one articles—the same search for 1988 returned eighty-nine articles. And it wasn't just newspapers: the number of references to furloughs in Congress also shot up in the aftermath of the 1988 campaign. Harris Wofford's victory in the special U.S. Senate election in Pennsylvania in 1990 helped to propel health care to the top of the national agenda in the early 1990s. Even the issues raised by defeated third-party candidates such as Ross Perot's focus on deficit reduction and campaign reform in 1992 can become key elements of the postelection political agenda.

If campaigns matter, then the proposals of campaign reformers warrant our considered attention. To fully assess the proposals for reform, however, we have to reflect further upon the nature of American democracy. Let us first consider the charge that negative advertising depresses voter turnout. While the evidence on this count is at best mixed (see chapter 3), on balance, the link between negativity and turnout is not persuasive. Some of the most negative campaigns have had some of the highest voter turnouts, for example the 1994 Virginia Senate campaign between Chuck Robb and Oliver North. The suggestion that there has been a precipitous drop in voter turnout, coinciding with the rise of campaign advertising is also suspect. In fact, a recent study found that the alleged decline in voter participation is principally the result of the misuse of the voting age population in calculating turnout. The voting age population includes a growing population of people not eligible to vote, including felons—America has incarcerated more of its citizens than any other nation on earth—and unnaturalized immigrants. When persons ineligible to vote are removed from the equation, there is no evidence of a systematic decline in voter turnout from negative advertising or anything else (McDonald and Popkin 2001). Nor does the evidence support a link between negative campaigning and an increase in negative evaluations of candidates or decreases in citizen interest in campaigns (Bartels 2000).

More fundamentally, if voter turnout was declining, would that necessarily be a problem? Recall that the framers restricted the right to vote rather narrowly, and that extensions of the franchise were the result not of any great theoretical reassessment, but rather the consequence of partisan political struggle. Neither of the two contending camps in the constitutional debates, the federalists and the antifederalists, embraced direct democracy or placed widespread voting at the center of their vision of the ideal form of government. Both considered themselves republicans, heirs to a tradition dating back to the ancient Greeks and especially the Romans. Classical republicanism espoused the virtues of a "mixed" government, which combined elements of monarchy (rule by one), aristocracy (rule by the few), and democracy (rule by the many). An undercurrent in this analysis was the conflict between the interests of the different elements of society, most fundamentally the wealthy, the middle class, and the poor. Indeed, the antifederalist Brutus (probably Robert Yates) denounced the constitutional framework for providing only sham representation and insuring that the rich would dominate, even in that branch supposed to be most representative of the common people, the U.S. House (Ball 1988:146–47). This debate turned on differing conceptions of the meaning of representation. The federalists embraced a notion of representatives as independent trustees, free to substitute their own better judgments for those of their constituents. Antifederalists advocated representatives who were like their constituents, demographically, and who acted in accordance with their constituents' preferences. For the antifederalists, it was the different "orders" or elements of society that needed to be represented (Ball 1988). For neither side was the role of voters overwhelmingly significant.

The two sides also differed in their assessment of the possibilities of an "extended" republic. Classically, republics had been limited to geographically small areas, indeed smaller than the larger colonies such as Pennsylvania and Virginia. It was Madison's great insight to see the expanded territorial sweep of the new nation as a blessing rather than a burden. The enlarged pool of potential leaders would be a source of strength, and the country's diversity would further limit the ability of any one faction or element of society to dominate. In terms of representation, Madison argued, an extended republic would actually be superior to a smaller republic. Yet representation was only one of the elements of republicanism. At its core, republicanism was concerned with virtue—the ability of citizens to rise above their narrow self-interest and act in ways that were in the public interest. Political participation, particularly in local affairs, was essential to cultivating civic virtue. And it is here that the antifederalist critique of Madison's extended republic may have been most prescient, for as the nation evolved, it began to drift from its republican moorings.

Neither the federalists nor the antifederalists considered themselves "democrats," that is, adherents to the notion that the people should rule directly. Indeed, when Jefferson and Madison bolted from Hamilton and the federalists as the eighteenth century drew to a close, their movement became known as the Republicans. But by limiting the role of direct citizen involvement with government to elections, the federalists had heightened the stakes on voting rights, and created the conditions where the appeal of calls for greater democracy could flourish (Hanson 1988:188). Eventually, as the contours of the political struggle changed and the appeal of democracy grew, some of the loosely affiliated organizations that rose in support of the egalitarian principles of the French Revolution began calling themselves Democratic-Republican societies, and finally, after Andrew Jackson inherited the leadership mantle of the Jeffersonian movement, it became known simply as the Democratic Party. And, as the debate over extending voting rights unfolded during the first two decades of the 1800s, individualism rose to the fore, supplanting the republican emphasis on virtue. But neither the rise of individualism nor the erosion of republican virtue led to changes in the constitutional design itself. That is, the newly enlarged democratic electorate would still be funneled indirectly through representative institutions. So neither the developmental function of participation of republicanism, nor the direct role in government of democracy, would exist at the national level. Given this hybrid system, it is difficult to see where lower voter turnout would be necessarily viewed as a serious threat to the Republic. Participation in state and local politics might serve to cultivate the virtues of republican citizenship in the absence of a forum for national action, but for Madison, local enclaves could erode one of the greatest strengths of the extended republic, the ability to channel diverse interests through constitutional means of resolving conflict (Sunstein 2001:96–97).

Indeed, in the aftermath of the emergence of twentieth-century totalitarian regimes, founded in part on high rates of mass participation, the enlarged, self-interested electorate would eventually prompt revisionist theorists to caution against the strains on a society from excessive popular demands (Berelson et al. 1954). Government simply could not effectively respond to such a wide range of disparate preferences. Carol Pateman summarized Berelson's conclusions this way: "Limited participation and apathy have a positive function for the whole system by cushioning the shock of disagreement, adjustment and change" (Pateman 1970:7). While Pateman and others reject Berelson's argument and urge greater and more meaningful participation, they do not base their proposals on the limited act of voting, or what Barber (1984) calls "thin" democracy.

What we are left with, then, is an institutional framework that severely limits popular participation and is not dependent upon high levels of participation in order to function. The many strong claims that can be made for enhancing citizen engagement with politics require much more than mere voting. Given such circumstances, it is hard to see how the heightened level of concern over lower voter turnouts, assuming that they are lower, is warranted.

Still, if we were concerned about lower participation in voting, it is unlikely that such concerns would be so powerful as to justify restrictions on "negative" advertising. Negative attacks are essential to democratic choice, especially when the choice of whether or not to turn out the party in power is the fundamental decision facing voters in American democracy. As the Declaration of Independence notes, "All experience hath shewn, that mankind are disposed to suffer, while evils are sufferable, than to right themselves by abolishing the forms to which they are accustomed." It takes a lot to motivate people to seek change. Only through vigorous, "negative" campaigning, can that case for change be made. Moreover, Jamieson (1992a:103) found that "negative" ads include more factual content than positive ads.

REASON AND EMOTION IN POLITICAL ADVERTISING

If there is one aspect of ads that has drawn even more fire than negativity, it may be the related perception, articulated by Paul Taylor above, that ads emphasize emotion and short-circuit reasoning (see also Jamieson 1992a). As Graber notes, however, emotions do not automatically impair reasoning. Decision making involves the brain's primary reasoning centers as well as parts of the brain that deal with emotion; indeed, emotions are an essential part of the ability to reason. She recounts the tale of Phineas Gage, a nineteenth-century railroad worker who had the portion of his brain that recorded emotion destroyed when it was accidentally pierced by an iron rod. The injury did not affect his cognitive capacities (such as speech and memory), but the loss of emotional capacity robbed him of the ability to feel joy or empathy, and prevented him from making sound, self-interested decisions (Graber 2001:36–37). In political terms, as we saw in chapter 3, the high point of voter turnout in the late 1800s was marked by highly emotional appeals. Today, emotional advertising may serve to draw the interest of citizens who might otherwise not be engaged, just as Graber suggests dramatic, visual, and emotionally compelling news stories grab the attention of otherwise disinterested viewers (Graber 2001). In fact, political scientists have begun to disentangle the processes by which emotionally evocative campaign ads affect political thinking. Building upon the work of Marcus, Neuman, and MacKuen (2000) and their theory of *affective intelligence*, Ted Brader conducted experiments demonstrating that the arousal of fear by ads may cause the brain to search for new information. Appeals to enthusiasm, by contrast, may motivate participation (Brader 2006).

Let us return for a moment to the James Byrd Jr. ad, which critics derided for its overly emotional appeal. Consider the following. At the dawn of the twenty-first century, black Americans faced racial profiling as they drove the nation's highways and byways. They paid more for car loans than whites, regardless of their credit histories (Henriques 2001). They paid higher home mortgage costs, even at high income levels, than whites with comparable incomes (Leonhardt 2002). They continued to pay more for life insurance than whites (Paltrow 2001). They received inferior health care to whites, even when their income and health insurance were the same; they were also more likely to receive less desirable procedures such as amputations than whites (Stolberg 2002). In state prisons, blacks make up 60 percent of those serving time for drug offenses, though blacks are only 15 percent of regular drug users; while roughly as many whites as blacks use crack cocaine, nearly 90 percent of the people locked up for crack under federal drug laws are black; in California, the nation's largest state, five black men of college age are locked up behind bars for every one in a college classroom (Egan 1999). For all this, critics fault the NAACP for an ad that is too emotional? Political advertising is successful when it communicates a combination of affect (emotion) and cognition (thought) that can trigger action (such as voting). In the final analysis, we may be able to better understand emotional political appeals, but it is unlikely they will ever be eliminated—nor should they.

PARTIES, PRESSURE GROUPS, AND ISSUE ADVOCACY

The Byrd ad is just one case. If we examine more comprehensive data, on at least some of the dimensions by which campaign advertising has been criticized above, issue ads actually come out fairly well. Issue ads are twenty times more likely than candidate advertising to provide information rather than to be aimed at "generating support," and 77 percent of issue ads focus on policy, while only 64 percent of candidate ads do (Krasno and Seltz 2000:21–23). During the Senate debate over the McCain-Feingold campaign finance reform bill, California Senator Diane Feinstein summarized the concerns of many critics of issue ads, when she said that "independent campaigns conducted by groups that are accountable to no one threaten to drown out any attempt by candidates or by the parties to communicate with voters" (Mitchell 2002). These critics fear that issue advertising will shift the focus of the campaign from the issues candidates, parties, and voters want to discuss to those of concern to special interests. Nearly two-thirds of all issue ads aired in 1998, however, were sponsored by political parties (Krasno and Seltz 2000:2). An analysis of the content of issue advertising prepared for the Brennan Center for Justice offers additional grounds for caution in accepting this "drowning out the debate" thesis. It found that the specific issue focus of candidate ads and issue ads is actually quite similar. In 1998, the top four issues in candidate advertising—taxes, education, social security, and health care—were also the top four issues in issue advertising. The same four issues were also among the top five issues in both candidate and issue advertising in 2000 (Krasno and Goldstein n.d.:5).

To be fair, the claim that issue advertising might distort the campaign discourse may not be the major objection of critics. They also target issue ads as funded almost completely outside of the campaign finance regime. Before the passage of McCain-Feingold (formally known as the Bipartisan Campaign Reform Act or BCRA), it was extremely difficult to identify who sponsored a given issue ad and how much money that had been raised to do it. The NAACP's Byrd ad was funded by a $9 million contribution from a single anonymous donor (Firestone 2000; Fletcher 2000). The BCRA's ban on issue ads aired within 60 days of a general election was struck down by the Supreme Court in 2007 (*Federal Election Commission v. Wisconsin Right to Life Inc.*, No. 06-969). Writing for the majority in a splintered 5-4 decision, Chief Justice John G. Roberts Jr. argued, "where the First Amendment is implicated, the tie goes to the speaker, not the censor." The Court found the ban on issue ads overly broad, upholding the ban only for ads "susceptible of no reasonable interpretation other than as an appeal to vote for or against a specific candidate." The ads involved in the case were targeted at voters in the days before the election and specifically mentioned by name Wisconsin Senator Russ Feingold, who was seeking reelection. The ads did not include the "magic words" ("vote for" or "vote against"). Campaign finance experts noted that while the Court did not address the BCRA's ban on "soft money," its ruling would permit the largely unlimited flow of money from corporate and union treasuries into sponsoring such "issue" ads (direct contributions to candidates remain prohibited). The four dissenting justices were joined by Justice Antonin Scalia in suggesting that in fact, the Court was effectively overruling its 2003 decision upholding the constitutionality of the BCRA "without saying so" (Greenhouse 2007).

Yet there are reasons to doubt the desirability of this approach. Setting aside for the moment the troublesome question of unequal campaign resources, political arguments must ultimately be judged against opposing views. The vigorous exchange of views is a crucial element of democratic politics. Our democracy thrives on contested debate, and candidates are free to choose what they will contest. The question then becomes, are voters up to the task of balancing politicians' competing appeals in order to make governing choices?

THE ROLE OF VOTERS IN THE AMERICAN REPUBLIC

Improving the content of campaign discourse and building better voters have been at the core of many debates about the performance of electoral democracy. Walter Lippmann was perhaps America's most influential journalist. Among his primary concerns was the prospect for democracy in the modern world. To Lippmann, democratic theory presented an idealized vision of omnicompetent citizens, capable of making informed decisions leading to wise laws and good government. Such citizens clearly were not the norm. His most prominent critic, John Dewey, rejected Lippmann's instrumental view of citizen participation, and viewed the omnicompetent citizen as a straw man. While Dewey agreed with much of Lippmann's indictment of the citizenry as uninformed, he saw that as a consequence and not a cause of the problems of modern society, and viewed individuals as capable of intellectual improvement and political life as a part of human fulfillment (Davis 1996:327–35).

The underlying tension between Dewey's optimistic vision of a democratic citizenry and Lippmann's bleak assessment would also be played out in the political science literature on voting behavior. *The American Voter*, originally published in 1960, found the electorate to be almost wholly without detailed information about decision making in government . . . (and) almost completely unable to judge the rationality of government actions (Campbell, Converse, Miller, and Stokes 1964:282). Instead of deliberating over the key issues of the day, *The American Voter* found an electorate straight-jacketed by partisan affiliations developed in childhood, long before serious political thinking was possible.

Responding to this unflattering portrait of the voters, V. O. Key's *Responsible Electorate* argued that "voters were not fools" (Key 1966:7). Contrary to the conventional wisdom that independent voters were less well-informed than rigid partisans, therefore leaving the flexibility of democracy in the hands of its least attractive voters, Key found switchers, those who voted for a different party presidential candidate in subsequent elections, were not necessarily less informed or less active than standpatters. The electorate as a whole, argued Key, was moved by central and relevant questions of public policy, of governmental performance, and of executive personality (Key 1966:7–8). For Key, democratic elections did not provide a clear indication of the electorate's policy preferences. After all, he noted, the people's verdict can be no more than a selective reflection from among the alternatives and outlooks presented to them. If the people can choose only from among rascals, they are certain to choose a rascal (Key 1966:2–3). What elections do reflect according to Key, is the electorate in its great, and perhaps principal, role as an appraiser of past events, past performance and past actions. It judges retrospectively; it commands prospectively only insofar as it expresses either approval or disapproval of that which has happened before. (Key 1966:61)

Not all subsequent research has sustained Key's conclusions, and *The American Voter's* essential findings of low sophistication are not without supporters (see especially Smith 1989). Additionally, the idea that retrospective evaluations reigned supreme in voter decision making has been questioned (Lewis-Beck 1988). The dire normative conclusions of the early voting studies have, however, been roundly challenged.[6]

Michael X. Delli Carpini and Scott Keeter (1996) describe three academic approaches which attempt to exonerate American politics from the evils attributed to voter ignorance: collective rationality (Page and Shapiro 1992), online information processing (Lodge, McGraw, and Stroh 1989; Boynton and Lodge 1994), and low information rationality (Popkin 1994). Page and Shapiro's notion of collective rationality suggests that the opinions of uninformed voters are randomly distributed and essentially cancel each other out, leaving the views of better informed citizens to provide the defining character of public opinion. Lodge and others discount the apparent ignorance of voters on specific details, seeing that as the result of a pattern of processing information where the evaluative impact of information is added to a running tally of opinion on an issue or candidate, while the substantive content of that information is discarded. Voters actively and continually update their assessment of politics, but forget many of the details that once informed that process. Faced with survey questions, they respond, though such responses are essentially rationalizations and not reasons. Finally, Popkin (1994) and others (Sniderman, Brody, and Tetlock 1991) argue that through cognitive shortcuts or heuristics, voters can use cues to adequately inform decisions without possessing elaborate or detailed knowledge.

Delli Carpini and Keeter find such notions of democratic participation thin, and seek higher levels of knowledge in the citizenry. Accordingly, they raise the bar on the knowledge requirements of democratic citizenship, and write:

> A general familiarity with (1) the rules of the game (the institutions and processes of elections and governance); (2) the substance of politics (the major domestic and international issues of the day, current social and eco-

nomic conditions, key policy initiatives, and so forth); and (3) people and parties (the promises, performances, and attributes of candidates, public officials, and the political parties) is critical to the maintenance of a healthy democracy. (Delli Carpini and Keeter 1996:14)

Still, existing approaches to the role of citizens in a democracy, whether promoting thin or thick notions of participation, eventually rest on citizen knowledge of major patterns of political conduct and information. They stop well short of requiring voters to become issue-obsessed policy wonks.

This bears directly upon the practice of ad watch journalism, discussed in chapter 4, and one of the reforms embraced by the Task Force for Campaign Reform. The case for ad watch journalism is normally made in part on the grounds that journalistic attention to the validity of political advertising deters candidates from airing egregiously misleading or deceptive spots. There is at least anecdotal evidence that this has been the case. Many ad watches focus on the truthfulness of the minor premises of campaign spots, however, and neglect broad patterns of policy and record. As we saw in chapter 4, this serious shortcoming in the ad watch's ability to better inform voters is one that can be readily addressed.

But at another level, perhaps the strongest rationale for ad watch journalism is to free candidates from having to respond to each of their opponent's attacks, regardless of their merits, for fear that a charge not rebutted is a charge believed. This was the central lesson Bill Clinton's campaign in 1992 learned from the success of George Bush's attacks in 1988. In 1992 and throughout his tenure, when opponents launched attacks against Clinton, his team would respond by providing reporters information and analysis rebutting the charges during the same "news cycle," insuring that no story would include only the attack and not their response. Candidates face a dilemma when responding to their opponent's attacks. Responding draws attention to the opponent's issues and away from the candidate's themes. Here, the independent voice of the media can contribute to a more productive campaign discourse. The Clinton team was able to weave the independent credibility of journalistic ad watches into its own responses to the Bush attacks, allowing the campaign to return more quickly to its own preferred themes and arguments. In 2000, pundits aggressively denounced the Byrd ad, freeing Governor Bush from that burden.

ATTACK ADVERTISING AND DEMOCRATIC POLITICS

Before we can fully assess the ad watch project and the role of campaign advertising in general, however, we must address one final question: Are "distortions" always illegitimate? The assumption of the reform position is that they are. Yet, a case can be made that "distortions" need not be seen as inherently toxic. To make that case, we can begin by placing political advertising in context of telling the stories of American politics.

In some ways, all storytelling is vulnerable to distortion, especially the way ad watchers define distortions to include exaggeration, selective presentation of information, emotional appeals, and so on. The point of telling stories, especially in politics, is to select from all the information that is out there that which, for one reason or another, the storyteller thinks is important. It also helps when the story is memorable. And emotional stories are memorable. While such considerations may strike many as the basis of irrationality, consider the perspective of someone seeking to initiate political change. How are they to break through the human tendency to suffer those ills that are sufferable, rather than try to right them, if not through emotion?

Just as political cartoons exaggerate the features of their subjects, so too do other forms of political argument take artistic liberties. The point is not so much that ad watchers should be prohibited from pointing out exaggerations, but rather that at least they should consider whether the exaggerator does in fact have a good point—despite the exaggeration. It should also be noted that, to some degree, exaggeration is in the eye of the beholder. For someone who has been burdened with rising prescription drug costs, Al Gore's alleged exaggeration about the prices to fill his mother-in-law's and his dog's prescriptions probably didn't go far enough. For someone traumatized by the fear of violent crime and impatient with the criminal justice system, George Bush's 1988 ads probably didn't go far enough either.

Of course, reformers will point out that such ads do not allow citizens to make truly informed choices. But again, consider exactly the choices voters are faced with. They ultimately decide whether they find the party in power worthy of reappointment—no more and no less. As Key (1966) and Graber (2001) point out, citizens do seem up to that task.

Political scientist John Geer (2006) has gone farther than most in his defense of attack politics. He argues that negative spots are more specific and provide more information than positive spots. His empirical analysis rebuts several criticisms of negative ads, finding no link between negative advertising and declining trust in government, less faith in elections, or lower voter turnout. Negative ads, moreover, are more likely to make the kind of retrospective claims that of greatest use to voters in the American political system.

Much of Geer's argument has also been made previously in this book. On one issue, however, Geer may overextend his analysis: his contention that "there is no such thing as *the* truth" (Geer 2006:134; emphasis in original). To be fair, most of Geer's argument is phrased in terms of the difficulty of reconciling different notions of truth in politics. His actual analysis of particular campaign ads accused of purveying mistruth, however, suggest a somewhat more literal reading of the statement.

Geer devotes an entire chapter to the 1988 campaign, one often cited as an exemplar of negativity gone wild (see especially Jamieson 1992a). Geer presents the script to the "Revolving Door" ad, followed by his assessment: "These claims are not false" (Geer 2006:126). Yet the ad script reads *"his* revolving door prison policy" (when the program was started under a previous Republican governor). Similarly, in discussing the ad "Tank Ride," Geer argues that while the ad clearly exaggerated, Bush advisers argued they had double checked every claim and "the overall message of the ad seems defensible" (Geer 2006:127). In fact, the ad states Dukakis opposed four missile systems when he only opposed two; the ad also erroneously states Dukakis opposed the Stealth bomber; nor did Dukakis "oppose virtually every defense system we developed" as the ad claims (Jamieson 1992a:7). I will leave it to the reader to judge whether two plus zero equals four and yes means no.

Geer (2006:127) suggests that a Republican claim to be stronger on defense is valid on its face (exonerating "Tank Ride" from indictment on charges of falsehood). Michael Dukakis sought to challenge precisely that premise of GOP credibility on security. His original media event at the tank factory was intended not just to show he was "strong on defense" as Geer notes (2006:128), but to dramatize the difference between his approach to security (emphasizing conventional weapons like tanks and helicopters) and Vice President Bush's emphasis on strategic nuclear weapons systems. A cynical press corps, biased to cover trailing candidates less favorably, would instead frame the event as inept campaigning by a desperate challenger and implicitly validate Bush's security credentials, paving the way for the more vitriolic

Bush ad. In fact, history would validate Dukakis's position. The M-1 tank he rode in was critical in Operation Desert Storm in 1991, as was the Apache attack helicopter—two weapons the Reagan–Bush administration sought to cut. Once elected, moreover, President Bush would abolish the MX and Midgetman missiles, two of the four the Bush ad claimed Dukakis opposed (Jamieson 1992a:7–8).

More significantly, Geer's analysis is based on a reading of the text of campaign ads, not their audiovisual elements. He does acknowledge in discussing "Revolving Door," that the ad's audiovisual juxtaposition invites the false inference that 268 first degree murderers not eligible for parole went on to commit other crimes like kidnapping and rape. In fact, only one first degree murderer escaped and went on to commit such crimes ("Willie" Horton). Geer refers to this as "stretching the truth" (Geer 2006:126).

Limiting his analysis to texts only significantly weakens the force of Geer's larger argument. As we have seen, often the most emotional and compelling elements of ads lie outside the script in the way ads use audiovisual elements to evoke particular responses in viewers. From this perspective, the impact of ads like "Revolving Door" is drawn not so much from the narrow policy claims about prison furloughs and mandatory sentences for drug dealers, but from the fear and fright prompted by audiovisual elements found in horror movies. If the work on terror management theory discussed in chapter 6 is true, the evocation of horror and the fear of death signified by the ominous musical score and "slasher" sound effects alone could substantially bias viewer response to the ad (and its textual claims). Perhaps that is why so many ads use such music in so many different contexts. Analysis limited to an ad's text cannot account for such effects.

It can be argued that evocation of fear and death is precisely appropriate to the politics of the moment. Perhaps. It may be helpful to place current challenges such as terrorism in a broader context. On September 11, 2001, nearly 3,000 Americans lost their lives in New York City, Washington, D.C., and Pennsylvania. The threat of terrorism is real and serious. For the sake of argument, however, let me briefly present a case that the terror fear is overheated and exaggerated and that other matters ought to draw our concern first. That is the position of political scientist John Mueller, who holds the Woody Hayes Chair of National Security Studies at the Mershon Center at Ohio State University. He argues that the response to 9/11 has been a "hyperbolic overreaction," leading to what Lief Weimar of the University of Sheffield has called "a false sense of insecurity" (Mueller 2004:43; see also Mueller 2006a, 2006b).

Mueller points out that September 11 is an extreme outlier among terrorist attacks, and that before and since, no more than 329 people have been killed in any other single terrorist incident. Writing in *The New Republic*, Greg Easterbrook deconstructed the threat of "weapons of mass destruction." He pointed out that "in actual use, chemical arms have proven less deadly than regular bombs, bullets, and artillery shells." The most deadly use ever of biological weapons occurred nearly 250 years ago when the British gave blankets infected with smallpox to Native Americans allied with the French during the Seven Years' War (Easterbrook 2002). Only nuclear weapons, concludes Easterbrook, truly warrant the designation "weapons of mass destruction"; even radioactive "dirty bombs" are unlikely to cause extremely large numbers of deaths. In the end, refusing to be terrified is the ultimate defense against terrorism. From a book by Senator John McCain (R-AZ): "calculate the odds of being harmed by a terrorist! It's still about as likely as being swept out to sea by a tidal wave. Suck it up, for crying out loud" (cited in Mueller 2004).

Mueller points out that the hyperbolic overreaction to terrorism also leads to neglect of more pressing and real threats. Consider the fact that the American Society of Civil Engineers estimates that each year, roughly one-third of the 40,000 plus deaths on the nation's highways are caused by substandard road conditions (Timiraos 2007). Or that each year tens of thousands of Americans die from the flu. Or that tens of thousands more die from infections they caught in hospitals. Or that soot particles in the air have been implicated in tens of thousands of deaths annually from respiratory and coronary disease. A single decision in 2006 by EPA Administrator Stephen L. Johnson to reject the recommendation of his staff to issue tougher soot regulations will lead to 3,000 premature deaths annually, according to Joel Schwartz, an epidemiologist at the Harvard School of Public Health (Barringer 2006). That decision alone amounts to a number of deaths equivalent to the September 11 attacks each and every year. Even discounting for the fact that a fair number of such deaths occur among individuals already weakened by age or illness, the numbers remain staggering, approaching or exceeding that of even worst-case terrorist scenarios.

In the five years after 9/11, no Americans died from terrorist attacks on U.S. soil. Hundreds of thousands died from poorly maintained roads, inadequate health care, and befouled air. A fairly compelling challenge can be made to the claim that the politics of terror represent a reasonable and appropriate response to our present predicament. Further still, it appears that the policies of the purveyors of the fear of terrorism (i.e., war in the Middle East) are actually making America less safe, not more so. That is the sobering conclusion of the nation's intelligence community (Mazzetti 2006).

In the end, readers may not feel as comfortable with an electorate vulnerable to being so easily misled as is Professor Geer.

Even if a large, extended electorate means that uninformed voters "cancel each other out," the 2000 election showed that only a few voters can have an enormous impact. Perhaps even more to the point, however, we may fear unscrupulous politicians who will actively seek to mislead the public, or, alternatively, to play to ill-informed popular prejudices. This, at least, was of great concern to James Madison, whose disdain for electoral politics focused on the evils of "unworthy candidates" who practiced the "vicious arts" (Ball 1988:149).

Here we must finally confront the inherent limitations of popular rule. As the muckraking journalist H. L. Mencken wrote, "democracy is the theory that the common people know what they want, and deserve to get it good and hard" (Mencken 1916:19). Between the optimism of the founding and the commitment to republican principles, the framers never quite had to confront the present conundrum. They imagined citizens schooled in republican virtues in a communal context that does not exist today, articulating the popular will in a much less directly influential manner than we have today. That is, they figured we'd have somewhat better voters (and politicians) in a position to do somewhat less damage to the public interest than the present circumstances allow.

What we do have today is a constitutional hybrid, a democratic republic, as it were, with an admixture of the virtues and vices of each form. It is, moreover, a constitutional order particularly protective of property—something Madison saw as the "first order of government." Throughout American history, the constitutional protection of property has limited movement toward social change on issues ranging from slavery to fundamental fairness, just as the framers intended.

Today, however, we face a growing level of inequality far greater than what the framers knew or could have imagined. It is an inequality that animates contemporary debates on issues ranging from taxes to education to health care to the environment and campaign finance. The framers were not of one mind on the threat to society as a whole posed by extended economic inequality. Thomas Jefferson saw inequality as breeding instability, and favored efforts by government such as progressive taxation to mitigate the gap between the wealthiest and poorest citizens. Madison saw the protection of the unequal accumulation of property as the fundamental instance of minority rights. Regardless of which side you agree with, you may very well come to appreciate the value in embracing the full range of communicative possibilities available to the combatants in this epic struggle, and grateful for the power of televised advertising to help tell the worthy stories of American politics. For in the final analysis, as the great Greek historian Pericles noted in his famous Funeral Oration, the purely private and silent citizen (known to the Greeks as *idiotes*) is not merely quiet or harmless, but "useless" (Livingstone 1968:113). Republicanism—and America is a republic—is, at its root, a politics of communication. The pluralism that for Madison protects essential liberty by matching ambition against ambition, passion against passion, is an armed pluralism. And throughout this nation's history, those who have communicated effectively in the mediums of their times, from James Madison and Alexander Hamilton to Abraham Lincoln, to Theodore and Franklin Roosevelt, to John F. Kennedy and Dr. Martin Luther King, Jr. to Ronald Reagan and Bill Clinton, have been the trumpeters of democracy and drum majors for justice. A free people should be blessed with no less.

In Madison's armed pluralism, "ad wars" are not to be feared but celebrated. They are manifestations of free speech and help hold government accountable. Surveys show that voters know very little about the candidates, parties and issues in congressional elections. Yet Congress rarely enacts unpopular legislation. In fact, members of Congress fear not what the voters know, but what they might learn after their opponents have combed their voting records for material to include in thirty-second campaign ads (Arnold 1990).

Responding to ads with ads, rather than restricting advertising, is perhaps the most appropriate redress to distorted charges. Governor Bush, for example, could have responded to the NAACP National Voter Fund's ad with his own commercial, defending his veto of the hate crimes act because it also extended protection to gays vicitimized by hate crimes, which he opposed. Or he could have simply taken umbrage at the ad's implicit charge that he was racially insensitive. It is quite clear everyone associated with the Kerry campaign now wishes they had responded more effectively to the "swift boat" attacks in 2004.

By using the recognizable stories and audiovisuals of popular culture, candidates can communicate more effectively with voters. Republican politics is a politics of communication, of storytelling, and popular culture tells stories people are familiar with. Used effectively, evoking popular culture can speed the processing of information, imbed political arguments with substantive and emotional richness, and increase the memorability of political information. All serve vital purposes in linking citizens and government through elections.

That popular culture is the culture of the familiar does not necessarily limit political communication to the well-worn and universally accepted. American popular culture is a diverse tapestry of many threads. It endures and evolves and in that balance are the moments of our lives. Popular culture helps to tell the stories of American politics in ways both coarse and elegant, utterly suiting a democratic republic, where the stories of politics are politics itself. There are many stories yet to be told.

NOTES

1. See for example Barfield 2000; "Byrd and Bush: Searing Ad Doesn't Make Case for Hate-Crimes Laws"; "Freedom of Speech and Attack Ads"; Huffington 2000; Kane 2000; Knight 2000; McGrath 2000; Perkins 2000; Woodson 2000.

2. Sullivan, for example, argues that while the Byrd ad speciously links George W. Bush to opposition to hate-crimes legislation, the Horton ad was logically connected to "Michael Dukakis's leniency on prisoner furloughs and the ability of a furloughed Horton to commit more crimes." In fact, the furlough program was initiated not by Dukakis, but by his Republican predecessor; Dukakis eventually cancelled the program. Also, while the Bush campaign may have "cynically disowned" the Horton ad as Sullivan suggests, Bush himself frequently referred to Horton in his campaign speeches, and Bush–Quayle advertising repeated the tale, albeit without using Horton's name or picture. The Byrd appeal was emotional, but no more so than other ads seeking support for tough on crime policies through tales of victims' suffering. (On Bush and Horton, see Jamieson 1992a, especially pp. 15–42.)

3. See also Markus 1992, Erickson 1989, Fiorina 1981.

4. Lewis-Beck and Rice 1992, Wlezien and Erickson 1996, Fair 1978, Hibbs 1987, Abramowitz 1988; Lockerbie 2000; Jones 2002.

5. Gelman and King 1993; Holbrook 1996; Campbell 2000.

6. Nie, Verba, and Petrocik 1976; Page and Shapiro 1992; Popkin 1994; Stimson, MacKuen, and Erikson 1995.

References

Abelson, Robert P. 1968. "Simulation of Social Behavior." In *The Handbook of Social Psychology*, 2d ed., vol. 2., ed. Gardner Lindzey and Elliot Aronson. Reading, MA: Addison-Wesley.

Abramowitz, Alan I. 1988. "An Improved Model for Predicting Presidential Election Outcomes." *PS: Political Science & Politics* 21:843–47.

Adams, Chris and Gardiner Harris. 2002. "Drug Makers Face Battle to Preserve Patent Extensions: Governors Join Businesses, Labor Unions in Effort to Hasten Generics to Market." *Wall Street Journal* (March 19), A24.

Althaus, Scott L., Peter F. Nardulli, and Daron R. Shaw. 2002. "Campaign Effects on Presidential Voting, 1992–2000." Revised version of paper presented at the Annual Meeting of the American Political Science Association, August 30–September 2, 2001, San Francisco, CA.

Anderson, John R. 1983. *The Architecture of Cognition*. Cambridge, MA: Harvard University Press.

Ansolabehere, Stephen and Shanto Iyengar. 1996. "Can the Press Monitor Campaign Advertising? An Experimental Study." *Harvard International Journal of Press/Politics* 1:72–86.

———. 1995. *Going Negative: How Political Advertisements Shrink and Polarize the Electorate*. New York: Free Press.

Ansolabehere, Stephen, Shanto Iyengar, and Adam Simon. 1999. "Replicating Experiments Using Aggregate and Survey Data: The Case of Negative Advertising and Turnout." *American Political Science Review* 93:901–9.

Arnold, R. Douglas. 1990. *The Logic of Congressional Action*. New Haven, CT: Yale University Press.

Associated Press. 2001. "New Drugs Such as Celebrex, Vioxx Are Responsible for Rising Prescription Costs, Study Says." *St. Louis Post-Dispatch* (May 8), A4.

Aufderheide, Pat. 1990. "Vietnam: Good Soldiers." In *Seeing Through Movies*, ed. Mark Crispin Miller. New York: Pantheon Books.

Baker, C. Edwin. 2002. *Media, Markets, and Democracy*. New York: Cambridge University Press.

Ball, Terrence. 1988. "A Republic—If You Can Keep It." In *Conceptual Change and the Constitution*, ed. Terence Ball and J. G. A. Pocock. Lawrence: University of Kansas Press.

Balz, Dan and Thomas B. Edsall. 2004. "Lawyer Quits Bush–Cheney Organization; Campaigns Spar Over Ties to Outside Funding Groups." *Washington Post* (August 24), A1.

Barbaro, Michael. 2006. "Wal-Mart Dismisses Adviser Who Created G.O.P. Ad." *New York Times* (October 28), A11.

Barbanel, Josh and Ford Fessenden. 2000. "Error-Prone Voting Machines Lowered the Minority Vote—and Gore's Chances." *New York Times* (November 29).

Barber, Benjamin. 1984. *Strong Democracy: Participatory Politics for a New Age*. Berkeley: University of California Press.

Barber, James David. 1972. *The Presidential Character: Predicting Performance in the White House*. Englewood Cliffs, NJ: Prentice-Hall.

Barfield, Deborah. 2000. "Ad Assails Bush on Hate Crimes." *Newsday* (New York, NY; October 25), A4.

Barringer, Felicity. 2006. "Top E.P.A. Official Rejects Recommendations on Soot." *New York Times* (September 22), A14.

Barry, Ann Marie Seward. 1997. *Visual Intelligence: Perception, Image, and Manipulation in Visual Communication*. Albany: State University of New York Press.

Barstow, David and Don Van Natta Jr. 2001. "How Bush Took Florida: Mining the Overseas Absentee Vote." *New York Times* (July 15).

Bartels, Larry M. 2000. "Campaign Quality: Standards for Evaluation, Benchmarks for Reform." In *Campaign Reform: Insights and Evidence*, ed. Larry M. Bartels and Lynn Vavrek. Ann Arbor: University of Michigan Press.

Bartels, Larry M. and Lynn Vavreck. 2000. *Campaign Reform: Insights and Evidence*. Ann Arbor: University of Michigan Press.

Bartels, Larry M. and John Zaller. 2001. "Presidential Vote Models: A Recount." *PS: Political Science & Politics* 34(1).

Bartlett, Frederic C. 1932. *Remembering: A Study in Experimental and Social Psychology*. Cambridge: Cambridge University Press.

Basil, Michael, Caroline Schooler, and Byron Reeves. 1991. "Positive and Negative Advertising: Effectiveness of Ads and Perceptions of Candidates." Pp. 245–62 in *Television and Political Advertising (Volume I): Psychological Processes*, ed. Frank Biocca. Hillsdale, NJ: Lawrence Erlbaum Associates.

Beer, Thomas. 1929. *Hanna*. New York: Alfred A. Knopf.

Bennett, W. Lance. 1988. *News: The Politics of Illusion*, 2d ed. New York: Longman.

Bennett, W. Lance, Regina G. Lawrence, and Steven Livingston. 2007. *When the Press Fails: Political Power and the News Media from Iraq to Katrina*. Chicago: University of Chicago Press.

Berelson, Bernard R., Paul F. Lazarsfeld, and William N. McPhee. 1954. *Voting: A Study of Opinion Formation in a Presidential Campaign*. Chicago: University of Chicago Press.

Berger, Arthur Asa. 1995a. *Essentials of Mass Communication Theory*. Thousand Oaks, CA: Sage Publications.

———. 1995b. *Cultural Criticism: A Primer of Key Concepts*. Thousand Oaks, CA: Sage Publications.

———. 1992. *Popular Genres: Theories and Texts*. Newbury Park, CA: Sage Publications.
Berger, Peter L. and Thomas Luckmann. 1966. *The Social Construction of Reality*. Garden City, NY: Doubleday.
Berke, Richard L. 2002. "Bush Adviser Suggests War as Campaign Theme." *New York Times* (January 19), A1.
Berntsen, Gary and Ralph Pezzullo. 2006. *Jawbreaker: The Attack on Bin Laden and Al-Qaeda: A Personal Account by the CIA's Key Field Commander*. New York: Three Rivers Press.
Biocca, Frank. 1991a. *Television and Political Advertising (Volume I): Psychological Processes*. Hillsdale, NJ: Lawrence Erlbaum Associates.
———. 1991b. *Television and Political Advertising (Volume 2): Signs, Codes and Images*. Hillsdale, NJ: Lawrence Erlbaum Associates.
Blakeslee, Sandra. 1994. "Tracing the Brain's Pathways for Linking Emotion and Reason." *New York Times* (December 6).
Bonanza News Service. 1999. "Former Gubernatorial Candidate Arrested." *North Lake Tahoe Bonanza* (January 22).
Bowker, R. R. 1880. "Political Responsibility of the Individual." *Atlantic Monthly* 46 (September): 320.
Boynton, G. R. 1995. "Computational Modeling: A Computational Model of a Survey Respondent." In *Political Judgment: Structure and Process*, ed. Milton Lodge and Kathleen M. McGraw. Ann Arbor: University of Michigan Press.
Boynton, G. R. and Milton Lodge. 1998. "Hot Cognition." *Political Communication* 15, 1998 (special volume on CD-ROM).
———. 1994. "Voter's Image of Candidates." In *Presidential Campaigns and American Self Images*, ed. Arthur H. Miller and Bruce E. Gronbeck. Boulder, CO: Westview Press.
Brader, Ted. 2006. *Campaigning for Hearts and Minds: How Emotional Appeals in Political Ads Work*. Chicago: University of Chicago Press.
Braudy, Leo. 1985. "From the World in a Frame. Genre: The Conventions of Connection." Pp. 411–33 in *Film Theory and Criticism*, 2d ed., ed. Gerald Mast and Marshall Cohen. Oxford: Oxford University Press.
Brock, David. 2004. *The Republican Noise Machine: Right-Wing Media and How It Corrupts Democracy*. New York: Crown Publishers.
Broder, David A. 1990. "A Five Point Plan to Return Campaigns to Voters." *Washington Post Service* (January 21).
Bumiller, Elisabeth and Allison Mitchell. 2002. "Traces of Terror: Congressional Races; Bush Aides See Political Plus in Security Plan." *New York Times* (June 15), A1.
Burnham, Walter Dean. 1965. "The Changing Shape of the American Political Universe." *American Political Science Review* 59, 7–28.
"Byrd and Bush: Searing Ad Doesn't Make Case for Hate-Crimes Laws." Editorial. *Houston Chronicle* (November 5, 2000), 2.
Calmes, Jackie and Edward P. Foldessy. 2001. "Final Tally: In Florida Recount, Supreme Court's Role Appears Less Decisive." *Wall Street Journal* (November 12), A1.

Campbell, Angus, Philip E. Converse, Warren E. Miller, and Donald E. Stokes. 1964. *The American Voter* (An abridgment). New York: John Wiley & Sons, Inc.

Campbell, Karlyn Kohrs and Kathleen Hall Jamieson, eds. 1978. *Form and Genre: Shaping Rhetorical Action*. Falls Church, VA: Speech Communication Association.

Campbell, Donald T. 1969. "Prospective: Artifact and Control." In *Artifact in Behavioral Research*, ed. Robert Rosenthal and Robert Rosnow. New York: Academic Press.

Campbell, James E. 2000. *The American Campaign: U.S. Presidential Campaigns and the National Vote*. College Station, TX: Texas A&M University Press.

Capella, Joseph N. and Kathleen Hall Jamieson. 1994. "Broadcast Ad Watch Effects: A Field Experiment." *Communication Research* 21(3):342–65.

Chandrasekaran, Rajiv. 2006. *Imperial Life in the Emerald City: Inside Iraq's Green Zone*. New York: Random House.

Clinger, James H. 1987. "The Clean Campaign Act of 1985: A Rational Solution to Negative Campaigning Which the One Hundredth Congress Should Reconsider." *Journal of Law and Politics* 3, 727–48.

Cohen, Florette, Daniel Ogilvie, Sheldon Solomon, Jeff Greenberg, and Tom Pyszczynski. 2005. "American Roulette: The Effect of Reminders of Death and Support for George W. Bush in the 2004 Presidential Election." 5 *Analyses of Social Issues and Public Policy* 1:177–87.

Coile, Zachary. 2006. "Desperate Campaigns Resort to Attack Ads; 91% of Republican Commercials and 81% of Democratic Spots Called Negative by Policy Center." *San Francisco Chronicle* (November 1), A1.

Conason, Joe and Gene Lyons. 2000. *The Hunting of the President: The Ten-Year Campaign to Destroy Bill and Hillary Clinton*. New York: Thomas Dunne Books.

Conover, Pamela Johnston and Stanley Feldman. 1984. "How People Organize the Political World: A Schematic Model." *American Journal of Political Science* 28:95–126.

———. 1986. "The Role of Inference in the Perception of Political Candidates." Pp. 127–58 in *Political Cognition*, ed. Richard R. Lau and David O. Sears. Hillsdale, NJ: Lawrence Erlbaum Associates.

Converse, Philip E. 1972. "Change in the American Electorate." Pp. 263–37 in *The Human Meaning of Social Change*, ed. A. E. Campbell and P. E. Converse. New York: Russell Sage Foundation.

Cook, Timothy E. (ed.) 2005. *Freeing the Presses*. Baton Rouge: Louisiana State University Press.

Coopersmith, Jonathan. 2000. "He didn't invent Internet, but he was its patron saint." *Milwaukee Journal Sentinel* (October 26).

Covington, Cary R., Kent Kroger, Glenn W. Richardson Jr., and J. David Woodard. 1993. "Ronald Reagan's 'Issue of the Day' Strategy and Differences in Its Impact on Television and the Print Media during the 1980 Election." *Political Research Quarterly* 46(4):483–98.

Coyle, David C. 1960. *Ordeal of the Presidency*. Washington, DC: Public Affairs Press.

Cundy, Donald T. 1986. "Political Commercials and Candidate Image: The Effect

Can Be Substantial." Pp. 210–34 In *New Perspectives on Political Advertising*, ed. Lynda Lee Kaid, Dan Nimmo, and Keith R. Sanders. Carbondale, IL: Southern Illinois University Press.

Damasio, Antonio R. 1994. *Descartes' Error: Emotion, Reason and the Human Brain.* New York: Grosset/Putnam.

Davis, Sue. 1996. *American Political Thought: Four Hundred Years of Ideas and Ideologies.* Englewood Cliffs, NJ: Prentice Hall.

Delli Carpini, Michael X. and Scott Keeter. 1996. *What Americans Know about Politics and Why it Matters.* New Haven, CT: Yale University Press.

Derrida, Jacques. 1980. "The Law of Genre." In *Glyph 7.* Baltimore: Johns Hopkins University Press.

Devlin, L. Patrick. 1986. "An Analysis of Presidential Television Commercials, 1952–1984." Pp. 21–54 in *New Perspectives on Political Advertising*, ed. Lynda Lee Kaid, Dan Nimmo, and Keith R. Sanders. Carbondale: Southern Illinois University Press.

Diamond, Edwin and Stephen Bates. 1988. *The Spot: The Rise of Political Advertising on Television* (rev. ed.). Cambridge, MA: MIT Press.

Dionne, E. J. 2004. "Tests of a Smear Campaign." *Washington Post* (August 24), A17.

Dobbs, Michael. 2004a. "Records Counter a Critic of Kerry; Fellow Skipper's Citation Refers to Enemy Fire." *Washington Post* (August 19), A1.

———. 2004b. "Swift Boat Accounts Incomplete; Critics Fail to Disprove Kerry's Version of Vietnam War Episode." *Washington Post* (August 22), A1.

Easterbrook, Gregg. 2002. "Term Limits." *The New Republic* (October 7), 22.

Edelman, Murray. 2001. *The Politics of Misinformation.* Cambridge: Cambridge University Press.

Edsall, Thomas B. and Mary D. Edsall. 1991. *Chain Reaction: The Impact of Race, Rights, and Taxes on American Politics.* New York: W. W. Norton.

Edwards, Catherine. 2000. "Political Ads with Show-Biz Appeal." *Insight Magazine* (November 20).

Egan, Timothy. 1999. "The War on Drugs Retreats, Still Taking Prisoners." *New York Times* (February 28).

Erickson, Robert S. 1989. "Economic Conditions and the Presidential Vote." *American Political Science Review* 83:567–73.

Espo, David. 2002. "GA War Hero Challenged on Security." *Associated Press Online* (October 13).

FactCheck.org. 2004a. "Republican-funded Group Attacks Kerry's War Record." August 6, 2004 (updated August 22, 2004). Online at: http://www.factcheck.org/article231.html. Accessed August 7, 2007.

———. 2004b. "Bush Ad Twists Kerry's Words on Iraq." September 27; Updated September 28. Online at: http://www.factcheck.org/article269.html. Accessed on August 9, 2007.

Fair, Ray C. 1978. "The Effect of Economic Events on Votes for President." *Review of Economics and Statistics* 60:159–73.

Felknor, Bruce L. 1966. *Dirty Politics.* New York. W. W. Norton and Company.

Fessenden, Ford and John M. Broder. 2001. "Study of Disputed Florida Ballots

Finds Justices Did Not Cast the Deciding Vote." *New York Times* (November 12), A1.
Files, John. 2006. "A Playboy Party at the Super Bowl, a Wink and an Invitation." *New York Times* (October 26), A22.
Fiorina, Morris P. 1981. *Retrospective Voting in American National Elections*. New Haven, CT: Yale University Press.
Firestone, David. 2000. "The 2000 Campaign: The Turnout: Big Push Starts to Lift Turnout of Black Vote." *New York Times* (October 29), 1.
Fiske, John. 1987. *Television Culture*. London: Methuen.
Fletcher, Michael A. 2000. "NAACP Makes Leap to Big-Money Political Activism; $7 Million Fund to Pay for Major Voter Effort." *Washington Post* (August 4), A14.
Freedman, Paul and Kenneth Goldstein. 1999. "Measuring Media Exposure and the Effects of Negative Campaign Ads." *American Journal of Political Science* 43(4), 1189–1208.
"Freedom of Speech and Attack Ads." Editorial. *Tampa Tribune* (November 4, 2000), 14.
Frontline. 2002. "The Persuaders." Online transcript at http://www.pbs.org/wgbh/pages/frontline/shows/persuaders/etc/script.html. Accessed August 4, 2007.
Frye, Northrop. 1957. *Anatomy of Criticism: Four Essays*. Princeton, NJ: Princeton University Press.
Garramone, Gina M. 1986. "Candidate Image Formation: The Role of Political Information Processing." In *New Perspectives on Political Advertising*, ed. Lynda Lee Kaid, Dan D. Nimmo, and Keith R. Sanders. Carbondale: Southern Illinois University Press.
———. 1984. "Audience Motivation Effects: More Evidence." *Communication Research* 10:59–76.
Garramone, Gina M., Michael E. Steele, and Bruce Pinkleton. 1991. "The Role of Cognitive Schemata in Determining Candidate Characteristic Effects." In *Television and Political Advertising (Volume I): Psychological Processes*, ed. Frank Biocca. Hillsdale, NJ: Lawrence Erlbaum Associates.
Geer, John G. 2006. *In Defense of Negativity: Attack Ads in Presidential Campaigns*. Chicago: University of Chicago Press.
Gelman, Andrew and Gary King. 1993. "Why Are American Presidential Election Campaign Polls So Variable When Votes Are So Predictable?" *British Journal of Political Science* 23:409–51.
Germond, Jack W. and Jules Witcover. 1989. *Whose Broad Stripes and Bright Stars: The Trivial Pursuit of the Presidency 1988*. New York: Warner Books.
Gigot, Paul A. 2007. "The Mark of Rove." *Wall Street Journal* (August 13), A15.
Goldstein, Kenneth and Joel Rivlin. 2003. *Political Advertising in the 2002 Elections*. Online at http://polisci.wisc.edu/tvadvertising/Political%20Advertising%20in%20the%202002%20Elections.htm; accessed August 4, 2007.
Graber, Doris. 2001. *Processing Politics: Learning from Television in the Internet Age*. Chicago: University of Chicago Press.
———. 1997. "Hardware and Software for Political Learning: New Discoveries about How Human Brains Process Audio-Visual Data." Paper presented at the Annual Meeting of the Midwest Political Science Association, Chicago, Illinois.

———. 1988. *Processing the News: How People Tame the Information Tide*. New York: Longman.

Greenberg, Jeff, Tom Pyscżcynski, and Sheldon Solomon. 1986. "The Causes and Consequences of the Need for Self-Esteem: A Terror Management Theory." In R. F. Baumeister, (Ed.). *Public and Private Self*. (pp. 189–207). New York: Springer-Verlag.

Greenberg, Jeff, Tom Pysczynski, Sheldon Solomon, Linda Simon, and Michael Breus. 1994. "Role Consciousness and Accessibility of Death-Related Thoughts in Mortality Salience Effects." 67 *Journal of Personality and Social Psychology* 4:627–637.

Greenfield, Meg. 1995. "It's Time for Some Civility: Good, Frontal, Rough Debate Is What We Should Be About." *Washington Post* (May 29), A15.

Greenhouse, Linda. 2007. "Justices Loosen Ad Restrictions in Campaign Law." *New York Times* (June 26), A1.

Gronbeck, Bruce E. 1994. "Negative Political Ads and American Self Images." In *Presidential Campaigns and American Self Images*, ed. Arthur H. Miller and Bruce E. Gronbeck. Boulder, CO: Westview Press.

Grunwald, Michael. 2006. "The Year of Playing Dirtier; Negative Ads Get Positively Surreal." *Washington Post* (October 27), A1.

Halicks, Richard. 2006. "Websites Give Political Ads Wider Audience." *Atlanta-Journal Constitution* (October 29), 4E.

Halperin, Mark and John F. Harris. 2006. *The Way to Win: Taking the White House in 2008*. New York: Random House.

Hamilton, D. L. and M. P. Zanna. 1972. "Differential Weighting of Favorable and Unfavorable Attributes in Impression Formation." *Journal of Experimental Research in Personality* 6:204–12.

Hanson, Russell L. 1988. "'Commons' and 'Commonwealth' at the American Founding: Democratic Republicanism as the New American Hybrid." In *Conceptual Change and the Constitution*, ed. Terence Ball and J. G. A. Pocock. Lawrence: University of Kansas Press.

Hart, Roderick P. 2000. *Campaign Talk: Why Elections are Good for Us*. Princeton, NJ: Princeton University Press.

Hefling, Kimberly. 2006. "Lawmaker-Vets Bring Military Credentials." *Associated Press Online*. November 9.

Henriques, Diana B. 2001. "Review of Nissan Car Loans Finds That Blacks Pay More." *New York Times* (July 4), A1.

Hibbs, Douglas A. Jr. 1987. *The American Political Economy: Macroeconomics and Electoral Politics*. Cambridge, MA: Harvard University Press.

Hilts, Philip J. 1995. "Brain's Memory System Comes into Focus." *New York Times* (May 30).

Holbrook, Thomas M. 1996. *Do Campaigns Matter?* Thousand Oaks, CA: Sage Publications.

Huffington, Ariana. 2000. "A Wasted Effort on Hate Crimes." *San Diego Union-Tribune* (November 1), B10.

Jamieson, Kathleen Hall. 1992a. *Dirty Politics: Deception, Distraction and Democracy*. New York: Oxford University Press.

———. 1992b. *Packaging the Presidency: A History of Criticism of Presidential Campaign Advertising*. New York: Oxford University Press.

———. 1992c. News Coverage of Political Ads: Annenberg Washington Program. C-SPAN videotape recorded February 26, 1992.

———. 1984. *Packaging the Presidency: A History of Criticism of Presidential Campaign Advertising*. New York: Oxford University Press.

Jamieson, Kathleen Hall and Karlyn Kohrs Campbell. 2001. *The Interplay of Influence: News, Advertising, Politics, and the Mass Media*. Belmont, CA: Wadsworth Thomson Learning.

Jamieson, K. H., P. Waldman, and S. Sherr. 2000. "Eliminate the Negative? Categories of Analysis for Political Advertisements." Pp. 44–64 in *Crowded Airwaves: Campaign Advertising in Elections*, ed. James A. Thurber, Candace J. Nelson, and David A. Dulio. Washington, D.C.: Brookings Institution Press.

Jasperson, Amy E. and David P. Fan. 2002. "An Aggregate Examination of the Backlash Effect in Political Advertising: The Case of the 1996 U.S. Senate Race in Minnesota." *Journal of Advertising* 31(1), Spring, 1–12.

Johnson-Cartee, Karen S. and Gary A. Copeland. 1997. *Manipulation of the American Voter: Political Campaign Commercials*. Westport, CT: Praeger.

———. 1991. *Negative Political Advertising: Coming of Age*. Hillsdale, NJ: Lawrence Erlbaum Associates.

Jones, Randall J. Jr. 2002. *Who Will Be in the White House? Predicting Presidential Elections*. New York: Longman.

Jurkowitz, Mark. 2004. "Media Buzz Aided Anti-Kerry Effort Ad Ran in Few States but Story was Nationwide." *Boston Globe* (August 21), A3.

Just, Marion R., Ann N. Crigler, Dean E. Alger, Timothy E. Cook, Montague Kern, and Darrell M. West. 1996. *Crosstalk: Citizens, Candidates and the Media in a Presidential Campaign*. Chicago: University of Chicago Press.

Kahn, Kim Fridkin and Patrick J. Kenney. 1999. "Do Negative Campaigns Mobilize or Suppress Turnout? Clarifying the Relationship between Negativity and Participation." *American Political Science Review* 93(4):877–90.

Kaid, Lynda L. and Anne Johnston. 1991. "Negative versus Positive Television Advertising in U.S. Presidential Campaigns, 1960–1988." *Journal of Communication* 41, Summer, 53–64.

Kaid, Lynda Lee and Dorothy K. Davidson. 1986. "Elements of Videostyle: Candidate Presentation through Television Advertising." Pp. 184–209 in *New Perspectives on Political Advertising*, ed. Lynda Lee Kaid, Dan Nimmo, and Keith R. Sanders. Carbondale: Southern Illinois University Press.

Kaid, Lynda L. and Anne J. Wadsworth, eds. 1985. *Political Campaign Communication: A Bibliography and Guide to the Literature: 1973–1982*. Metuchen, NJ: Scarecrow Press, Inc.

Kalb, Marvin. 2001. *One Scandalous Story: Clinton, Lewinsky, and the Thirteen Days that Tarnished American Journalism*. New York: Free Press.

Kamber, Victor. 1997. *Poison Politics: Are Negative Campaigns Destroying Democracy?* New York: Insight Books.

Kane, Gregory. 2001. "Hate-crime Ad's Truth Was Meant to Mislead." *Baltimore Sun* (November 4), 1B.

Kellerman, Kathy. 1984. "The Negativity Effect and Its Implications for Initial Interaction." 51 *Communication Monographs* (March):37–55.

Kellner, Douglas. 2001. *Grand Theft: Media Spectacle and a Stolen Election*. Lanham, MD: Rowman & Littlefield.

Kennedy, John F. 1960. "Remarks of Senator John F. Kennedy, Wichita Falls, Tex., November 3, 1960." Pre-Presidential Papers, Box #914, John F. Kennedy Library.

Kepplinger, Hans Mathias. 1991. "The Impact of Presentation Techniques: Theoretical Aspects and Empirical Findings." Pp. 173–94 in *Television and Political Advertising (Volume I): Psychological Processes*, ed. Frank Biocca. Hillsdale, NJ: Lawrence Erlbaum Associates.

Kern, Montague. 1989. *30-Second Politics: Political Advertising in the Eighties*. New York: Praeger.

Kernell, Samuel. 1977. "Presidential Popularity and Negative Voting: An Alternative Explanation of the Midterm Congressional Decline of the President's Party." *American Political Science Review* 71, 44–66.

Key, V. O. Jr. 1966. *The Responsible Electorate: Rationality in Presidential Voting, 1936–1960*. New York: Vintage Books.

Kinder, Donald R. and Thomas R. Palfrey. 1993. "On Behalf of an Experimental Political Science." In *Experimental Foundations of Political Science*, ed. Donald R. Kinder and Thomas R. Palfrey. Ann Arbor: University of Michigan Press.

Knight, Al. 2001. "Shame on the NAACP." *Denver Post* (October 29), M3.

Koff, Stephen. 2006. "Troops' Armor is Focus of Senate-Race Fracas; Brown Backer Calls GOP Ads a Smear." (Cleveland) *Plain-Dealer* (September 30), A5.

Kornblut, Anne E. 2005. "Bush and Party Chief Court Black Voters at 2 Forums." *New York Times* (July 15), A12.

Kranish, Michael. 2004. "Kerry in Vietnam: Attack and Counterattack." *Boston Globe* (August 20), A30.

Krasno, Jonathan and Kenneth Goldstein. n.d. "The Facts about Television Advertising and the McCain-Feingold Bill." Unpublished manuscript.

Krasno, Jonathan and Daniel E. Seltz. 2000. *Buying Time: Television Advertising in the 1998 Congressional Elections*. New York: Brennan Center for Justice.

Kuklinski, James H., Robert C. Luskin, and John Bolland. 1991. "Where Is the Schema? Going Beyond the 'S' Word in Political Psychology." *American Political Science Review* 85:1341–56.

Kurtz, Howard. 1997. E-mail to author, March 27, 1997.

———. 1996a. "Ad Watch: Evaluating the Political Message. *Washington Post* (October 22), A14.

———. 1996b. "The Air Wars: Television and the Candidates. From Wish List to Political Pork." *Washington Post* (September 27), A16.

———. 1993. "Yesterday's News: Why Newspapers are Losing Their Franchise." In *Reinventing the Newspaper*, ed. Frank Denton and Howard Kurtz. New York: Twentieth Century Fund Press.

Landau, Mark J., Sheldon Solomon, Jeff Greenberg, Florette Cohen, Tom Pyszczynski, Jamie Arndt, Claude H. Miller, Daniel M. Ogilvie, and Alison Cook. 2004. "Deliver Us from Evil: The Effects of Mortality Salience and Reminders of

9/11 on Support for President George W. Bush." 30 *Personality and Social Psychology Bulletin* 9:1136–50.

Lang, Annie. 1991. "Emotion, Formal Features, and Memory for Televised Political Advertisements." Pp. 221–43 in *Television and Political Advertising (Volume I): Psychological Processes*, ed. Frank Biocca. Hillsdale, NJ: Lawrence Erlbaum Associates.

Lau, Richard R. 1986. "Political Schemata, Candidate Evaluations and Voting Behavior." In *Political Cognition: The 19th Annual Carnegie Symposium on Cognition*, ed. Richard R. Lau and David O. Sears. Hillsdale, NJ: Lawrence Erlbaum Associates.

———. 1985. "Two Explanations for Negativity Effects in Political Behavior." *American Journal of Political Science* 29:119–38.

———. 1982. "Negativity in Political Perception." *Political Behavior* 4:353–77.

Lau, Richard R. and David O. Sears, eds. 1986. *Political Cognition: The 19th Annual Carnegie Symposium on Cognition*. Hillsdale, NJ: Lawrence Erlbaum Associates.

Lau, Richard R., Lee Sigelman, Caroline Heldman, and Paul Babbitt. 1999. "The Effects of Negative Political Advertisements: A Meta-Analytic Assessment." *American Political Science Review* 93:851–76.

LeDoux, Joseph E. 1996. *The Emotional Brain: The Mysterious Underpinnings of Emotional Life*. New York: Simon and Schuster.

Leonhardt, David. 2002. "Wide Racial Disparities Found in Costs of Mortgages." *New York Times* (May 1).

Lewis, Neil A. 2002. "Final Report by Prosecutor on Clintons is Released." *New York Times* (March 21), A30.

Lewis-Beck, Michael S. 1988. *Economics and Elections: The Major Western Democracies*. Ann Arbor: University of Michigan Press.

Lewis-Beck, Michael S. and Tom Rice. 1992. *Forecasting Elections*. Washington, DC: CQ Press.

Livingstone, Sir Richard. 1968. *Thucydides: The History of the Peloponnesian War*. London: Oxford University Press.

Lockerbie, Brad. 2000. "Election Forecasting: A Look to the Future." In *Before the Vote: Forecasting National Elections*, ed. James E. Campbell and James C. Garand. Thousand Oaks, CA: Sage Publications.

Lodge, Milton. 1995. "Toward a Procedural Model of Candidate Evaluation." In *Political Judgment: Structure and Process*, ed. Milton Lodge and Kathleen M. McGraw. Ann Arbor: University of Michigan Press.

Lodge, Milton, Kathleen M. McGraw, Pamela Johnston Conover, Stanley Feldman, and Arthur H. Miller. 1991. "Where Is the Schema? Critiques." *American Political Science Review* 85(4):1357–80.

Lodge, Milton, Kathleen M. McGraw, and Patrick Stroh. 1989. "An Impression Driven Model of Candidate Evaluation." *American Political Science Review* 83:399–419.

March, William. 2000. "Crist stops ad mentioning DUI." *Tampa Tribune* (November 4), 4.

Marcus, George E., W. Russell Neuman, and Michael MacKuen. 2000. *Affective Intelligence and Political Judgment*. Chicago: University of Chicago Press.

Marks, Peter. 2000. "The 2000 Campaign: The Ad Campaign; Campaigns Set a Brisk, Focused TV Pace." *New York Times* (October 17).

Markus, Gregory B. 1992. "The Impact of Personal and National Economic Conditions on Presidential Voting, 1956–1988." *American Journal of Political Science* 36:829–34.

Mazzetti, Mark. 2006. "Spy Agencies Say Iraq War Worsens Terrorism Threat." *New York Times* (September 24), 1.

McChesney, Robert. 2004. *The Problem of the Media: U.S. Communication Politics in the 21st Century*. New York: Monthly Review Press.

McDonald, Michael P. and Samuel L. Popkin. 2001. "The Myth of the Vanishing Voter." *American Political Science Review* 95(4):963–75.

McGerr, Michael E. 1986. *The Decline of Popular Politics: The American North, 1865–1928*. New York: Oxford University Press.

McGinniss, Joe. 1969. *The Selling of the President 1968*. New York: Trident Press.

McGrath, Jim. 2000. "NAACP Has Hit a Low Point with Anti-Bush Ad." *Houston Chronicle* (November 3), A37.

McGraw, Kathleen M. and Marco Steenbergen. 1995. "Pictures in the Head: Memory Representations of Political Candidates." In *Political Judgment: Structure and Process*, ed. Milton Lodge and Kathleen M. McGraw. Ann Arbor: University of Michigan Press.

McGraw, Kathleen M., Neil Pinney, and David Neumann. 1991. "Memory for Political Actors: Contrasting the Use of Semantic and Evaluative Organizational Strategies." *Political Behavior* 13:165–89.

Mencken, H. L. 1916. *A Little Book in C Major*. New York: John Lane.

Mendelberg, Tali. 2001. *The Race Card: Campaign Strategy, Implicit Messages and the Norm of Equality*. Princeton, NJ: Princeton University Press.

Messaris, Paul. 1997. *Visual Persuasion: The Role of Images in Advertising*. Thousand Oaks, CA: Sage Publications.

Milbank, Dana. 2003. "Upbeat Tone Ended with War; Officials' Forecasts are Questioned." *Washington Post* (March 29), A1.

Miller, Arthur H. 1986. "Partisan Cognitions in Transition." Pp. 203–31 in *Political Cognition*, ed. Richard R. Lau and David O. Sears. Hillsdale, NJ: Lawrence Erlbaum Associates.

Minsky, Marvin. 1975. "A Framework for Representing Knowledge." In *The Psychology of Computer Vision*, ed. Patrick H. Winston. New York: McGraw-Hill.

Mitchell, Alison. 2002. "Trying to Keep Money, Politics and Free Speech Honest." *New York Times* (March 24).

Mueller, John. 2006a. *Overblown: How Politicians and the Terrorism Industry Inflate National Security Threats, and Why We Believe Them*. New York: Free Press.

———. 2006b. "Is There Still a Terrorist Threat? The Myth of the Omnipresent Enemy." 85 *Foreign Affairs* 5 (September/October).

———. 2004. "A False Sense of Insecurity?" 27 *Regulation* 3 (Fall).

Natchez, Peter B. 1985. *Images of Voting/Visions of Democracy*. New York: Basic Books.

Nelson, John S. and G. R. Boynton. 1997. *Video Rhetorics: Televised Advertising in American Politics*. Urbana: University of Illinois Press.

Nelson, John S. 1993. "Genres in the Rhetorics of Political Ads." Pp. 379–87 in *Argument and the Postmodern Challenge*, ed. Raymie McKerrow. Annandale, VA: Speech Communication Association.

Newhagen, John E. and Byron Reeves. 1991. "Emotion and Memory Responses for Negative Political Advertising: A Study of Television Commercials Used in the 1988 Presidential Election." Pp. 197–220 in *Television and Political Advertising (Volume I): Psychological Processes*, ed. Frank Biocca. Hillsdale, NJ: Lawrence Erlbaum Associates.

———. 1989. "Emotion and Memory Response for Negative Political Advertising: A Study of the 1988 Campaign." Paper presented to the Association for Education in Journalism and Mass Communication, Washington, D. C. (cited in Jamieson, *Dirty Politics*, 1992a).

Nie, Norman H., Sidney Verba, and John R. Petrocik. 1976. *The Changing American Voter*. Cambridge, MA: Harvard University Press.

Nimmo, Dan and Arthur J. Felsberg. 1986. "Hidden Myths in Televised Political Advertising: An Illustration." Pp. 248–67 in *New Perspectives on Political Advertising*, ed. Lynda Lee Kaid, Dan Nimmo, and Keith R. Sanders. Carbondale: Southern Illinois University Press.

Now. 2004a. August 20. Transcript online at http://www.pbs.org/now/transcript/transcript334_full.html. Accessed on August 8, 2007.

———. 2004b. December 17. Transcript online at http://www.pbs.org/now/printable/transcript351_full_print.html. Accessed on August 9, 2007.

Oakland Tribune. 1999. "Libertarian Candidate for Governor Arrested in Marijuana Investigation" (January 21).

Oppenheimer, Bruce I. 2005. "Deep Red and Blue Congressional Districts: The Causes and Consequences of Declining Party Competitiveness." In Lawrence C. Dodd and Bruce I. Oppenheimer (eds.), *Congress Reconsidered* (8th ed.). Washington, DC: CQ Press.

Page, Benjamin I. and Robert Y. Shapiro. 1992. *The Rational Public: Fifty Years of Trends in Americans' Policy Preferences*. Chicago: University of Chicago Press.

Paltrow, Scot J. 2001. "In Black and White: Old Memos Lay Bare Metlife's Use of Race to Screen Customers." *Wall Street Journal* (July 24), A1.

Parry, Robert. 2000. "He's No Pinocchio: How the Press Has Exaggerated Al Gore's Exaggerations." *Washington Monthly* 32(4), April 23–28.

Pateman, Carol. 1970. *Participation and Democratic Theory*. Cambridge, MA: Cambridge University Press.

Patterson, Thomas and Robert McClure. 1976. *The Unseeing Eye: The Myth of Television Power in National Elections*. New York: Putnam.

Perkins, Joseph. 2000. "A Desperate Campaign Sinks to Its Last Resort." *San-Diego Union-Tribune* (November 3), B9.

Pew Research Center for the People and the Press. 2000. "The Tough Job of Communicating with Voters." Released: February 5, 2000. Online at http://people press.org/reports/display.php3?ReportID=46, May 24, 2002.

Pfau, Michael and Allan Louden. 1994. "Effectiveness of Adwatch Formats in Deflecting Political Attack Ads." *Communication Research* 21(3):325–41.

Pitkin, Hanna F. 1969. "The Concept of Representation." In *Representation*, ed. Hanna F. Pitkin. New York: Atherton Press.

PollingReport.com. 2004. "White House 2004: Miscellany (p. 2)." Online at: http://www.pollingreport.com/wh04misc2.htm. Accessed August 7, 2007.

Popkin, Samuel L. 1994. *The Reasoning Voter: Communication and Persuasion in Presidential Campaigns* (2d ed.). Chicago: University of Chicago Press.

Preston, Jennifer. 1996. "The Ad Campaign: Torricelli Takes on Zimmer on Medicare." *New York Times* (October 25).

Protess, David and Rob Warden. 1998. *A Promise of Justice: The Eighteen-Year Fight to Save Four Innocent Men*. New York: Hyperion.

Rado, Diane. 2000. "Republican pulls ad critical of arrest with time running out." *St. Petersburg Times* (November 4), A1.

Reeves, Byron, Esther Thorson, and J. Schleuder. 1986. "Attention to Television: Psychological Theories and Chronometric Measures." In *Perspectives on Media Effects*, ed. J. Bryant and D. Zillman. Hillsdale, NJ: Lawrence Erlbaum Associates.

Richardson, Glenn W. Jr. 2007. "Anatomy of a Smear: John Kerry, Vietnam and the Swift Boat Veterans for Truth: The Contest for Meaning in the 2004 Presidential Campaign." Paper presented at the 65th Annual National Conference of the Midwest Political Science Association, Chicago, Illinois, April 12–15, 2007.

———. 2006. "Ad Watch 3.0: Developing Audiovisual Techniques for Engaging the Audiovisual Content of Political Advertising." Prepared for Presentation at the Foundations of Political Theory Workshop on Political Myth, Rhetoric and Symbolism at the 102nd Annual Meeting of the American Political Science Association, Philadelphia, Pennsylvania, August 31–September 3, 2006.

———. 2002. "Visual Storytelling and the Competition for Political Meaning in Political Advertising and News in Campaign 2000." *American Communication Journal* 5:3 (Spring); online at: http://www.acjournal.org/holdings/vol5/iss3/articles/visual/visual.htm

———. 2001. "Looking for Meaning in All the Wrong Places: Why 'Negative' Advertising Is a Suspect Category." *Journal of Communication* 51(4), Winter.

———. 2000. "Pulp Politics: The Genres of Popular Culture in Political Advertising." *Journal of Rhetoric and Public Affairs* 3(4), Winter, 603–26.

———. 1998a. "The Popular Culture Context of Political Advertising: Linkages and Meanings in Political Information Processing." 15 *Political Communication* [special electronic volume on CD-ROM].

———. 1998b. "Building a Better Adwatch: Talking Patterns to the American Voter." *Harvard International Journal of Press/Politics* 3(3), 76–95.

———. 1995. "Genre and Political Information Processing: How Political Advertising Works." Unpublished Ph.D. Dissertation, University of Iowa.

Richardson, Glenn W. Jr. and Amy E. Jasperson. 2001. "Connecting with What's Inside of Peoples' Heads: Humor and Culture in Political Advertising." Paper prepared for delivery at the 2001 Annual Meeting of the American Political Science Association, San Francisco, August 30–September 2, 2001.

Ricks, Thomas E. 2006. *Fiasco: The American Military Adventure in Iraq*. New York: Penguin Press.

Robertson, Andrew W. 1995. *The Language of Democracy: Political Rhetoric in the United States and Britain, 1790–1900*. Ithaca, NY: Cornell University Press.

Robinson, Walter V. 2000. "Gore Misstates Facts in Drug-Cost Pitch." *Boston Globe* (September 18), A6.
Rosenblatt, A., J. Greenberg, S. Solomon, T. Pyszczynski, and D. Lyon, 1989. "Evidence for Terror Management Theory I: The Effects of Mortality Salience on Reactions to Those Who Violate or Uphold Cultural Values." *Journal of Personality and Social Psychology* 57:681–90.
Rothbart, M., M. Evans, and S. Fulero. 1979. "Recall for Confirming Events: Memory Processes and the Maintenance of Social Stereotyping." *Journal of Experimental Social Psychology* 15:343–55.
Schattschneider, E. E. 1960. *The Semisovereign People*. New York: Holt, Rinehart and Winston.
Schatz, Amy. 2002. "Bush Team Goes All Out in Strategic Senate Races." *Atlanta Journal-Constitution* (June 15), A6.
Schroen, Gary C. 2005. *First In: An Insider's Account of How the CIA Spearheaded the War on Terror in Afghanistan*. New York: Presidio Press.
Schudson, Michael. 1998. "The Public Journalism Movement and Its Problems." In *The Politics of News: The News of Politics*, ed. Doris Graber, Dennis McQuail, and Pippa Norris. Washington, DC: CQ Press.
Seelye, Katharine Q. 2000. "The 2000 Campaign: The Vice President; Under Attack, Gore Reshapes Censure of Drug Industry." *New York Times* (September 21), A26.
Shapiro, Michael A. and R. H. Rieger. 1992. "Comparing Positive and Negative Political Advertising on Radio." *Journalism Quarterly* 69:135–45.
Sher, Andy and Herman Wang. 2006. "RNC Pulls 'Call Me' Ad." *Chattanooga Times Free Press* (October 26).
Sher, Richard K. 1997. *The Modern Political Campaign: Mudslinging, Bombast and the Vitality of American Politics*. Armonk, NY: M. E. Sharpe.
Shrum, Robert. 2007. *No Excuses: Concessions of a Serial Campaigner*. New York: Simon and Schuster.
Simon, Herbert A. 1979. *Models of Thought*. New Haven, CT: Yale University Press.
Simons, Herbert W. 1978. "'Genre-alizing' About Rhetoric: A Scientific Approach." In *Form and Genre: Shaping Rhetorical Action*, ed. Kathleen Hall Jamieson and Karlyn Kohrs Campbell. Falls Church, VA: Speech Communication Association.
Skaperdas, Stergios and Bernard A. Grofman. 1995. "Modeling Negative Campaigning." *American Political Science Review* 89:49–61.
Slevin, Peter. 2003. "Bush to Cast War as Part of Regional Strategy; In Speech Tonight President to Portray Iraq Effort as 'Battle for the Future of the Muslim World.'" *Washington Post* (February 26), A19.
Smith, Eric R. A. N. 1989. *The Unchanging American Voter*. Berkeley: University of California Press.
Smith, Larry D. and Anne Johnston. 1991. "Burke's Sociological Criticism Applied to Political Advertising: An Anecdotal Taxonomy of Presidential Commercials." Pp. 115–31 in *Television and Political Advertising (Volume II) Signs, Codes and Images*, ed. Frank Biocca. Hillsdale, NJ: Lawrence Erlbaum Associates.
Smith, Page. 1963. *John Adams II: 1784–1828*. Westport, CT: Greenwood Press.
Sniderman, Paul M., Richard A. Brody, and Philip E. Tetlock, eds. 1991. *Reasoning*

and Choice: Explorations in Political Psychology. Cambridge: Cambridge University Press.

Snyder, M. and S. W. Uranowitz. 1978. "Reconstructing the Past." *Journal of Personality and Social Psychology* 36:941–50.

Solomon, Sheldon, Jeff Greenberg, and Tom Pysczyznski. 1991. "A Terror Management Theory of Social Behavior: The Psychological Functions of Self-Esteem and Cultural Worldviews." In M. P. Zanna (Ed.), *Advances in Experimental Social Psychology* (Vol. 24, pp. 93–159). San Diego, CA: Academic Press.

Stewart, Charles J. 1975. "Voter Perception of Mudslinging in Political Communication." *Central States Speech Journal* 26:279–86.

Stimson, James A., Michael B. MacKuen, and Robert S. Erikson. 1995. "Dynamic Representation." *American Political Science Review* 89(3):543–65.

Stohlberg, Sheryl Gay. 2002. "Minorities Get Inferior Care, Even if Insured, Study Finds." *New York Times* (March 21), A1.

Sullivan, Andrew. 2000. "Drag Race." *The New Republic.* TRB from Washington, 6 (December 18).

Sunstein, Cass R. 2001. *Designing Democracy: What Constitutions Do.* Oxford: Oxford University Press.

Suprynowicz, Vin. 2002. "Pot Activist Held for Three Days in Canada." *Las Vegas Review-Journal* (April 28).

Surlin, Stuart H. and Thomas F. Gordon 1977. "How Values Affect Attitudes Toward Direct Reference Political Advertising." *Journalism Quarterly* 54, 89–98.

Suskind, Ron. 2006. *The One Percent Doctrine: Deep Inside America's Pursuit of Its Enemies Since 9/11.* New York: Simon and Schuster.

Taylor, Paul. 1998–2001. "Q & A." The 30-second Candidate (http://www.pbs.org/30secondcandidate/qanda/taylor1.html)

Teinowitz, Ira. 2006. "Political Ads Shatter Records on Way to $2B." *Advertising Age.* November 6: p. 1.

Tharpe, Jim. 2002. "Election 2002: Chambliss: Pass Bush Security Bill." *Atlanta Journal-Constitution* (October 1), 3D.

The Hotline. 2002. "Georgia: Cleland's 'One' Ad." September 10.

Thorson, Esther, William G. Christ, and Clarke Caywood. 1991. "Effects of Issue-Image Strategies, Attack and Support Appeals, Music and Visual Content in Political Commercials." *Journal of Broadcasting and Electronic Media* 35 (Fall): 465–86.

Timiraos, Nick. 2007. "Aging Infrastructure: How Bad Is It?" *Wall Street Journal* (August 4–5), A5.

Toner, Robin. 2006. "In Tight Senate Race, Attack on Black Candidate Stirs Furor." *New York Times* (October 26), A1.

Trent, Judith S. and Robert V. Friedenberg. 1991. *Political Campaign Communication: Principles and Practices,* 2d ed. New York: Praeger.

Tufte, Edward R. 1997. *Visual Explanation: Images and Quantities, Evidence and Narrative.* Cheshire, CT: Graphics Press.

Valentino, Nicholas A., Vincent L. Hutchings, and Ismail K. White. 2002. "Cues That Matter: How Political Ads Prime Racial Attitudes during Campaigns." 96 *American Political Science Review* 1 (March):75–90.

Vargas, Jose Antonio and Howard Kurtz. 2007. "Watching Big Sister; '1984' Takeoff on YouTube Is a Sign of Why 2008 Won't be Like 2004." *Washington Post* (March 21), C1.

Viguerie, Richard A. 2006. *America's Right Turn: How Conservatives Used New and Alternative Media to Take Power.* Los Angeles: Bonus Books.

Wasson, David. 2000. "Gore Touts His Drug Plan in Florida." *Tampa Tribune* (August 29), 1.

Wattenberg, Martin P. and Craig Leonard Brians. 1999. "Negative Campaign Advertising: Mobilizer or Demobilizer?" *American Political Science Review* 93:891–900.

West, Darrell M. 1997. *Air Wars: Television Advertising in Election Campaigns, 1952–1996*, 2d ed. Washington, DC: CQ Press.

———. 1992. "Reforming Campaign Ads." *PS: Political Science & Politics* 25 (March):74–77.

Wilfong, Cathy. 2002a. "Chambliss TV Ad Links Cleland to Terrorism." *Chattanooga Times Free Press* (October 12), B3.

———. 2002b. "Chambliss Camp Reworks TV Ad." *Chattanooga Times Free Press* (October 18), B3.

Wlezien, Christopher and Robert S. Erickson. 1996. "Temporal Horizons and Presidential Election Forecasts." *American Politics Quarterly* 24:492–505.

Wood, Gaby. 2007. "Review: From the Web to the White House: . . ." *The Observer* (England): July 8.

Woodson, Robert L. Sr. 2000. "The NAACP Sells Out." *Wall Street Journal* (November 1), A26.

Woodward, Bob. 1992. "The Anatomy of a Decision: Six Words That Shaped—and May Sink—the Bush Presidency," *Washington Post National Weekly Edition* (October 12–18).

Woodward, Bob and Dan Eggen. 2002. "Aug. Memo Focused on Attacks in U.S.: Lack of Fresh Information Frustrated Bush." *Washington Post* (May 18), A1.

WSB-TV. 2002. "GA: NRSC Targeting Ads To Help Chambliss Against Cleland, Irvin." June 4 (Summarized in *The Bulletin's Forerunner*, June 5, 2002).

Zaller, John R. 1998. "Monica Lewinsky's Contribution to Political Science." *PS Political Science and Politics* 33:182–89.

Zernike, Kate and Jim Rutenberg. 2004. "Friendly Fire: The Birth of an Attack on Kerry." *New York Times* (August 20), A1.

Index

24 (TV action drama), 138–141

activation, spreading, 34–35
Acxiom Corporation, 133
Adams, John, 78
Adams, John Quincy, 78
adjacency, 121–22
advertising. *See* audiovisuals; negative advertising
ad watch journalism: advent of, 89; audiovisuals and, 96–98, 99–100, 101–3, 104–7; Bill Clinton and, 98–101, 103; broadcast ads generally, 96–103; democracy and, 167–68; effectiveness of, 89–90, 98–103; election of 1992 and, 97–98, 98–101, 102–3, 167; election of 1994 and, 98; election of 1996 and, 91–93, 93–96, 103; election of 2000 and, 25; exaggeration and, 168; George H. W. Bush and, 98–101, 102; grammar for, 84–85, 96–98, 101–2, 104–7, 113, 122–23; horror and, 105–6; improvement of, 7, 85, 96–98, 101, 103–9; Medicare and, 91–93; narration and, 104; pattern analysis by, 103–4, 109; policy focus of, 15–16, 90–96, 98–103, 103–4, 109; popular culture and, 104–5; print ads generally, 93–96; purposes of, 98, 167–68; space and time for, 107–9; viewers and, 104, 107; voters and, 98, 101; wholistic processing and, 90–92, 104. *See also* negative advertising
Afghanistan, 126–27
African Americans, 162–63
Ailes, Roger, 5

American National Election Study (ANES), 62, 67–70
The American Voter, 165–66
Annenberg School of Communication, 2, 96–98, 101
Ansolabehere, Stephen, 64, 98, 101
Aristotle, 13–14
"Arkansas" ad, 40, 68–70
assault ads, 65, 73–74. *See also* attack ads; negative advertising
associative networks: audiovisuals and, 45; cognition and, 34–36; election of 2000 and, 112–15, 115–17; genre and, 11–13, 34–36; horror and, 5, 12, 20, 35, 50–52; popular culture and, 4–5, 11–13; satire and, 43; science fiction and, 52–53; Vietnam War and, 54–57, 58–59; wholistic processing and, 35. *See also* cognition
attack ads, 64–65, 68–70, 134–37. *See also* assault ads; negative advertising
audiovisual grammar, 84–85, 86–87, 101–2, 104–7. *See also* visual grammar
audiovisuals: ad watch journalism and, 96–98, 99–100, 101–3, 104–7; associative networks and, 45; emotions and, 45, 46, 47–48; grammar for, 84–85, 101–2, 104–7; importance of, 3, 173–74; reasoning and, 122–23; terror, 125–53. *See also* music; narration; sound effects; visuals
Aufderheide, Pat, 57

Barber, Benjamin, 161
Barber, James D., 66

Barnes, Roy, 130
Barry, Ann. M. S., 122
Baudrillard, Jean, 31
Berelson, Bernard R., 161
Berger, Arthur A., 12
bin Laden, Osama, 127, 129–30, 143
Biocca, Frank, 14–15, 16
Bolland, John, 35
Boston "Harbor" ad. *See* "Harbor" ad
Bowden, Bobby, 83
Boynton, G. R., 13, 34
brain, 3–4, 32, 33. *See also* cognition
Brancaccio, David, 137
Braudy, Leo, 12
Brennan Center for Justice, 108, 163
Brown, Sherrod, 145
Bryan, William Jennings, 78
Buchanan, Pat, 20–21, 27, 102
Bush, George H. W: ad watch journalism and, 98–101, 102; "Arkansas" ad, 40, 68–70; Boston "Harbor" ad, 20, 38; comparative ads by, 19; genre and, 20, 27; image of, 15; negative advertising and, 68–70; "Read my lips" promise, 4–5; "Revolving Door" ad, 5, 12, 20, 27, 35, 85, 104, 108, 169; "Tank Ride" ad, 15–16, 27, 42, 43, 53, 76, 85, 96, 97; Willie Horton ad, 2, 104, 108, 174n2. *See also* election of 1988
Bush, George W.: ads about Al Gore, 113–23; ads about John Kerry, 138–43; Al Gore ads about, 115, 116; drunk driving by, 1–2, 3; James Byrd Jr. ad, 155–56, 162–63, 173; margin of victory of, 8n2; negative advertising by, 24–25; "Peace and Security" ad, 140, *141*; Ralph Nader ads about, 24; "Risk" ad, 138, *139*; "Searching" ad, 140, *142*, 143. *See also* election of 2000; election of 2004
Byrd, James, Jr., 156, 162–63

campaign finance, 156, 163–64
Campaign Media Analysis Group (CMAG), 108
campaigns, 157–61
Campbell, Karlyn K., 28n1
Capella, Joseph N., 98
Chambliss, Saxby, 128–30
chapter overviews, 6–8
character, 66, 76, 111, 112–13, 117–20. *See also* honesty
Cheney, Dick, 131
Cicero, Marcus T., 61
Cleland, Max, 128–30, 156
Clinton, Bill: ad watch journalism and, 98–101, 103; "Arkansas" ad, 40, 68–70; genre and, 21, 27; image of, 78, 111, 112; negative advertising and, 68–70; scandals of, 24–25, 112–13, 113–15, 115–17, 123n1
Clinton, Hillary, 149–50
cognition, 3–4, 32–36, 163. *See also* associative networks; brain
Cohen, William S., 146
collective rationality, 166
communications revolution, 125–26
comparative ads: adjacency and, 121–22; genre and, 19, 44–45, 54–59; as negative advertising, 65, 71–73, 75. *See also* negative advertising
confederate battle flag, 130
Congress, 173
Copeland, Gary A., 26, 27
Corker, Bob, 146
Crist, Charlie, 1–2, 3

Darman, Richard, 5
Davis, Gray, 21–22, 23
Dean, Howard, 132
"Del Ad," 132–33
Delli Carpini, Michael X., 166, 167
Democracy: ad watch journalism and, 167–68; campaign finance and, 156, 163–64; campaigns and, 157–61; emotions and, 156, 162–63; issue ads and, 156, 162–63; negative advertising and, 7, 63, 70, 77, 80–82, 85–86, 161, 168–69; popular culture and, 5, 173–74; reasoning and, 165–67; republicanism and, 159–61, 172–74;

voters and, 8, 11, 158–61, 165–67, 172–74. *See also* politics
Derrida, Jacques, 25
De Vellis, Phil, 151
Devlin, L. Patrick, 27
Dewey, John, 165
DeWine, Mike, 145
distortions, 75–76, 96, 102, 119–21, 168. *See also* exaggeration
Dole, Bob, 21, 27, 103. *See also* election of 1996
Dukakis, Michael: Boston "Harbor" ad, 20, 38; genre and, 19, 20; image of, 15–16; "Revolving Door" ad, 5, 12, 20, 27, 35, 85, 104, 108, 169; "Tank Ride" ad, 15–16, 27, 42, 43, 53, 76, 85, 96, 97; Willie Horton ad, 2, 104, 108, 174n2. *See also* election of 1988

"Earth" ad, 40–41, 52–53
economy, 111, 172–73
Edelman, Murray, 158
Edwards, John, 83, 152
election of 1984, 19–20
election of 1988: Boston "Harbor" ad, 20, 38; genre and, 20; negative advertising and, 89; popular culture and, 15–16, 19; "Read my lips" promise, 4–5; "Revolving Door" ad, 5, 12, 20, 27, 35, 85, 104, 108, 169; "Tank Ride" ad, 15–16, 27, 42, 43, 53, 76, 85, 96, 97; Willie Horton ad, 2, 104, 108, 174n2. *See also* specific candidates
election of 1992: ad watch journalism and, 97–98, 98–101, 102–3, 167; "Arkansas" ad, 40, 68–70; genre and, 20, 27; negative advertising and, 67–70. *See also* specific candidates
election of 1994, 98
election of 1996, 20–21, 27, 91–93, 93–96, 103. *See also* specific candidates
election of 2000: adjacency and, 121–22; ad watch journalism and, 25; associative networks and, 112–15, 115–17; character and, 111, 112–13, 117–20; Charlie Crist ads and, 1–2, 3; exaggeration and, 111, 117–21; Florida and, 3; forecast for, 111–12; genre and, 22–25; graphics and, 121–22; Internet and, 117–18; James Byrd Jr. ads and, 155–56, 162–63; late-night television and, 113–15; popular culture and, 22–25, 113–15; prescription drugs and, 118–21; result of, 3, 8n2, 111–12; scandals and, 7, 24–25, 112–13, 113–15, 115–17; television screens and, 113–15, 116–17; visuals and, 113–23; White House images and, 115–16; wholistic processing and, 112–15, 115–17, 120. *See also* specific candidates
election of 2002: confederate battle flag, 130; "Global War on Terror," 126–28; Max Cleland ads and, 127–28; result of, 130–31; Saxby Chambliss ads and, 129–30
election of 2004: George W. Bush ads about John Kerry, 138–43; Iraq War, 131–33; profiles, 133; result of, 143–44; swift boat ads, 132–36
election of 2006, 144–48
election of 2008, 148–53
embellishment, 6–7, 54, 55–56. *See also* exaggeration
emotions: audiovisuals and, 45, 46, 47–48; cognition and, 32; democracy and, 156, 162–63; horror and, 49–50; negative advertising and, 63, 64–65, 77, 83; reasoning and, 6, 13–14, 156, 162–63; satire and, 57–58; Vietnam War and, 57–58
environmental decay, 37–38, 39–40, 49–51, 52–53
Ettinger, Amber Lee, 151
exaggeration, 111, 117–21, 168. *See also* embellishment; honesty
experimental research: design of, 35–37, 45–46, 60n6, 60n9, 71; horror

ads, 37–40, 46–52; negative advertising, 70–77; satire ads, 41–43, 71, 72, 73–74, 75–76; science fiction ads, 40–41; Vietnam War ads, 44–45, 71–75, 77

Faircloth, Lauch, 83
fear, 49–50, 77. *See also* horror
Feinstein, Diane, 163
Felknor, Bruce L., 78
Fitzpatrick, Mike, 144
Ford, Harold E., Jr., 145–47
Fox News, 134–35
freedom of speech, 81
Friedenberg, Robert, 17
Fund for a Conservative Majority, 20

Gage, Phineas, 162
Geer, John, 146, 148
genre: associative networks and, 11–13, 34–36, 43, 50–52, 52–53, 54–57, 58–59; Bill Clinton and, 21, 27; classification of, 25–28; comparative ads and, 19, 44–45, 54–59; definition of, 25, 28n1; election of 1984 and, 19–20; election of 1988 and, 20; election of 1992 and, 20, 27; election of 1996 and, 20–21, 27; election of 2000 and, 22–25; George H. W. Bush and, 20, 27; incongruent, 19–20; literary, 29n2; Michael Dukakis and, 19, 20; popular culture and, 11–13, 16–17, 17–18, 25–28, 28n1; science fiction, 37, 40–41, 47–48, 52–53; tabloid television, 20; talking head, 44–45, 54–59; Vietnam War, 44–45, 47–48, 54–59, 71–75, 77; viewer response to, 45–59, 71–77. *See also* experimental research; horror; popular culture; satire
Gephardt, Richard, 132
Germond, Jack W., 96
Gigot, Paul, 127
Ginsberg, Benjamin, 135
Gore, Al: ads about George W. Bush, 115, 116; character of, 111, 112–13, 117–20; election forecasts for, 111–12; George W. Bush ads about, 113–15, 115–23; Internet and, 117–18; margin of defeat of, 3, 8n2; prescription drugs and, 118–21; Ralph Nader ads about, 24; scandals and, 25, 112–13, 113–15, 115–17; White House images and, 115–16. *See also* election of 2000
Graber, Doris: on cognition, 3, 4, 33–34; on emotions, 6, 162; on memory, 32; on visual communication, 108; on voters, 168
grammar: for audiovisuals, 84–85, 86–87, 101–2, 104–7; visual, 84–85, 96–98, 101, 113, 122–23
graphics, 121–22. *See also* visuals
Greenberg, Jeff, 126
Greenfield, Meg, 61–62
Gronbeck, Bruce, 26, 27, 65, 71

Hanna, Mark, 77–78
"Harbor" ad, 20, 38
heuristics, 166
Hillsman, Bill, 17, 18–19, 24
Holtz, Lou, 83
honesty, 75–76, 89, 103, 117–20. *See also* character; exaggeration
horror: ad watch journalism and, 105–6; associative networks and, 5, 12, 20, 35, 50–52; emotions and, 49–50; experimental research on, 36–40, 46–53; negative advertising and, 49–50, 67, 80, 85; viewer response to, 46–53; visuals, 39–40, 49; wholistic processing and, 67. *See also* fear; science fiction
"Horror" ad, 36–40, 46–52
Horton, William J., Jr., 2, 104, 108, 174n2. *See also* "Revolving Door" ad
"Hott-4-Hill" music video, 151
humor, 17–18, 73–74. *See also* satire
Hussein, Saddam, 129–30

"I Feel Pretty" video, 152
"I Got a Crush on Obama" music video, 151–52

implicative ads, 65. *See also* negative advertising
information tide, 3–4
Internet, 117–18
Iraq War, 130–32, 139, 144
issue ads, 156, 162–63
Iyengar, Shanto, 64, 98, 101

Jackson, Andrew, 78
Jackson, Brooks, 98–100
Jamieson, Kathleen H: on ad typologies, 25; on ad watch journalism, 89, 96–98, 101; on genre, 28n1; on negative advertising, 2, 62, 80, 136–37, 161; on visual grammar, 84, 96–98
Janklow, William, 121
Jefferson, Thomas, 78, 172
jibjab.com, 151
Johnson-Cartee, Karen S., 26, 27
journalism, 93, 101–2, 125–6. *See also* ad watch journalism
Just, Marion R., 28, 68

Kahn, Kim F., 65–66
Kaid, Lynda L., 79
Kamber, Victor, 61
Kaplan, Howard, 97–98
Keeter, Scott, 166, 167
Kendall, David E., 124n1
Kennedy, John F., 78–79
Kenney, Patrick J., 65–66
Kern, Montague, 26, 27, 66–67
Kerry, John: George W. Bush ads about, 138–43; swift boat ads, 132–36
Key, V. O., Jr., 109, 165–66, 168
Kubby, Steve, 21–22, 23, 29n6
Kuklinski, James H., 35
Kurtz, Howard, 93, 94–96, 108

late-night television, 113–15
Lau, Richard R., 33, 79
Letterman, David, 113–15
Levin, Carl, 37, 41–45, 53–54, 71, 75–76
"Levin of Arabia" ad: description of, 41–43, 71; viewer response to, 53–54, 57–58, 72, 73–74, 75–76; wholistic view of, 85
Lincoln, Abraham, 78
Lippmann, Walter, 165
Lodge, Milton, 34
Louden, Allan, 98
low-information rationality, 4, 166
Lundgren, Dan, 21–22, 23
Luskin, Robert C., 35

Madison, James, 160, 161, 172
Mastercard, 24
McCain, John, 22–24, 163, 164
McClure, Robert, 2
McGinniss, Joe, 78
McKinley, William, 77–78
Medicare, 91–93
Mehlman, Ken, 146, 148
Mellman, Mark, 132, 134
meltdown phenomena, 2–3
memory, 32–33. *See also* brain; cognition
Mencken, H. L., 172
messages and, 46–47
Messaris, Paul, 122
military ads. *See* "Levin of Arabia" ad; "Never Again" ad; swift boat ads; "Tank Ride" ad
"Mission Accomplished" banner, 132
money, 156
mugwumps, 63, 80–81, 81–82
Mullins, Renee, 156
Murdoch, Rupert, 125
Murphy, Patrick, 144–45
music: ad watch journalism and, 99–100; horror, 38–39, 48–49; science fiction, 40–41, 52–53; tone and, 64–65; Vietnam War, 44–45, 54–55. *See also* sound effects

NAACP National Voter Fund, 155–56, 173
Nader, Ralph, 24
narration, 39, 41, 43, 54, 104
"narrowcasting," 130, 133, 152–53
National Endowment for the Arts (NEA), 102

National Republican Senatorial Committee (NRSC), 145
National Security Political Action Committee (NSPAC), 2
negative advertising: alternative analysis of, 83–87; American National Election Study (ANES), 62, 67–70; apparent, 65–66; assault ads, 65, 73–74; attack ads, 64–65, 68–70, 134–37; Bill Clinton and, 68–70; Charlie Crist and, 1–2, 3; comparative ads as, 65, 71–73, 75; conventional approaches to, 64–67; defining, 62–63; democracy and, 7, 63, 70, 77, 80–82, 85–86, 161, 168–69; "Earth" ad as, 53; election of 1988 and, 89; election of 1992 and, 67–70; emotions and, 63, 64–65, 77, 83; experimental research on, 70–77; George H. W. Bush and, 68–70; George W. Bush and, 24–25; grammar for, 84–85, 86–87, 96–98, 101, 113, 122–23; hard-sell, 66–67; history of, 61–62, 77–80; horror and, 49–50, 67, 80, 85; as misleading, 15–16, 75–76, 96, 102, 119–21; pathological analysis and, 83–84; *"Playboy"* ad as, 145–48; policy and, 73; politics and, 63, 76, 80–82, 82–83; popular culture and, 85–87; reasoning and, 63, 80–82; research concerning, 64–67, 83–87; soft-sell, 66–67; typologies of, 27, 65, 66–67, 74–77; as unbalanced, 74–75; viewer response to, 67–77; voters and, 5–6, 80–82, 85–86; wholistic processing and, 64, 67, 85–87. *See also* ad watch journalism
Nelson, John S., 13
Nelson, Terry, 148
"Never Again" ad, 44–45, 54–59, 71–75, 77
newspapers, 125–26
Nixon, Richard M., 78, 78–79
Noonan, Peggy, 5
North, Oliver, 20
Northwestern University, 109

Obama, Barack, 144, 149, 151–52
"One America" ad, 129
on-line information processing, 166
overviews, 6–8

Page, Benjamin I., 166
Pateman, Carol, 161
pathological analysis, 83–84
patriotism, 54–56
pattern analysis, 103–4, 109
Patterson, Thomas, 2
"Peace and Security" ad, 140, *141*
Pericles, 173
Perot, Ross, 26, 27, 68, 69
Persian Gulf War, 131
persuasion, 13–14
Pfau, Michael, 98
physiological response, 46, 47–48
"Playboy" ad, 145–48
policy: ad watch journalism and, 15–16, 90–96, 98–103, 103–4, 109; negative advertising and, 73; voters and, 90–91
political action committees (PACs), 2. *See also* campaign finance
political parties, 80–81, 86
politics: competition in, 82–83; negative advertising and, 76; reform of, 63, 80–82, 85–87, 157. *See also* democracy
Popkin, Samuel, 4, 166
popular culture: ad watch journalism and, 104–5; associative networks and, 4–5, 11–13; cognition and, 32, 34; democracy and, 5, 173–74; election of 1984 and, 19–20; election of 1988 and, 4–5, 15–16, 19; election of 1996 and, 20–21; election of 2000 and, 22–25, 113–15; genre and, 11–13, 16–17, 17–18, 25–28, 28n1; Jesse Ventura campaign, 17–18; late-night television, 113–15; negative advertising and, 85–87; "Read my lips" promise, 4–5; reality and, 31; schemas and, 4–5; *South Park*, 21–22, 23; wholistic processing and, 4. *See also* genre

prescription drugs, 118–21
Preston, Jennifer, 93
prison furloughs. *See* "Revolving Door" ad
profiles, 133
Pyszczynski, Tom, 126

racist cues, 145–48
rapid response, 166
Rassman, Jim, 132–33
Ray, Robert W., 124n1
"Read my lips" promise, 4–5
Reagan, Ronald, 19–20
reality, 31
reasoning: audiovisuals and, 122–23; democracy and, 165–67; emotions and, 6, 13–14, 156, 162–63; negative advertising and, 63, 80–82
republicanism, 159–161, 172–74
research, experimental. *See* experimental research
"Revolving Door" ad: ad typologies and, 27; ad watch journalism and, 108; associative networks and, 35; effect of, 169; horror and, 5, 12, 20, 85; wholistic processing and, 104. *See also* Horton, William J., Jr
Rice, Condoleezza, 128
"Risk" ad, 138, *139*
Robb, Charles, 20
Roosevelt, Franklin D., 78
Roosevelt, Theodore, 77–78
Rove, Karl, 127, 130–31
Rowley, Colleen, 127

Sandusky, Del, 132
satire: associative networks and, 43; emotional response to, 57–58; messages and, 46–47; physiological response to, 47–48; "*South Park*" ad, 21–22, 23; viewer response to, 46–47, 47–48, 53–54, 57–58, 71, 72, 73–74, 75–76; visuals, 42, 53–54. *See also* humor; "Levin of Arabia" ad; "Tank Ride" ad
scandals: election of 2000 and, 7, 24–25, 112–13, 113–15, 115–17; Whitewater, 123n1
schemas, 4–5, 32–34, 35
Schuette, Bill, 37, 41–45, 54–56, 71
science fiction, 37, 40–41, 47–48, 52–53. *See also* horror
Scott, Ridley, 148
"Searching" ad, 140, *142*, 143
Sears, David O., 33
semantics, 14–15
September 11 terrorist attacks, 128–29, 138–39
Sestak, Joe, 144
Shapiro, Robert Y., 166
Sheldon, George, 1–2
Shelton, Hilary, 146
Shinseki, Eric K., 131
Shrum, Robert, 131–32, 143
Simons, Herbert W., 29n1
Solomon, Sheldon, 126
sound effects: ad watch journalism and, 99–100; grammar for, 105; horror, 49; "Levin of Arabia" ad, 43, 53, 54; "Tank Ride" ad, 43, 53. *See also* music
Soundtracks. *See* music
South Park, 21–22, 23
special effects. *See* graphics; sound effects
spreading activation, 34–35
Springsteen, Bruce, 19–20
Strasma, Kenneth, 133
Sullivan, Andrew, 156, 174n2
suppressing context, 103, 119–20
swift boat ads, 132–37
"Swift Boat Veterans for Truth" (SBVT), 132–37

talking head ads, 44–45, 54–59
"Tank Ride" ad: ad typologies and, 27; ad watch journalism and, 96, 97; as misleading, 15–16, 76, 96; as satire, 15–16, 42, 85; sound effects in, 43, 53
Task Force on Campaign Reform, 157, 167
Taylor, Paul, 156–57, 162

television, 80, 113–15, 116–17, 119–20. *See also* visuals
"terror management theory" of social behavior, 126
tone, 64–65
"Tongues Untied" ad, 102
top-down processing. *See* wholistic processing
Torricelli, Robert G., 93–94
Trent, Judith, 17
Tufte, Edward, 106, 107, 119, 122
typologies, 25–28, 65, 65–67, 74–77

user-posted video, 151–52

Ventura, Jesse, 17–18, 21, 26, 27
Vietnam War ads, 44–45, 47–48, 54–59, 71–75, 77
viewers: ad watch journalism and, 104, 107; horror and, 46–53; measuring responses of, 45–46; negative advertising and, 67–77; physiological responses of, 46, 47–48; satire and, 46–47, 47–48, 53–54, 57–58, 71, 72, 73–74, 75–76; science fiction and, 47–48, 52–53; Vietnam War and, 47–48, 54–59, 71–75, 77. *See also* voters
viral videos, 148, 150–52
visual grammar, 84–85, 96–98, 101, 113, 122–23. *See also* audiovisual grammar
visuals: adjacency, 122; ad watch journalism and, 96–98, 99–100, 101–3, 104–7; election of 2000 and, 113–23; grammar for, 84–85, 86–87, 101–2, 104–7; graphics, 121–22; horror, 39–40, 49; satire, 42, 53–54; tone and, 64–65; Vietnam War, 44, 54–56; wholistic processing and, 121–22. *See also* audiovisuals
"Vote Different" ad, 148–149, *150,* 151
voters: ad watch journalism and, 98, 101; democracy and, 8, 11, 158–61, 165–67, 172–74; negative advertising and, 5–6, 80–82, 85–86; policy and, 90–91; young, 22. *See also* reasoning; viewers

Wadsworth, Anne J., 79
Webb, Jim, 145, 151
Weldon, Curt, 144–45
West, Darrell M., 25, 26, 27
White House, 115–16
Whitewater scandal, 123n1
wholistic processing: ad watch journalism and, 90–92, 104; associative networks and, 35; election of 2000 and, 112–15, 115–17, 120; embellishment and, 6–7, 54; horror and, 67; incongruent genres and, 19; negative advertising and, 64, 67, 85–87; popular culture and, 4; schemas and, 4–5, 33–34; semantics and, 14, 16; Vietnam War and, 55–56; visuals and, 121–22
Witcover, Jules, 96
Wofford, Harris, 158
Wood, Gaby, 149

youth, 22
YouTube, 148–51

Zimmer, Dick, 93
Zimmer, Richard A., 20

About the Author

Glenn W. Richardson Jr. is associate professor of political science at Kutztown University of Pennsylvania. His research on political advertising and the media has appeared in the *Journal of Communication, Harvard International Journal of Press/Politics, Rhetoric and Public Affairs, Political Research Quarterly*, and the *American Communication Journal*, where his article on political advertising and the media in the 2000 campaign received the 2002 American Communication Journal Article of the Year Award.

```
JK          Richardson, Glenn W.
2281
.R53        Pulp politics.
2008

                        35019000033844
```

DATE			

BAKER & TAYLOR